作者简介

陈　宁　福建师范大学协和学院教授，硕士生导师，高级经济师，福建省翻译协会常务理事。

陈鹏南　福建理工大学人文学院讲师，第13届"外教社杯"全国高校外语教学大赛福建赛区一等奖获得者，福建省翻译协会会员。

"十四五"职业教育国家规划教材

"十三五"职业教育国家规划教材

21世纪全国应用型人才培养规划教材

21世纪实用国际商务英语口语（第四版）

陈宁　陈鹏南　◎著

北京大学出版社
PEKING UNIVERSITY PRESS

内容简介

本书深入贯彻党的二十大精神，以习近平新时代中国特色社会主义思想为指导，准确把握教育事业发展面临的新形势、新任务，以培养学生的商务英语口语能力为核心，把英语语言能力培养与商务知识学习有机结合起来，突出知识掌握、能力培养与价值塑造的协同发展。全书以国际商务交际活动为中心，展示如何处理实际交易环节中出现的各类问题，内容涉及国际贸易的各个实战环节和相关商务活动两大主线，涵盖客户介绍、寻找贸易机会、商务安排、参加交易会、商务拜访、营销策略、商务会议、商务促销、商务谈判、技术创新和自主品牌战略等。

本书精心设计了与国际商务有关的话题，从国际贸易实务的各个实战环节入手，让学生在逼真的贸易情景中学习国际商务知识、模仿体验如何开展国际贸易，书中融入了展示中华文明等内容，通过情景对话、角色扮演、专题讨论、经典句型操练、交际技巧、实践操练等训练，让学生在不同的商务语境中应用国际商务英语口语，提高商务交际技能，提升民族自豪感，增强国际视野。本书配有课文范读和教学课件。

本书可作为高等院校经贸和英语专业的教材，也可作为相关从业人员的参考书。

图书在版编目(CIP)数据

21世纪实用国际商务英语口语 / 陈宁，陈鹏南著. 4版. -- 北京：北京大学出版社，2024.8. -- (21世纪全国应用型人才培养规划教材). -- ISBN 978-7-301-35417-9

Ⅰ.F740

中国国家版本馆CIP数据核字第202431CM07号

书　　名	21世纪实用国际商务英语口语（第四版） 21 SHIJI SHIYONG GUOJI SHANGWU YINGYU KOUYU（DI-SI BAN）
著作责任者	陈　宁　陈鹏南　著
责任编辑	吴坤娟
标准书号	ISBN 978-7-301-35417-9
出版发行	北京大学出版社
地　　址	北京市海淀区成府路205号　100871
网　　址	http://www.pup.cn　新浪微博：@北京大学出版社
电子邮箱	编辑部 zyjy@pup.cn　总编室 zpup@pup.cn
电　　话	邮购部 010-62752015　发行部 010-62750672　编辑部 010-62756923
印 刷 者	北京溢漾印刷有限公司
经 销 者	新华书店
	787毫米×1092毫米　16开本　18.5印张　629千字
	2007年4月第1版　2012年8月第2版　2018年3月第3版
	2024年8月第4版　2024年8月第1次印刷
定　　价	59.00元

未经许可，不得以任何方式复制或抄袭本书之部分或全部内容。
版权所有，侵权必究
举报电话：010-62752024　电子邮箱：fd@pup.cn
图书如有印装质量问题，请与出版部联系，电话：010-62756370

第四版前言

新时代，新形势，实施科教兴国战略，强化社会主义现代化建设人才支撑，加快建设教育强国、科技强国、人才强国，这对商务英语口语课程的学习提出了新的更高的要求。本书深入贯彻党的二十大精神，以习近平新时代中国特色社会主义思想为指导，准确把握教育事业发展面临的新形势、新任务，以培养学生的商务英语口语能力为核心，把英语语言能力培养与商务知识学习有机结合起来，希望为高等院校的商务英语、国际贸易和经济等专业的学生以及外贸工作者提供一本有针对性和实用价值的商务英语口语教材。

本书在编写过程中，坚持培育和践行社会主义核心价值观，坚持深化教育改革创新，坚持用社会主义核心价值观立德树人，书中融入了展示中华文明等内容，突出知识掌握、能力培养与价值塑造的协同发展。从第一版到第四版，编者不断在书中充实新知识、完善新内容，体现与时俱进，与时代发展同步。

本书具有以下特色：

1. **理论与实践一体化结合。**

本书集商务和英语理论知识、实际运用及实训于一体。本书以能力培养为目标，以国际贸易实际工作项目为载体，以学生为中心，以交易磋商任务驱动学生完成知识和技能的学习，以国际贸易交易实际操作环节为章节，每个章节都是独立的商务活动场景，把理论知识的学习与语言能力的培养放在具体的商务情景中，形成了适应一体化教学的模式。本书将理论学习与实践相结合，可促进学生认知能力的发展和商务英语口语的提高。第三版在教材Part C部分强化了理论与实践一体化结合的内容。

2. **融入思政元素，体现鲜明的时代特色。**

本书应用现代流行、生动地道的国际商务英语口语的表达方式，摒弃过时的商务知识和行话，便于开展互动式商务英语口语训练；融合于各章节中的国际商务观念和技巧贴近时代脉搏，具有强烈的时代感；涉及的内容贴近现代国际商务实际，满足了当前国际商务的交际需求。本书结合时代发展，通过例句融入思政元素，拓展学生关于"一带一路"、国际进口博览会、开放合作、中华民族伟大复兴、北京奥运会、小康社会等新思维，以及数字经济等新话题，以调动学生的学习兴趣和求知欲望，用潜移默化的方式培养学生的国际视野和中国情怀，提高学生的学习效果。

3. **架构完整，内容丰富。**

本书以国际商务交际活动为中心，展示如何处理实际交易环节中出现的各类问题，内容涉及国际贸易的各个实战环节和相关商务活动两大主线，涵盖客户介绍、寻找贸易机会、商务安排、参加交易会、商务拜访、营销策略、商务会议、商务促销、商务谈判、技术创新和自主品牌战略等。从开展国际贸易实务，如询盘、报盘、还价、接受、签约、支付、包装、商检、发货和索赔等各个实战环节入手，其中还涉及许多外贸的知识细节，如商标、专利、保险、普惠制和独家经营等，让学生在逼真的贸易情景中学习国际商务知识和模仿体验如何开展国际贸易，应用国际商务英语口语，提高商务交际技能。

4. 突出实用性和实战技能。

本书所包含的国际商务知识、英语口语技能、商务业务技巧、商务礼仪和流行口语、情景对话、经典句型等，让学生接触到生动真实的国际商务英语口语信息；通过模拟操练、角色扮演、讨论和辩论等方法，可调动学生学习的积极性，培养学生熟练运用英语从事商务活动的能力，启迪学生在逼真的贸易情景中学习国际商务知识，模仿体验如何开展国际贸易，应用国际商务英语口语，提高商务交际技能。

本书由具有丰富教学和外贸实践经验的资深教师精心撰写，许多章节情景就是现实国贸业务的片段再现。课文的音频材料由外国专家朗读，便于学生模仿和进行听说练习。学生可用微信扫描二维码获取学习材料。本书教学课件可提供给教师教学参考。本书可供一学年商务英语口语学习，若只安排一学期教学，教师可根据商务程序和课文的深浅酌情选择学习内容。

最后，衷心希望读者能学有所获。另外，书中还有很多不尽如人意之处，恳请专家、学者、同行等批评指正。

编　者

2024年7月

本教材配有教学课件和其他相关教学资源，如有老师需要，可扫描右边的二维码关注北京大学出版社微信公众号"北大出版社创新大学堂"（zyjy-pku）索取。

·课件申请
·样书申请
·教学服务
·编读往来

Contents

Chapter 1 Welcoming Clients ··1
    Part A Situational Dialogue ··2
        Communicative Scene 1 ··2
        Communicative Scene 2 ··3
        Communicative Scene 3 ··3
    Part B Practical Key Sentences ···7
    Part C Integration of Theory and Practice ···8
    Part D Practice ···11

Chapter 2 Seeking Business Opportunities ···15
    Part A Situational Dialogue ···16
        Communicative Scene 1 ··16
        Communicative Scene 2 ··17
        Communicative Scene 3 ··18
    Part B Practical Key Sentences ···23
    Part C Integration of Theory and Practice ···25
    Part D Practice ···27

Chapter 3 Making Inquiries ··31
    Part A Situational Dialogue ···32
        Communicative Scene 1 ··32
        Communicative Scene 2 ··33
        Communicative Scene 3 ··34
    Part B Practical Key Sentences ···39
    Part C Integration of Theory and Practice ···41
    Part D Practice ···43

Chapter 4 Business Appointment and Arrangement ··47
    Part A Situational Dialogue ···48
        Communicative Scene 1 ··48
        Communicative Scene 2 ··49
        Communicative Scene 3 ··50
    Part B Practical Key Sentences ···54
    Part C Integration of Theory and Practice ···56
    Part D Practice ···58

Chapter 5 Offer and Counter-offer ··61
    Part A Situational Dialogue ···62
        Communicative Scene 1 ··62

	Communicative Scene 2	63
	Communicative Scene 3	64
Part B	Practical Key Sentences	67
Part C	Integration of Theory and Practice	69
Part D	Practice	71

Chapter 6 At China Import and Export Fair

Part A	Situational Dialogue	74
	Communicative Scene 1	74
	Communicative Scene 2	75
	Communicative Scene 3	76
Part B	Practical Key Sentences	79
Part C	Integration of Theory and Practice	80
Part D	Practice	82

Chapter 7 Business Visit

Part A	Situational Dialogue	86
	Communicative Scene 1	86
	Communicative Scene 2	87
	Communicative Scene 3	88
Part B	Practical Key Sentences	92
Part C	Integration of Theory and Practice	93
Part D	Practice	96

Chapter 8 Innovative and Power Brand Strategy

Part A	Situational Dialogue	100
	Communicative Scene 1	100
	Communicative Scene 2	101
	Communicative Scene 3	102
Part B	Practical Key Sentences	107
Part C	Integration of Theory and Practice	109
Part D	Practice	111

Chapter 9 Packing and Quality Inspection

Part A	Situational Dialogue	116
	Communicative Scene 1	116
	Communicative Scene 2	117
	Communicative Scene 3	118
Part B	Practical Key Sentences	121
Part C	Integration of Theory and Practice	123
Part D	Practice	125

Chapter 10 Acceptance and Orders

Part A	Situational Dialogue	130
	Communicative Scene 1	130

	Communicative Scene 2	131
	Communicative Scene 3	132
Part B	Practical Key Sentences	136
Part C	Integration of Theory and Practice	137
Part D	Practice	140

Chapter 11 Business Telephone Calls — 143

- Part A Situational Dialogue — 144
  - Communicative Scene 1 — 144
  - Communicative Scene 2 — 145
  - Communicative Scene 3 — 146
- Part B Practical Key Sentences — 148
- Part C Integration of Theory and Practice — 150
- Part D Practice — 152

Chapter 12 Terms of Payment — 155

- Part A Situational Dialogue — 156
  - Communicative Scene 1 — 156
  - Communicative Scene 2 — 157
  - Communicative Scene 3 — 158
- Part B Practical Key Sentences — 163
- Part C Integration of Theory and Practice — 165
- Part D Practice — 166

Chapter 13 Business Negotiation — 169

- Part A Situational Dialogue — 170
  - Communicative Scene 1 — 170
  - Communicative Scene 2 — 171
  - Communicative Scene 3 — 172
- Part B Practical Key Sentences — 176
- Part C Integration of Theory and Practice — 178
- Part D Practice — 180

Chapter 14 Sign a Contract — 185

- Part A Situational Dialogue — 186
  - Communicative Scene 1 — 186
  - Communicative Scene 2 — 187
  - Communicative Scene 3 — 188
- Part B Practical Key Sentences — 192
- Part C Integration of Theory and Practice — 193
- Part D Practice — 195

Chapter 15 Cargo Delivery — 199

- Part A Situational Dialogue — 200
  - Communicative Scene 1 — 200

Communicative Scene 2	201
Communicative Scene 3	201
Part B　Practical Key Sentences	205
Part C　Integration of Theory and Practice	206
Part D　Practice	209

Chapter 16　Business Conference　213

Part A　Situational Dialogue	214
Communicative Scene 1	214
Communicative Scene 2	215
Communicative Scene 3	216
Part B　Practical Key Sentences	221
Part C　Integration of Theory and Practice	222
Part D　Practice	225

Chapter 17　Sales Promotion　229

Part A　Situational Dialogue	230
Communicative Scene 1	230
Communicative Scene 2	231
Communicative Scene 3	233
Part B　Practical Key Sentences	237
Part C　Integration of Theory and Practice	239
Part D　Practice	240

Chapter 18　Interview　243

Part A　Situational Dialogue	244
Communicative Scene 1	244
Communicative Scene 2	244
Communicative Scene 3	245
Part B　Practical Key Sentences	249
Part C　Integration of Theory and Practice	251
Part D　Practice	254

Chapter 19　Complaints　257

Part A　Situational Dialogue	258
Communicative Scene 1	258
Communicative Scene 2	259
Communicative Scene 3	259
Communicative Scene 4	260
Part B　Practical Key Sentences	265
Part C　Integration of Theory and Practice	266
Part D　Practice	267

Chapter 20　Banquet and Parting　271

Part A　Situational Dialogue	272

　　　　Communicative Scene 1 ··272
　　　　Communicative Scene 2 ··274
　　　　Communicative Scene 3 ··274
Part B　Practical Key Sentences ··278
Part C　Integration of Theory and Practice ···279
Part D　Practice ··281

Chapter 1

Welcoming Clients

Learning Objectives
Upon completion of this chapter, you will be able to

- get familiar with the process of customs formality.
- welcome the guests at the airport.
- to introduce yourself and someone else politely.
- perform the functions of skills of communication.
- conduct the activities related to greetings and introductions.
- understand orienting yourselves to modernization, the world and the future.[1]

1　理解面向现代化、面向全世界、面向未来。

Part A Situational Dialogue

Communicative Scene 1

Going through Formalities (Going Abroad on Business)

(Mr. Peng is a manager of China Machinery Import & Export Company. He goes to the United States for the first time. Having claimed the luggage, he goes to the customs service desk.)

Officer: Good afternoon. May I have a look at your passport and customs declaration form?

Peng: Certainly. Here you are.

Officer: Thank you. And your health declaration form, please?

Peng: All right. Just a moment. Oh, here it is.

Officer: What nationality are you?

Peng: I am Chinese.

Officer: Would you mind telling me the purpose of your visit?

Peng: No, not at all. We are going to have business negotiations with some machinery companies. We are planning to import some equipment from your country.

Officer: I see. How long do you plan to stay in the United States?

Peng: Only a couple of weeks.

Officer: Is this all your baggage, sir?

Peng: That's right.

Officer: Have you anything particular to declare?

Peng: I suppose not, except a digital camera, some samples and personal effects. Are they duty free?

Officer: You needn't pay duty on samples and personal belongings.

Peng: I am taking USD 20,000 with me. Do I need to declare?

Officer: Yes. Please fill out this Currency Declaration Form.

Peng: OK. I'll do it.

Officer: Thank you.

Peng: <u>Is that all for customs formalities?</u>[1]

Officer: Yes, sir. You are through now. Go ahead. This way, please.

Peng: Thanks.

Chapter 1　Welcoming Clients

　Communicative Scene 2

Meeting at the Airport

(Sherry, the secretary of China Import and Export Corporation, is at the airport to meet Mr. Jones from Brazilian Company)

Sherry: Excuse me. Aren't you Mr. Jones from Brazilian Company?
Jones: Yes, you are right. I don't believe we've met before.
Sherry: No, I don't think so. Allow me to introduce myself to you. I am Sherry, the secretary of China Import and Export Corporation.
Jones: How nice to meet you!
Sherry: Glad to meet you too. Welcome to Beijing!
Jones: Thank you. It's my pleasure to have an opportunity to visit China again.
Sherry: Our CEO was planning to pick you up at the airport in person, but it is a pity that he is tied up in important business affairs today.
Jones: That's all right. I know he is somebody.²
Sherry: You may well say so. He has been very successful in his job. What is more, he is never flashy and he is really a team player, too.³
Jones: He is doing a great job for our business. I am dying to meet him.⁴
Sherry: How was the flight? You must be very tired after such a long travel.⁵
Jones: Oh, no, the flight was comfortable and I had a very pleasant journey. But I could not sleep on the plane. I am feeling a little jet lag now.
Sherry: Please take a good rest before we have a business negotiation.
Jones: Things couldn't be better.
Sherry: We have made a reservation at a very nice hotel near a beautiful lake. I hope you'll have a pleasant stay in Beijing.
Jones: It's very kind of you to do so.
Sherry: Let's go to the hotel, shall we?
Jones: Terrific.

　Communicative Scene 3

Introducing Each Other

(Zheng Dongxiao is meeting Milton Walter, the president of a multinational corporation. He also wants to make the acquaintance of marketing manager, Mr. Sam Auden.⁶)

Zheng: Good morning. If I'm not mistaken, you must be Mr. Walter, president of the multinational

3

corporation. May I take the liberty to introduce myself to you?⁷ My name is Zheng Dongxiao.

Walter: How do you do? I'm Milton Walter.

Zheng: How do you do? I have often heard about you. I've been looking forward to meeting you for a long time.

Walter: By the way, how to spell your name? It's hard for me to remember Chinese names.

Zheng: Z-h-e-n-g D-o-n-g-x-i-a-o. It's right here on my card. Here's my name card.

Walter: Good. I remember now. And here's mine.

Zheng: Thank you. Will you introduce me to your marketing manager over there?

Walter: Haven't you met yet?

Zheng: No, I don't think so.

Walter: I'm glad to introduce him to you.

Zheng: Yeah. Why not?

Walter: Sam, come and meet Dongxiao. This is Sam, my colleague.

Zheng: Hello, Mr. Sam Auden. It's a pleasure to finally meet you after so many e-mails, telephone calls and fax contacts.

Auden: Wow! In the flesh!⁸ It's good to meet you.

Zheng: Let me help you with the baggage.

Auden: Thank you so much.

Zheng: It's my pleasure. I'd like to make an arrangement for tomorrow.

Walter: Suppose we meet at 10 a.m. tomorrow.⁹

Zheng: Here is a copy of the agenda I have worked out for you and Mr. Auden. I hope it will meet your requirements.

Walter: Fine. I'll have a look at it in the hotel.

Zheng: It was nice meeting all of you.¹⁰ See you!

Walter: See you!

Words and Expressions

1. claim the luggage		领取行李
2. the customs service desk		海关服务台
3. declaration form		申报单
declare	v.	向海关申报进口应纳税物品
Currency Declaration Form		货币申报单
4. digital camera		数码相机
5. personal effects		个人用品
6. fill out		填写
7. CEO *abbr.* Chief Executive Officer		首席执行官，执行总裁
8. flashy	*adj.*	华而不实的，浮华的
9. be tied up		无法脱身，忙碌

10. terrific	*adj.*	好极了的
11. jet lag		飞行时差反应
12. reserve	*v.*	预定，make a reservation 预定
13. meet the requirements of		满足要求
14. have a business negotiation		商务谈判，商洽
15. a multinational corporation		跨国公司
16. agenda/agendas	*n.*	议事日程（复数形式）
agendum	*n.*	议事日程（单数形式）
17. work out		制定，制订

Notes

1. Is that all for customs formalities?
    海关手续办完了吗？
    ① go through formalities 办理手续
    ② customs formality and requirement 报关手续和规定
    ③ export formality 出口手续
    ④ transit formality 过境手续
    You are through now. 您的手续办好了。

2. He is somebody.
    他可是个人物。
    ① somebody 有影响力的重要人物
    ② VIP即very important person 贵宾或重要人物
    ③ nobody 平庸之辈

3. He is really a team player.
    他确实是个容易合作的人。

4. I am dying to meet him.
    很久以来一直期望与他相见。
    be dying for 非常渴望
    例句：
        People around the world are dying for a complete success of Beijing 2022 Winter Olympic Games.
        世界人民期盼着北京2022年冬季奥运会的圆满成功。
        We are dying for the good cooperation with multinational companies.
        我方非常渴望与跨国公司的良好合作。

5. You must be very tired after such a long travel.
    长途旅行后您一定很累了。
    must 此处表示肯定的猜测，必定、非常可能发生，表示逻辑推断的可能性和必然性。
    例句：
        You must be Mr. Walter.

您一定是沃尔特先生吧。

If the light was on, Dr. Bailey must have been in the office.

如果灯亮着,贝利博士一定在办公室。

表示否定用can not be,而could not have done 表示对过去否定的猜测。

6. He also wants to make the acquaintance of marketing manager, Mr. Sam Auden.

他还想结识公司的营销部经理山姆·奥登先生。

① make the acquaintance of sb. 结识某人

② make sb.'s acquaintance 结识某人

③ pick acquaintance with 偶然结识

④ have no acquaintance with 不熟悉,不了解

⑤ have a nodding acquaintance with sb./ the subjects 与某人有点头之交/对某学科略知一二

7. May I take the liberty to introduce myself to you?

我可以冒昧地自我介绍吗?

① liberty *n*. 冒昧,自由

② take the liberty to do sth. / take the liberty of doing sth. 冒昧行事

例句:

May we take the liberty of asking you to make out the business negotiation agenda?

我们可以冒昧地请您制订谈判的议事日程吗?

8. Wow! In the flesh!

啊!终于见到真人了!

① in flesh 肥胖的

② in the flesh (习惯用语)活生生的,亲自

例句:

Wow! In the flesh! You know she has not shut up about you ... you did something to impress her.

哇,终于见到真人了!她总是谈到你……她对你的印象很好。

9. Suppose we'll meet at 10 a.m. tomorrow.

我建议明天上午十点相会。

suppose常用祈使语气表示:让我建议……

例句:

Suppose we make an investment plan together.

我建议我们一起制订投资计划。

10. It was nice meeting all of you.

很高兴认识你们!(通常在临别时用)

而在见面介绍时通常用:

It is nice to meet you.

很高兴认识您!

Chapter 1 Welcoming Clients

Part B Practical Key Sentences

1. **request the guests to show something**

    May I see your passport and customs declaration form?
    请您出示护照和报关申请表。
    Certainly, here you are.
    当然可以，给您。
    替换表达：
    Show me your passport, please.
    Here it is.
    Passport and declaration, please.
    Certainly.
    Would you show me your documents, please?
    Sure.

2. **introduce oneself**

    May I take the liberty to introduce myself to you? I am ... (Formal usage)
    我可以冒昧地自我介绍吗？我是……
    替换表达：
    Allow me to introduce myself to you. My name is ... (Formal usage)
    May I introduce myself to you? I am ... (Basic usage)
    Hello! I am Peter. (Informal usage)
    Let me introduce myself to you. (Basic usage)

3. **introduce others**

    Sam, come and meet Dongxiao. This is Sam, my colleague.
    山姆，来见见东晓。这位是山姆，我的同事。(Informal usage)
    替换表达：
    I'd like you to meet our manager. (Basic usage)
    Hello, this is Mr. Forest. (Informal usage)
    I'd like to introduce our manager to you. (Formal usage)
    Please let me introduce Mr. James to you. (Formal usage)
    Allow me to present my colleague to you. (Formal usage)
    I am honored to introduce... (Formal usage)
    It is with great pleasure to present Mr. Brown, our CEO. (Formal usage)

4. **respond to an introduction**

    How do you do? 您好！（初次见面招呼用语）
    How do you do? 您好！（回应用语）
    替换表达：
    How nice to meet you.

Glad to meet you.

It's good to meet you, too. (Basic usage)

It's a pleasure to know you.

Pleased to meet you.

I am happy to have the opportunity to meet you. (Formal usage)

I am delighted to make your acquaintance. (Formal usage)

5. **get acquainted**

Have you met before?

你们见过面吗？（介绍别人相识）

No, I don't think we have.

不，我想没有。

Yes, I think so.

是的，我们见过面。（此表达比No, I don't. 或 Yes, I do. 更委婉）

替换表达：

Do you know each other?

Have we been introduced? (basic usage)

Your name, please?

May I have your name, please?

Haven't you met before?

Yes, I think we have, haven't we?

I think I have seen you somewhere. You look familiar.

Part C Integration of Theory and Practice

【知识点】介绍是国际贸易中一个非常重要的环节，是商务交际之桥。介绍缩短了人际交流间的距离。得体的介绍将引导和缓和业务伙伴之间的沟通，塑造良好的第一印象，从而促进交易的成功。

1. **first impression 第一印象**

【知识点】在商务活动中，第一印象的好坏关系到未来业务的开展。恰当得体的介绍将给贸易伙伴留下美好印象，主动自我介绍是自信的表现。不断认识新的贸易客户，良好的第一印象和介绍会给客户留下宝贵的形象，有利于开创新的贸易商机。

【技能训练句型】

Allow me to introduce myself to you. My name is ...

请允许我自我介绍，我叫……

May I take the liberty to introduce myself to you?

我可以冒昧地自我介绍吗？

2. **order of introduction 介绍顺序**

【知识点】介绍别人时，介绍顺序应遵循的原则是尊者居后。有礼貌的介绍顺序是，把主人介绍给客人，将男士介绍给女士，把年轻人介绍给长者，把职位低者介绍给职务高者。

【技能训练句型】

Miss Taylor, may I introduce my friend Mr. Lee to you?

泰勒小姐，我能否向您介绍我的朋友李先生？

在商务活动中应先将职务低的人介绍给职务高的人。例如：

Mr. President, I'm glad to introduce her to you.

总裁先生，我很高兴将她介绍给您。

3. order of introduction for group people　集体相见介绍顺序

【知识点】在商务活动中，双方公司成员集体相见介绍时，先介绍主方成员，之后客方作介绍。顺序以职位高为先。

【技能训练句型】

Hosting side: Song Dalian, Design Manager; Wang Ming, President of ABC Computer Company; Ma Yuelin, Design Engineer（主方：宋大连，设计部经理；王明，ABC计算机公司总裁；马越林，设计工程师）

Introduce hosting side first to the visiting side（向客方介绍主方）：

This is Wang Ming, President of ABC Computer Company, and this is Song Dalian, Design Manager, and this is Ma Yuelin, Design Engineer. He has been very successful in his job.

这位是王明，ABC计算机公司总裁；这位是宋大连，设计部经理；这位是马越林，设计工程师，他的工作做得非常出色。

Then the visiting side will do the self-introduction to the hosting side in turn.（客方一一作自我介绍）

4. welcome new clients　迎接新客户

【知识点】迎接新客户时，迎宾人员通常在迎宾处高举写着公司名称和客户姓名的牌子，如看到有人像是要迎接的客户，可向前询问并加以确认。

【技能训练句型】

If I'm not mistaken, you must be Mr. Walter from artificial intelligence company.

如果我没搞错的话，您一定是来自人工智能公司的沃尔特先生吧。

Excuse me. Aren't you Mr. Jones from Brazilian Company?

请问，您是来自巴西公司的琼斯先生吗？

You are Milton Walter, president of the company, aren't you?

您是公司总裁密尔顿·沃尔特，对吗？

5. introduction　引见

【知识点】在商务活动中，要积极主动地认识新客户和商务界人士，为避免唐突，不妨请客户帮助介绍。

【技能训练句型】

Will you introduce me to your marketing manager over there?

请替我引见那位营销部经理好吗？

I would like to meet Chairman of Council for the Promotion of International Trade.

我想结识一下国际贸易促进委员会的会长。

6. express the willingness of getting acquainted　表达想结识的意愿

【知识点】表达想结识的意愿，可增进亲切友好的感觉，自然地缩小与客户的距离，有助于开展业务。

【技能训练句型】

I've heard a lot /so much about you.
久仰大名。

I have often heard of you.
久闻大名。

He always talks about you.
他常提及您。

I've been looking forward to meeting you for a long time.
久仰。

Your company is very reputed. I heard many praises for it.
贵公司信誉很好，我久仰大名。

I am dying to meet him.
我真想见到他。

It's nice to finally meet you.
终于见面了！见到您真好。

7. remember other's names　听清并记住对方的姓名

【知识点】被介绍人要听清并记住对方的姓名，否则叫错客户姓名，有失礼仪。若未听清楚，可马上请求对方再说一遍。

【技能训练句型】

I beg your pardon. What is your name again?
请再说一遍。

如对方的姓名很长而且难记，可询问拼写方法。例如：

By the way, how do you spell your name? It's hard for me to remember Chinese names.
顺便问一下，如何拼读你的名字？对我来说很难记住中国人的姓名。

8. popular greeting　地道流行的招呼语

【知识点】熟人见面打招呼问好，如果只会用在以往教科书中最常用的How are you? I am fine. Thank you. And you? 显然过时了。

当今美语流行How are you doing?（近来好吗？）

【技能训练句型】

回答可根据实际情况用：

I am doing good. 或I am pretty good.
我很好。

Not so good.
不怎样。

Uh, nothing much.
哦，老样子。

英美国家人士还常喜欢用：

What's up? (Informal usage)

嗨，怎么样？

How's everything?

一切都好？

What's new?

有什么新鲜事？

What's happening?

在忙什么？

How is it going?

近来好吗？

Part D Practice

I. Complete the Following Dialogues

(1)

Zhang: May I introduce ____1____ to you? My name is Zhang Hua.

George: Glad to meet you. I am George. How do you ____2____ your name? It is difficult for me to remember Chinese ____3____.

Zhang: Z-h-a-n-g H-u-a. Here's my name ____4____.

George: Good. I ____5____ now. Here is my card. By the way, do you know Zhang Ziyi?

Zhang: Yes, I know a lot about her. Why do you ____6____?

George: That is impossible. You are kidding, I am afraid. Do you ____7____ know her?

Zhang: Certainly. Zhang Ziyi is a famous film star.

George: How do you know her? Can you ____8____ her to me?

Zhang: Oh, I realize that I ____9____ a mistake. Just now my answer to your question means "Do you ____10____ who Zhang Ziyi is?"

(2)

A: Excuse me. ____1____ and your vaccination certificate, please?

B: Yeah, here is my passport. But what do you mean ____2____ vaccination certificate?

A: Vaccination certificate ____3____ the report of health condition.

B: I see. Oh, here ____4____ is.

A: Is this all your baggage, Sir?

B: That's right.

A: Do you have anything to ____5____?

B: No, Sir. I am just bringing in personal ____6____ and some fruits.

A: Sorry, rotten fruit is not allowed to bring ____7____.

B: But it is not rotten. Would you ___8___ allow me to bring in Lichi? It is my wife's favorite ___9___.

A: I am afraid not. Perishables are ___10___, too.

B: Oh, my poor wife!

II. Interaction Activities

Task 1

The teacher divides students into groups. Each group is suggested to be 5 students. Students make dialogues and role-play them.

Introduce the delegation to the hosts according to the following hints. Give the title of each person and make a brief introduction. Try to use the introductory phrases in the unit and respond to the introduction. The words or phrases suggested below might be helpful.

(1) Mr. Steve Singer, Sunshine Group Ltd.
(2) Mr. Robinson, Chief Executive Officer, a somebody
(3) Mr. Bright, export manager, a team player
(4) Miss Howard, attractive, smile
(5) Ms Morley, secretary, kind-hearted

Task 2

Short conversations.

(1)

Suppose you meet your client whom you have never met before at the airport. Introduce each other, express your welcome on behalf of your company and leave a good impression on the client.

(2)

Meet your old clients with an informal greeting.

III. Actual Practice

Work in pairs.

Use the business card to practice the following situation with your partner.

> Fruits & Vegetable Corp.
> Henry Brown
> Managing Director
> 10 Hero Street, Toronto, Canada
> Tel: (416)480-480
> Fax: (416)480-481

(1) Introducing yourself to Jake Tompkins

(2) Greeting

(3) Exchanging business cards

(4) Exchanging information about the company

IV. Creative Discussion

The teacher divides the class into groups and asks them to discuss, then choose the representatives of each group after discussion. The student who expresses well will be the winner.

Topic:

It is said that the first impression is very important, especially in business activity. What do you think of the first impression? Do you think it does matter? Please discuss with your partners about how to create a good impression on the customers that you first meet.

Chapter 2

Seeking Business Opportunities

Learning Objectives
Upon completion of this chapter, you will be able to

- [x] get to know the channels through which importers and exporters establish business relations.
- [x] learn the ways to get ready for getting into business relations.
- [x] acquire the skills of communication.
- [x] conduct the activities related to seeking business opportunities.
- [x] understand promoting the Belt and Road Initiative.[1]

---

1 理解推进一带一路建设。

Part A Situational Dialogue

Tips for Seeking Business Opportunities

(*Miss Fan Xin has just graduated from the university. She works in China Tea Export Corporation and is desirous of starting business. She is asking Liu Tao, a veteran businessman for some advice.*)

Liu: Fan Xin, you seem troubled. Is anything the matter?

Fan: Oh, Mr. Liu. I'd like to ask you some questions.

Liu: Yes, go ahead.[1]

Fan: You see, I'm really green.[2] I lack experience here. I wonder if you could give me some advice about how to seek business opportunities.

Liu: By all means,[3] there are tricks in every trade.[4]

Fan: I am eager to learn.[5]

Liu: Since we entered into the 21st century, great changes have taken place in the way of doing business. We may establish business relations with companies thousands of miles away through many channels.

Fan: It sounds interesting.

Liu: I'd like to introduce to you some main channels. From my point of view, nowadays the most effective way to find clients is surfing the Internet. Its advantage is fast and inexpensive. You may make a search on the web for prospective clients.

Fan: It is a good idea. It's a pity that I haven't learnt much about it in the classroom.

Liu: E-commerce plays an important part in modern business. It is easier and time-saving to find potential customers from the Internet. We needn't travel here and there to find customers and we still know a lot.

Fan: Oh, I can't wait to try it.

Liu: A Chamber of Commerce is an important channel to get the information and contact businessmen.

Fan: What is Chamber of Commerce?

Liu: Chamber of Commerce is an organization of businessmen. One of the main tasks for this organization is to help the companies or members get the business information and seek opportunities.

Fan: I remember now. Anything more?

Liu: Looking up in the *Trade Directory* is helpful, too.

Chapter 2 Seeking Business Opportunities

Fan: What shall I do?

Liu: You will find companies by checking the specific categories. Then you'll get the name, address and telephone number of the desired companies.

Fan: I learned from a textbook that banks usually supply the names and addresses of companies for businessmen.

Liu: Actually, it's not always the case. <u>Banks help companies for credit investigation, but they should keep the information of customers confidential, too.</u>[6] As a matter of fact, you can't rely on their finding clients for you in the foreign trade now.

Fan: Oh, really?

Liu: Some points in the trade books published long time ago may be out of date. You should be careful when you read and don't follow the old idea.

Fan: <u>You said it.</u>[7]

Liu: Necessary information can be obtained from <u>Commercial Counselor's Office stationed abroad</u>[8] and advertisement in the newspapers and magazines. Going to business fairs may be a good way to get in touch with customers but the cost is too high.

Fan: Um, I see your point.

Liu: After you get the desired names and addresses, you may begin to send e-mail, fax or telephone to start business.

Fan: Oh, yes.

Liu: Thanks to the development of the means of communication we no longer need to go to post office to send telegram or telex.

Fan: Yeah, the modern development ends its function.

Liu: Nowadays the most common and quickest way of communication is by sending e-mail, fax and telephone call.

Fan: True enough.

Liu: We can get in touch with whomever we want within seconds by using the Internet and computer.

Fan: It seems that we can probably make sure of business in the office. I am confident to start the business now.

Communicative Scene 2

Contact the Client

(Miss Fan Xin is contacting a foreign company for business opportunities.)

Fan: Hello, May I speak to the import manager?

Rance: <u>This is Mr. Rance of the Import Department. Who is it, please?</u>[9]

Fan: This is Fan Xin of China Tea Export Corporation.

Rance: What can I do for you?

Fan: I have come to know your company by making a search on the Internet. Your website shows that you are one of the leading importers of tea business in the European market. <u>I am glad to introduce my corporation to you as a professional one, specializing in the line of tea products.</u>[10]

Rance: Oh, I am interested. Would you tell me more about your business scope?

Fan: Certainly, we are exporters of high reputation, trading in various kinds of Black Tea, White Tea, Green Tea, Oolong Tea and Jasmine Tea. We have been in this line of business for more than fifty years.

Rance: Nice to hear that. How about the quality of tea?

Fan: <u>You may rest assured.</u>[11] Our tea products are very popular for their superb quality. We have our own processing factory and a lot of experienced technicians. Our Grade-A Jasmine Tea has won international high quality medals.

Rance: That's very inspiring. <u>So far the teabags cater to modern consumption habit.</u>[12] Can you supply them?

Fan: Yes, we are going all out to exploit new markets and push our new products. We are producing teabags in order to meet the need of world market.

Rance: What a coincidence! It seems to be what we are looking for.

Fan: We are also producing ice tea and Oolong liquor. They gain the character of quick and convenient drinking.

Rance: Fine. It would be very helpful if you could send us your catalogues or brochures for our further study.

Fan: <u>In order to let you have a general idea of all our products, I am going to send you our latest illustrated catalogue by EMS for your perusal.</u>[13]

Rance: Please send some samples of your teabags and new tea products.

Fan: No problem.

Rance: We'll let you know the result as soon as we have studied them.

Fan: I am looking forward to your favorable news soon.

Communicative Scene 3

Establish Business Relations

(Mr. Rance is contacting Miss Fan Xin for establishing business relations.)

Rance: Hello, Miss Fan. This is Rance speaking.

Fan: Oh, hi, Mr. Rance.

Rance: We have got your pamphlet, samples of your teabags and new tea products sent by express mail.

Fan: What do you think of our items?

Rance: After careful examination, we find that your tea is excellent in quality and beautifully packed as you described in the last talk.

Fan: Exactly. We always adhere to the principle of keeping the promise and honoring the contract.

Rance: <u>We made a market research on your teabags and new tea products and find there is a ready market for them.</u>[14]

Fan: It's quite good.

Rance: As your tea products fall within the range of our business activities, we would like to express our wish to set up trade relations with your corporation.

Fan: <u>Your desire to establish business relations coincides with ours.</u>[15] Building up direct business relations between our companies will be to our mutual benefit.

Rance: I have no doubt that it will bring about closer ties between our two companies.

Fan: It is our policy to trade with businessmen all over the world on the basis of equality and mutual benefit.

Rance: I know what you mean. We are considering expanding our business with you.

Fan: I'd be so pleased if you would.

Rance: Oh, yes. <u>We are prepared to trade with you in this line.</u>[16]

Fan: Sounds great!

Rance: I think I'll discuss with you more details about our business by e-mail.

Fan: I am for you. Our mutual understanding and cooperation will certainly result in more business.

Rance: Good-bye.

Fan: Bye.

Words and Expressions

1. lack of experience		缺乏经验，不熟练
lack	n.	常与 of 连用，表示缺乏，也可作动词
2. veteran	n.	老手，经验丰富的人
	adj.	经验丰富的，熟练的
3. trick	n.	诀窍，窍门，诡计
	v.	欺骗
4. from my point of view		依我的观点看来
5. effective	adj.	有效的，生效的，显著的
6. client	n.	客户，顾客
prospective clients		预期的客户
potential customers		潜在的客户
7. surf the Internet		网络搜索
8. prospective	adj.	预期的，未来的
9. Trade Directory		同业名录，行名录

10. specific categories		具体的行业分类
11. credit investigation		资信调查
12. as a matter of fact		实际上
13. professional	*adj.*	专业的，职业的
	n.	专业人员
14. telegram	*n.*	cable电报
15. telex	*n.*	电传
16. cater	*v.*	迎合，满足需要
17. go all out		全力以赴
18. Oolong Tea		乌龙茶
Oolong liquor		乌龙浓缩液
19. Jasminc Tea		茉莉花茶
20. superb	*adj.*	极好的，超等的
21. processing	*n.*	加工，处理
22. exploit	*v.*	开发，开拓
23. push out		推出，使突出
24. gain the character of		博得……名声
25. catalogue	*n.*	目录
26. brochure	*n.*	小册子（常包括推销材料或产品信息）
27. pamphlet	*n.*	小册子，手册
28. sample	*n.*	样品
29. bring about		使发生，致使，造成

Notes

1. **go ahead**

① 可以，干吧，表示毫不犹豫地开始做某事。

例句：

I'd like to ask you some questions.

我想问你几个问题。

Yes, go ahead.

请说吧。

② 常单独用于口语。当某人讲话欲言又止时，可用来催促大胆地说。

例句：

Go ahead and tell us what you want.

大胆说，告诉我们你要什么。

③ 前进，走在前面

例句：

Go ahead. This way, please.

请往前走，这边请。
另外还有press ahead 继续前进
例句：
> We sweated and we toiled as we pressed ahead with concrete efforts for achievements.
> 我们用汗水浇灌收获，以实干笃定前行。

2. I'm really green.
   我是新手。
   green 除众所周知绿色的意思之外，还有未成熟的、无经验的含义。
   green hand 新手，刚入门某一行的人被称为green hand.

3. by all means
   ① 当然可以
   ② 一定，务必
   相似的词组：
   by means of 借助于
   by any means 用一切手段和办法
   by some means 通过某种办法
   by this means 用这种办法
   by no means 决不
   not by any means 绝对不
   by what means 怎样

4. There are tricks in every trade.
   行行都有诀窍。
   trick 诀窍，窍门，诡计

5. I am eager to learn.
   我渴望着学会。
   相似的词组：
   be eager for success
   be eager about one's progress

6. Banks help companies for credit investigation, but they should keep the information of customers confidential，too.
   银行帮助公司进行资信调查，但应该对客户的信息保密。
   ① keep confidential, be confidential, in confidence 保密
   例句：
   > Any information that you supplied to us would be held in strict confidence.
   > 您为我们提供的任何信息都将严格保密。
   ② confident adj. 有信心的
   例句：
   > I am confident to start the business now.
   > 我现在对开展贸易充满了信心。

We are making confident strides on the path toward the great rejuvenation of the Chinese nation.

我们正昂首阔步行进在实现中华民族伟大复兴的道路上。

7. You said it.

   说得是！（表示随声附和。）

8. Commercial Counselor's Office stationed abroad

   驻外使馆商务处

9. This is Mr. Rance of Import Department. Who is it, please?

   我是进口部的兰斯，请问谁找我？

   中文里一般不自称我是某先生。用英语自我介绍时，在名字前冠以Mr., Mrs., Miss 等称呼，便于辨别性别或身份。

10. I am glad to introduce my corporation to you as a professional one, specializing in the line of tea products.

    我很高兴地向您介绍本公司，我们是专业从事茶叶产品生产和出口的公司。

    specializing in 是现在分词短语作定语，修饰a professional one，specializing 与in搭配表示专营某产品。

11. You may rest assured.

    您尽可放心。

    assured *adj.* 放心的，确信的

    例句：

    You can rest assured that our business relationship will be expanded continuously.

    您尽可放心，我们的业务关系将不断扩展。

12. So far the teabags cater to modern consumption habit.

    目前袋泡茶很适应现代消费的习惯。

    cater to/for 迎合,投合

    例句：

    The producers are catering to the taste of consumers.

    生产者正设法迎合消费者需求。

13. In order to let you have a general idea of all our products, I am going to send you our latest illustrated catalogue by EMS for your perusal.

    为了让贵方对我方的产品有个大概的了解，特打算寄上我方最新附图目录，以供细阅。

    have a general idea 有个大概的了解

14. We made a market research on your teabags and new tea products and find there is a ready market for them.

    我方就贵方的袋泡茶和茶叶新产品做了市场调查，发现很受市场欢迎。

    ① make a market research 开展市场调查

    ② There is a ready market. 很受市场欢迎。

15. Your desire to establish business relations coincides with ours.

    贵公司同我方建立业务关系的愿望与我们是一致的。

    ① coincide with 一致，完全相应，相符

    例句：

What he said coincided with the facts.

他所说的事情与事实相符合。

② coincidence *n.* 巧合，同时发生，一致

例句：

What a coincidence! 真巧！

16. We are prepared to trade with you in this line.

我方愿意在这行业与贵司开展业务。

be prepared to 表示愿意并且能够做好

例句：

We are prepared to set up business relations with your company.

我方愿意与贵司建立业务关系。

*17. be desirous of

渴望的

例句：

Many clients are desirous of establishing business relationship with you.

许多客户渴望与贵方建立业务关系。

相似的词组：

① be desirous to do sth.

② be desirous that...

*18. EMS *abbr.* Express Mail Service 邮政特快专递

世界四大著名快递公司：DHL敦豪速递；Fedex（Federal Express）联邦快递；TNT（TNT Express）TNT快递；UPS（Universal Postal Service）联合包裹服务

① illustrated catalogue 附图目录

② for your perusal 供细阅

Part B Practical Key Sentences

1. **asking for advice**

I wonder if you could give me some advice about how to seek business opportunities.

您可否告诉我如何寻找贸易机会？

替换表达：

I was wondering if you could possibly give me some ideas.

Do you have any suggestions?

Would you recommend me whether it is a good way to make a business contact?

I hope you don't mind my asking your opinion.

I need your good suggestions.

What do you reckon I should do next?

What is your view about seeking business opportunities?

Would you be so kind as to give us some advice?

2. giving suggestions

From my point of view, nowadays the most effective way to find more clients is surfing the Internet.
依我看来，当今寻找更多客户最有效的方法是通过网络查寻。

替换表达：

Looking up in the Trade Directory is helpful too.

I advise you strongly to find companies by checking the specific categories.

I'd like to suggest that you make a market research.

If I were you, I would send a fax instead of telephone call.

Perhaps you'd better make a search on the net for prospective clients.

Why not adhere to the principle of keeping the promise and honoring the contract?

3. agreement

（1）entire agreement

True enough. 太对了。

替换表达：

It is a good idea.

I am for you.

You said it.

It's quite good.

That's quite true.

What you said is true.

You are right.

I couldn't agree more!

（2）partial agreement

I know what you mean but I need your samples right now.
我明白您的意思，但我急需您的样品。

替换表达：

I more or less agree with you.

I agree with much of your idea but ...

I don't entirely agree with you.

To a certain degree, yes, but ...

4. communicating with businessmen

We can get in touch with whoever we want within seconds by using the Internet and computers.
我们可以通过国际互联网和电脑在片刻间与任何人联系。

替换表达：

Miss Fan Xin is contacting a foreign company for business opportunities.

Mr. Robinson communicates with his new business partner by e-mail.

I'll convey my manager's intention of establishing business relations to him.

Would you connect me with the Marketing Department for Mr. Robert?

5. line of business

We are exporters of high reputation, trading in various kinds of Black Tea, White Tea, Green Tea, Oolong Tea and Jasmine Tea. We have been in this line of business for more than 50 years.

我们的公司是信誉卓越的出口企业，经营各种各样的红茶、白茶、绿茶、乌龙茶和茉莉花茶。公司在此行业已有50多年的经营历史。

We are prepared to trade with you in this line.

我方愿意在这行业与贵司开展业务。

替换表达：

> As the item falls within the line of our business, we shall like to enter into business relations with your firm.
>
> Our range of business coincided with yours.
>
> We have learnt that you are the exporter of Chinese Tea, which comes within the frame of our business scope.

Part C Integration of Theory and Practice

【知识点】商务人员可以通过许多渠道寻找贸易机会，一般是通过网络、商会、通讯录、跨境电商平台、驻外使馆商务处、报纸杂志的广告、朋友或公司介绍等途径获得必要的信息；介绍自己公司的情况，了解对方，发现彼此间的共同点；参加交易会则可能有机会与客户直接会面。

1. the channel to get acquainted   告知认识对方的渠道

【知识点】初次与新客户联系，为了避免唐突，应告知对方自己是通过何种方式知道对方的，尽可能给对方留下一个较好的印象。

【技能训练句型】

(1) by making a search on Internet

I have come to know your company by making a search on Internet. Your website shows that you are one of the leading importers of tea business in European market.

通过国际互联网搜索，我结识了贵公司。您的网站显示贵公司是欧洲市场主要的茶叶进口商之一。

(2) by looking up in the Trade Directory

We have obtained your name and address by looking up in the Trade Directory.

我们是通过查看商业名录获知贵方的姓名与地址。

(3) through the courtesy of Chamber of Commerce

Through the courtesy of Chamber of Commerce, we have learnt your corporation.

承蒙商会的介绍，获悉了贵公司。

(4) by Commercial Counselor's Office

Your company has been recommended from the Commercial Counselor's Office of the Chinese

Embassy in Singapore.

中国驻新加坡大使馆的商务处向我方推荐了贵公司。

(5) by ads in the newspapers and magazines

Having had your name and address from ads in the newspapers and magazines, we avail ourselves of the opportunity to contact you.

从报纸杂志的广告得知你们的名字和地址,借此机会与贵方联系。

(6) by the introduction of friends or companies

Your name and address have been kindly introduced to us by Mr. Cade.

承蒙凯德先生的介绍,我们得知贵公司的名称和地址。

(7) by Cross-Border Electronic Commerce platforms

Foreign consumers often buy Chinese merchandise from Alibaba's, Amazon and Ebay's platforms.

外国消费者常通过阿里巴巴、亚马逊、易趣等跨境电商平台购买中国产品。

Founded in 2004, Dunhuang is a leading B2B cross-border e-commerce trading service platform in China.

敦煌网成立于2004年,是中国领先的B2B跨境电商交易服务平台。

2. introducing company and business scope 介绍公司的经营情况和经营范围

【知识点】公司双方了解彼此的经营情况、经营能力和资信状况以及产品情况后,再进行实质性业务探讨。

【技能训练句型】

I am glad to introduce my corporation to you as a professional one, specializing in the line of tea products.

我很高兴地向您介绍本公司是专门从事茶叶产品生产和出口的专业公司。

We are exporters of high reputation, trading in various kinds of Black Tea, White Tea, Green Tea, Oolong Tea and Jasmine Tea. We have been in this line of business for more than 50 years.

我们的公司是信誉卓越的出口企业,经营各种各样的红茶、白茶、绿茶、乌龙茶和茉莉花茶。公司在此行业已有50多年的经营历史。

Our tea products are very popular for their superb quality. Our Grade-A Jasmine Tea has won international high quality medals.

我方经营的茶叶以其优异的品质深受广大消费者的喜爱。我方的一级茉莉花茶荣获国际优质奖。

3. establishing trade relations 建立业务关系

【知识点】在相互了解的基础上,公司双方的经营范围一致,可以确定贸易对象,建立业务关系。建立业务关系可促进双方密切合作,顺利进行交易。

【技能训练句型】

As your tea products fall within the range of our business activities, we would like to express our wish to set up trade relations with your corporation.

由于贵方的茶叶产品与我方的经营范围一致,我们愿意同贵公司建立业务关系。

Your desire to establish business relations coincides with ours. Building up direct business relations between our companies will be to our mutual benefit.

你方想同我方建立业务关系的愿望与我方是一致的。建立直接的业务关系，双方将互利互惠。

We are willing to establish direct business relationship with your company on the basis of equality and mutual benefit.

我们愿在平等互利的基础上与贵公司建立直接的业务关系。

We shall be pleased to enter into business relations with you.

我们很乐意同贵公司建立业务关系。

4. sending catalogues and samples 寄产品目录和样品等

【知识点】为了进一步了解对方经营的产品具体品种，需要对方提供附图目录等材料，寻找合适的品种、型号或规格。如对方有展示介绍产品的网站，可要求其提供网址，可免去邮寄。如光看图片不能了解产品的品质，还需邮寄样品。

【技能训练句型】

In order to let you have a general idea of all our products, I am going to send you by air our latest catalogue for your perusal.

为了让贵方对我方的产品有个大概的认识，特打算航空邮寄我方最新附图目录，以供细阅。

Please send some samples of your teabags and new tea products.

请寄一些袋泡茶和茶叶新产品的样品。

It would be very helpful if you could send us your catalogue or brochures and give us your website for our further study.

如果你能寄给我们产品目录或小册子并提供网址供我们进一步研究将很有帮助。

5. expressing wishes 表达愿望

【知识点】在信件最后，表达对今后贸易的希望和期待。

【技能训练句型】

Our mutual understanding and cooperation will certainly result in more business.

我们之间的相互了解与合作必将促成今后的生意。

We look forward to trading with you and exchange of needed goods.

希望与贵方开展贸易，互通有无。

Part D Practice

I. Complete the Following Dialogues

A: Good afternoon. Import Department. Can I help you?

B: Hello, Can I ____1____ to Mr. Smith?

A: This is ____2____. Who is calling?

B: This is Pan Guoqiang speaking. We have obtained your name and address by ____3____ up in the Trade Directory.

A: Oh, hello. May I ask you what ____4____ of business you are ____5____?

B: I am glad to introduce my company to you as a ___6___ one, ___7___ in glass products. Our main ___8___ are constructive glass and pile glassware.

A: Oh, I think some of them will be of ___9___ to us.

B: Great! As your glass products ___10___ within the range of our business activities, we are ___11___ to establish ___12___ business relationship with your esteemed company on the ___13___ of equality and mutual benefit.

A: That's a good ___14___. We always ___15___ to the principle of keeping the promise and honoring the contract.

II. Interaction Activities

Divide students into pairs. Students make short dialogues and role-play them.

Task 1

Asking for advice on how to communicate with businessmen.

Ask for and get the advice from your partner politely and express your agreement or partial agreement. Use the following expressions:

(1) I hope you don't mind...

(2) Could you give me some advice about...

(3) Get in touch

(4) From my point of view...

(5) To a certain degree, yes, but...

(6) I know what you mean but...

(7) What is your view about...

(8) If I were you...

(9) That's quite true.

Task 2

Talking about how to ask for sending samples politely.

Ask for and get the advice from your partner and express your agreement or partial agreement. Use the following expressions:

(1) I need...

(2) What's your opinion about...

(3) Don't hesitate to...

(4) I agree with much of your idea but...

(5) Ask for samples

(6) True enough.

(7) What do you reckon I...?

(8) I'd like to suggest that...

(9) I don't entirely agree with you but...

III. Actual Practice

Work in pairs and role-play the conversation.

You work in a trade company. You are contacting the exporter in order to seek business opportunities.

By what means can you successfully establish business relations?

Use the hints below to practice with your partner:

(1) Inform the seller how you get to know the firm.

(2) Tell your intention.

(3) Tell the line of your business.

(4) Get some more information from prospective client.

(5) Express the desire to establish business relationship.

(6) Ask for catalogues and samples.

IV. Creative Discussion

The teacher divides the class into groups, and the students make a discussion with their partners and share their opinions with other groups.

Topic:

Suppose you are working in an export department. You and your colleagues are desirous of seeking new business opportunities.

There are many channels to find the business opportunities. Discuss which one you prefer and show the reasons. If possible, discuss the advantages and disadvantages of each channel.

V. Debate

The students are expected to give their own opinions freely on the following topic.

Topic:

Which channel is the best to find potential clients?

Chapter 3
Making Inquiries

Learning Objectives
Upon completion of this chapter, you will be able to

- understand that inquiries are made to seek the supply of products, services and information.
- learn the ways of making general inquiries and specific inquiries.
- acquire the skills of making inquiries.
- conduct the activities related to making inquiries.
- understand contemporary China.[1]

---

1 了解当代中国。

Part A Situational Dialogue

Communicative Scene 1

Making General Inquiries

(Mrs. Hanna, the Import Manager of Robinson Textiles Import Company, is making a general inquiry with Textiles Limited Corporation.)

Hanna: Good afternoon. Is this Textiles Limited Corporation?

Xue: Yes, it is. May I help you?

Hanna: This is Anna Hanna from Robinson Textiles Import Company. We have seen your advertisement in *China Daily*. Your textile products in the advertisement look really marvelous.

Xue: Oh, really?

Hanna: We are importers of fabrics. We have made a market research and found a promising market in our country for the textiles you listed in your advertisement.[1] So we are considering to broaden our business in Chinese market.[2]

Xue: Um. What a great idea! May I ask what kinds of products you are interested in?

Hanna: We are interested in the piece goods and made-up goods.[3]

Xue: Er, you know, we are a large textiles manufacturing corporation turning out high quality dyed fabric, printed fabric and 100% cotton garments.[4] We are making a variety of garments such as jackets, shirts, skirts, pants, jeans, pajamas and sport suits for men, women and children.[5]

Hanna: Wow! That's really something![6]

Xue: After China entered the WTO, our textiles have become more and more competitive in the world market.

Hanna: This is the reason we are getting in touch with you.

Xue: We are willing to enter into business relations with your firm.

Hanna: I think so, too. I believe that our trade relationship will be expanded continuously through our joint efforts.

Xue: I couldn't agree more.

Hanna: Would you please send us catalogues and necessary information for our reference?

Xue: Certainly. We are going to send you illustrated catalogues and some free samples by EMS for your consideration.

Hanna: We shall appreciate it if you will give us your price list for these garments.

Xue: OK. We are glad to do that. But these prices are subject to our final confirmation because the prices of raw materials keep rising.⁷

Hanna: Oh, goodness! We hope they are reasonable prices.

Xue: Don't worry, Mrs. Hanna. Our prices are still very competitive in spite of the rising prices of raw materials.

Hanna: I wouldn't mind knowing about your normal export terms.

Xue: We usually make an offer on the basis of FOB on our price list.⁸ If we know your destination, we'll quote CIF or CFR as the clients required.

Hanna: Fine. Do you allow commission?

Xue: No problem.

Hanna: OK. Let's get the ball rolling.⁹

Communicative Scene 2

Making Specific Inquiries

(Mr. Penn, who comes from a Canadian Import Company, is making a specific inquiry.)

Penn: Miss Yang, I'd like to thank you for your leaflet together with the sample which I received on Monday.

Yang: My pleasure.

Penn: We are particularly interested in well-favored electric irons.

Yang: Very good. Which model do you prefer?

Penn: We are in the market for your Model E013 and Model E016. Its power source is AC 220V, 1000W, but I am not clear about the type of steam generation.

Yang: They are drip type.

Penn: Do you have them in stock now?¹⁰

Yang: Yeah. They are available for export.

Penn: That is exciting! As Thanksgiving Day is drawing near, we need these products urgently. When will you be able to make shipment for these goods?

Yang: Don't worry. We'll make prompt shipment according to your requirement.

Penn: Fine. I'll be grateful to you for quoting me competitive prices CIF Vancouver, for these two models.

Yang: Okay. But could you tell me the quantity you want so that we can work out the quotation for you?

Penn: We are going to order 100,000 sets of electric irons, that is, 50,000 pieces each of the two models.¹¹

Yang: I see. The total electric irons you need are 100,000 sets.

Penn: Exactly.

Yang: I guess you must have noticed the soaring prices of raw materials in the world market recently.

Penn: Oh goodness! I hope you're not kidding. Can you keep competitive prices?

Yang: I'm not going to kid you. However, in view of our newly established good relationship, we'll keep our prices unchanged in spite of the rising prices of raw material.

Penn: I'm delighted to hear it. By the way, could you kindly send us a Proforma Invoice for electric irons?

Yang: Oh, you need Proforma Invoice?

Penn: Yeah. It will enable us to make the necessary preliminary import arrangements.

Yang: I understand.

Penn: We're looking forward to your reply to our inquiry soon.

Yang: I will.

Communicative Scene 3

A First Inquiry

(Mr. Hart is making a first inquiry to the supplier whom he has not previously dealt with.)

SEC: Good afternoon. Furniture Enterprise Company.

Hart: Hello. Could I speak to Mr. Fu, please?

SEC: Just a sec., please.

Fu: Hello, Fu speaking.

Hart: This is Hart speaking. Chamber of Commerce in our country has recommended your name and firm to us. We are glad to note that you specialize in handling new types of furniture.

Fu: Yes, that's good. What particular items do you need?

Hart: We are very interested in your rattan furniture.

Fu: Good. We have been in this line for 25 years. We are making new designs of wood, rattan, bamboo and wicker furniture and products. Our rattan furniture enjoys good reputation in the world market.

Hart: Yes, I believe your rattan furniture may find a ready market in our area.[12]

Fu: I feel the same way.[13]

Hart: We shall be pleased if you quote us competitive prices in Eurocurrency CFR EMP for rattan furniture.

Fu: Thank you for your inquiry.

Hart: We'd like to stress the importance of the competitive prices since our customers are very sensitive to the prices.[14]

Fu: We assure you that the prices we quote are competitive enough to induce business.

Hart: Thanks. If the prices are workable, we are planning to place a trial order with you for the first time.[15]

Fu: I see.

Hart: The large orders will follow when our clients see your rattan furniture.

Fu: I hope so.

Hart: <u>Could you do me a favor by sending us more copies of your relevant brochures?</u>[16] We need them to send out to our customers.

Fu: Certainly.

Hart: We are expecting your offer.

Fu: We'll calculate and let you know as soon as possible.

Words and Expressions

1. dyed fabric		色布
2. printed fabric		花布
3. garment	n.	服装，cotton garments 全棉服装
4. pajama	n.	睡衣
5. FOB (Free on Board)		船上交货价
6. quotation	n.	报价
7. CIF (Cost, Insurance and Freight)		成本加保险费和运费
8. CFR (Cost and Freight)		成本加运费
9. leaflet	n.	活页说明
10. well-favored		漂亮的，吸引人的
11. electric iron		电熨斗
12. steam generation		蒸汽发生方式
13. drip type		滴下式
14. Proforma Invoice		形式发票
15. preliminary arrangements		预先安排
16. SEC (Secretary)		秘书
17. EMP (Europe Main Port)		欧洲主要港口
18. rattan furniture		藤制家具
19. wicker	n.	柳条
	adj.	柳条编的
20. calculate	v.	计算
21. fabric	n.	织物，布

Notes

1. We have made a market research and found a promising market in our country for the textiles you listed in your advertisement.

近来我们做了市场调查，发现你方广告中刊登的纺织品在我国市场前景广阔。

promising market 市场前景广阔

相关表达：

booming market　市场繁荣

brisk market　市场景气

bull market　多头市场，市场行情看涨

bullish market　牛市

declining market　市场衰退

depressed market　市场萧条

dull market　市场呆滞

2. We are considering to broaden our business in Chinese market.

我们想把生意扩大到中国市场。

① broaden vt. & vi. 扩大，拓宽，扩大影响。主要指拓宽、增长（知识）等。

例句：

The college students broadened their experience by taking part-time job.

大学生通过兼职工作增长经验。

Good films broaden / widen our outlook / mind / horizon.

好影片使我们视野开阔。

② broad adj. 宽广的

例句：

The two countries make efforts to pursue stronger political trust, broader practical cooperation and closer cultural exchanges.

两国要努力夯实政治互信，扩大务实合作，密切人文交流。

③ widen vt. & vi. 使变宽，扩大

但 widen the opportunity（扩大机会）不能用broaden the opportunity。

④ expand v. 扩展（主要指范围、数量、重要性、尺寸、体积方面的扩大）

例句：

We discuss the plan to expand business.

我们商议扩展业务的计划。

3. We are interested in the piece goods and made-up goods.

我们对布匹和纺织成品很感兴趣。

① made-up goods　本文指纺织成品

② made-up　性格，气质；组成，构成；化妆（品）

4. We are a large textiles manufacturing corporation turning out high quality dyed fabric, printed fabric and 100% cotton garments.

我们是一家大型纺织品生产公司，生产高质量的色布、花布和全棉服装。

① turn out　生产，证实，发觉是，原来是，关闭

② manufacture / produce / make　生产

例句：

The survey shows that Chinese families prefer electrical appliances turned out by Chinese companies rather than foreign-made ones.

调查表明中国家庭喜欢购买国产家电而不是国外制造的产品。

③ to be found to be 证实是，发觉是

例句：

That kind gentleman turned out to be an industry analyst.

那个慈祥的绅士原来是个行业分析家。

④ turn off 关闭

例句：

Please make sure to turn off the computer before you leave.

在离开时请务必关机。

5. We are making a variety of garments such as jackets, shirts, skirts, pants, jeans, pajamas and sport suits for men, women and children.

我们生产多种男女服装和童装，例如：夹克衫、衬衫、裙装、裤子、牛仔服、睡衣和运动装。

a (considerable, great, wide) variety of 品种繁多

相关表达：

various kinds of

all kinds of

a range of

6. Wow! That's really something!

哇，真了不起！

be something 了不起，重要

口语中something 表示重要的人物或事情（非正式用法）。

例句：

He thinks he is something but actually he is nothing.

他自以为是个重要的人物，可是其实没啥了不起。

7. But these prices are subject to our final confirmation because the prices of raw material keep rising.

但由于原料价格不断上涨，这些价格应以我方最后确认为准。

be subject to 依……而定的，以……为准

例句：

The price of the export commodity is subject to the fluctuation exchange rate.

出口商品的价格视外汇波动而决定。

8. We usually make an offer on the basis of FOB on our price list.

我们在价格单上通常报FOB价格。

on the basis of FOB/on FOB basis 在FOB的基础上

例句：

It is our usual practice to do business on the basis of L/C.

在信用证的基础上做生意是我方的惯例。

9. Let's get the ball rolling.

那就开始干吧。

Get the ball rolling. 这是一句谚语，意思是开始某事并使之运作起来。

例句：

Let's get the ball rolling on the performance.

让我们开始表演吧。

一旦有了良好的开端，则可使用Keep the ball rolling表示继续的意愿。

10. Do you have them in stock now?

你现在有现货吗？

in stock 现货，库存

例句：

The new type of computer is out of stock, but the similar one is in stock.

这种新型电脑缺货，但类似的型号有现货。

相似词组：

from stock 现货供应

come into (to) stock 库存有货

a stock of 一批……现货

out of stock 缺货，无货

no stock on hand 手头无存货

11. We are going to order 100,000 sets of electric irons, that is, 50,000 pieces each of the two models.

我们打算订100,000台电熨斗，即两种型号各50,000台。

① that is 即，也就是

例句：

Could I have your firm price quotation CFR Oslo, that is, the final and firm offer?

何时能得到贵方到奥斯陆（挪威首都，港口）的CFR实盘，即最后一次有效的报盘？

② 同义词：namely, specifically, that is to say 即，那就是说，明确地

12. I believe your rattan furniture may find a ready market in our area.

我相信贵方的藤制家具在我国市场会旺销。

① find a ready market 旺销，畅销

② be in the market for 想购买

例句：

We are in the market for your electronic appliances.

我们想购买贵方的家用电器。

13. I feel the same way.

我有同感。

当你完全同意别人的观点，可以用I feel the same way这句话，不但让你避免把同样的话再重复一次，帮你省了不少口舌，还可以让对方感受到自己的意见被尊重。

14. We'd like to stress the importance of the competitive prices since our customers are very sensitive to the prices.

需要特别强调的是竞争性的价格，因为我方客户对价格特别敏感。

① sensitive 敏感的

例句：
> She is sensitive to what people think of her.
> 她对别人如何想她很敏感。

② sensitive 易波动的（价格，行情）
sensitive price 价格波动
sensitive stocks 行情起落的股票

15. If the prices are workable, we are planning to place a trial order with you for the first time.
若价格可行，我们准备首次向贵方下试订单。
① place a trial order with sb. 向某人下试订单
② place an initial order with sb. 初次向某人下订单

16. Could you do me a favor by sending us more copies of your relevant brochures?
能否帮忙寄上更多相关宣传小册子，以便我们分发给客户？
请人帮忙时比较正式而礼貌的表达，常用Could you do me a favor?/ Could you give me a hand? / May I ask a favor of you?
有时候请别人帮忙不太好意思说时，可以婉转地说：
Could you do me a little favor? 能不能帮我一个小忙？

Part B Practical Key Sentences

1. **asking for some information in a formal way**

I wouldn't mind knowing about your normal export terms.
我想知道你们一般采取什么出口条件。
"I wouldn't mind ..."是客套语，婉转表达本人的想法、愿望和请求。常用于表达想获取某种信息。译成"我希望了解……""我想要……""要是知道……就好了"。
I wouldn't mind learning the facts. 我想了解真相。

替换表达：
> May I ask what kinds of products you are interested in?
> I wonder which model you prefer.
> I'd particularly like to find out the correct answer.

"I wonder if ..."表示说话人以试探的口气婉转表达本人的想法和请求。当不知道对方是否愿意提供某种信息时，动词用过去时或过去进行时，试探性更强。
I wonder if you can give me some idea about the purpose of Proforma Invoice now.
您现在可否告知形式发票的用途。
I was wondering if you could send me some information about your credit standing now.
不知您现在能否发送一些关于贵方资信的信息。

替换表达：
> I wondered if you could give me a rough price of the oil in your market now.
> I was wondering if you could tell us about the plan of this business project now.

2. **expressing curiosity in an informal way**

　　I am most curious about the new sales plan.

　　我非常想知道新的销售计划。

　　好奇是人之常情，可以询问想了解的事情，但不要涉及别人的隐私，如年龄、婚姻、工资和财产等。

　　替换表达：

　　　　Hey, I wish I knew more about your trip.

　　　　I could hardly wait to know the result.

3. **showing interest**

　　May I ask what kinds of products you are interested in?

　　请问您对什么产品感兴趣？

　　We take interest in Internet of Things Engineering.

　　我们对物联网工程很感兴趣。

　　We are in the market for your high quality products.

　　我们欲购贵方高质量的产品。

　　Are you particularly interested in cloud computing?

　　你们对云计算特别感兴趣吗？

　　试用下列短语造句：

　　　　take (an) interest in

　　　　show (an) interest in

　　　　have an interest in

　　　　hold sb.'s interest

　　　　in the interest(s) of

　　　　with interest

　　　　be keen on

　　　　be crazy about

4. **showing no interest**

　　Nothing interests me less than going shopping.

　　我最不感兴趣的就是逛街买东西。

　　Business management isn't all that interesting as far as I am concerned.

　　工商管理对我来说没意思。

　　替换表达：

　　　　find ... rather uninteresting

　　　　lose interest

　　　　have no interest in

　　　　have no interest to

5. **expressing thanks in a formal way**

　　We shall be pleased if you quote us competitive prices in Eurocurrency CFR EMP for rattan furniture.

如果您能报藤制家具欧洲主要港口成本加运费有竞争性的价格，我们会感到十分高兴。
本句型是传统商务活动时，正式表达谢意的常见方式。

替换表达：

I'll be grateful to you for quoting me competitive prices CIF Vancouver, for these two models.

We shall appreciate it if you will give us your pricelist for these garments.

I'll be obliged if you would give the matter your close attention.

It would be appreciated if you would give us some catalogues for our reference.

I'd like to express my gratitude for your help.

6. expressing disagreement in a direct way with familiar persons

I hope you are not kidding. Can you keep competitive prices?
我想您不会开玩笑吧。能保持具有竞争力的价格吗？

替换表达：

Are you kidding?

You must be joking!

Sorry, I can't go along with your view.

On the contrary.

Do you really mean it?

Part C Integration of Theory and Practice

【知识点】询盘是国际贸易的重要环节之一，买方在交易之初需要了解许多与贸易相关的信息，因此，一般由买方不受约束地提出询盘。询盘可通过面谈、电话、电子邮件等方式进行。询盘分为一般（普通）询盘和具体询盘。

1. general inquiries　一般（普通）询盘

【知识点】买方告知对某类商品感兴趣，通过询盘，简明扼要地向卖方了解一般的商品信息和生产经营情况，以及进一步询问有关交易的信息。

【技能训练句型】

We take interest in Chinese electromobile.
我们中国生产的电动汽车很感兴趣。

I wouldn't mind knowing about your normal export terms.
我想知道你们一般采取什么出口条件？

Do you allow commission?
可以付佣金吗？

2. specific inquiries　具体询盘

【知识点】买方具体询问某种产品信息，不仅询问商品名称（name of the commodity），而且通过具体询盘，向卖方了解商品规格（specifications）、装船期（time of shipment）、付款方式（terms of payment）等细节。买方可告知购买的数量（quantity），请求卖方报价（make an offer）。

【技能训练句型】

We are in the market for your backup powers.

我们欲购买充电宝。

When will you be able to make shipment for these goods?

贵方何时可以装运?

I'll be grateful to you for quoting me competitive prices CIF Vancouver, for these two models.

请报这两种型号的CIF温哥华竞争性价格，我们将不胜感激。

3. a first inquiry　初次询盘

【知识点】首次向新客户询价，为了避免唐突，最好告知对方通过何种方式认识对方，并介绍自己公司的情况，以便双方了解彼此的经营情况以及产品情况，以寻找商机。

【技能训练句型】

Chamber of Commerce in our country has recommended your name and firm to us. We are glad to note that you specialize in handling new types of furniture.

我国的商会把您的大名和公司介绍给我们。我们高兴地注意到贵方专门经营新型家具。

4. inquiry guide　询盘指南

【知识点1】初次询盘既可以作一般询盘，也可具体询盘。

为了更好地了解对方经营的产品或分发给潜在的客户，询盘可要求索取商品资料，如附图目录（illustrated catalogues）、报价单（price-list）、宣传小册子（brochures）以及样品（samples）等。

【技能训练句型】

Would you please send us catalogues and necessary information for our reference?

请寄给我们产品目录和所需信息，供我们参考。

Could you do me a favor by sending us more copies of your relevant brochures to us? We need them to send out to our customers.

可否帮忙寄上更多相关宣传小册子，以便我们分发给客户？

【知识点2】询盘要具体（specific）、简洁（brief）和得体（to the point）。虽然询盘无法律约束，但不要轻易许下订货承诺，以免未订购而引起麻烦。但可加上某种条件，若卖方给予价格优惠等，将向其订货。

【技能训练句型】

If the prices are workable, we are planning to place a trial order with you for the first time.

若价格可行，我们准备首次向贵方下试订单。

【知识点3】卖方对询盘的反应要快（prompt）、诚恳（sincere）和有助（helpful）。详细告知经营情况和具体的产品，可了解买方的具体要求，尽快计算出合理的价格，促使交易获得成功。

【技能训练句型】

We'll calculate and let you know as soon as possible.

我们计算后尽快通知您。

5. Proforma Invoice　形式发票

【知识点】在国际贸易中，形式发票是一种为了形式而发送的发票，形式发票的内容可与商业发票相同，常包含商品名称、规格、数量、价格等，但形式发票的名称为Proforma Invoice而不是Invoice或Commercial Invoice。形式发票与商业发票的主要区别在于对买卖双方皆无约束力。

形式发票的主要作用：

（1）进口方申请进口许可证等；

（2）办理进口手续；

（3）作为正式报价。

注意：并不是每笔交易都要形式发票，其实大部分交易不需要形式发票。可在形式发票上注明有效期。

Part D Practice

I. Complete the Following Dialogues

(1)

Fill in the blanks with the proper words.

A: Mr. Wang, we take ___1___ in your electric meters.

B: Fine, we ___2___ out a considerable ___3___ of electric meters. They are both good in ___4___ and reasonable in price. Our company has ___5___ a market research and found it may be a promising ___6___ in your area.

A: That is why we are thinking to ___7___ our trade in Chinese market.

B: Yeah, indeed.

A: We would like to make an ___8___ for detecting instruments.

B: Which price term do you prefer?

A: We'd like you to ___9___ the price CIF Melbourne.

B: OK, we'll do it on the ___10___ of CIF Melbourne.

(2)

Fill in the blanks with the following expressions.

keep rising	interested in	in view of	wouldn't mind
place an order	in the market	in spite of	a great pleasure to
firm offers	conclude business	be helpful	subject to
in particular	get the ball rolling	from stock	

A: It is ___1___ have the opportunity of meeting you. I do hope to ___2___ with you.

B: What is it ___3___ you are ___4___ ?

A: We are ___5___ for your jackets and shirts for young men. Can you supply the goods soon after we ___6___ ?

B: I believe the jackets and shirts for young men can be supplied ___7___ recently.

A: Good. Er, I ___8___ knowing price terms of your products.

B: Thank you for your inquiry. Here are our FOB price lists. We hope they will ___9___ to you.

A: Are all prices on the list ___10___?

B: No, these prices are ___11___ our final confirmation because nowadays the prices of raw material ___12___ greatly.

A: Can I have your lowest prices?

B: Sure, ___13___ our new established good relationship, we'll keep our prices unchanged ___14___ the rising prices of raw material.

A: I am glad to hear it. Let's ___15___ immediately.

II. Interaction Activities

Divide students into pairs. Make short dialogues and role-play them.

Task 1

Inquire about the availability of the air conditioners.

The following expressions should be included in your dialogue:

(1) I wouldn't mind knowing about

(2) enjoy good reputation

(3) in the market for

(4) inquire about

(5) that is

(6) in stock

(7) out of stock

(8) Do you really mean it?

(9) Could you do me a favor by ...

(10) We shall appreciate it if you will ...

Task 2

Make an inquiry about the prices.

Use all of the following expressions in your dialogue:

(1) inquiry list

(2) You will find that the required items including ...

(3) I was wondering if ...

(4) competitive prices

(5) stress the important of

(6) find ... attractive

(7) place an order

(8) price list

III. Actual Practice

Work in pairs and role-play the conversation.

Suppose you show interest in importing mobile phones. You may make a specific inquiry for the following items with a new trade company:

(1) the specification of mobile phones

(2) competitive price

(3) superior quality

(4) terms of price

(5) shipment time

IV. Creative Discussion

The teacher divides the class into groups, and the students make a discussion with their partners and share their opinions with other groups.

Topic:

Inquiries are usually made by the importers without engagement to get the information about the commodity to be ordered. Price is one of the most important items to be inquired. Ordering large quantity usually makes prices cheaper. Some buyers may exaggerate their quantity for lower prices and promise to make substantial orders in order to get the lowest quotation.

Do you think it is a good way to get reasonable prices? Please discuss the issue with the members in your group.

Chapter 4

Business Appointment and Arrangement

Learning Objectives
Upon completion of this chapter, you will be able to

- make appointments with your clients.
- know how to make arrangements for your clients.
- make friends with your clients.
- know the importance of business appointment and arrangement.
- practice the core socialist values.[1]

---

1 践行社会主义核心价值观。

Making a Business Appointment

(Miss Lin is calling Mr. Wade to make an appointment at Canton Fair.)

Lin: Hello, Mr. Wade. This is Lin, calling from Fuzhou, China.

Wade: Hello, Miss Lin. Pleased to hear from you.

Lin: As Canton Fair is approaching, I'd like to know if you have any plan to visit the fair this spring.

Wade: Yes, we are planning to visit the fair. We would appreciate it if you could meet us there.

Lin: I'm eager to meet you because we have a lot of things to discuss with you face to face.[1] Do you have any opening? Could you tell me the schedule of your visit so that we can make arrangement beforehand?[2]

Wade: Yes. We'll be there from April 14 to 25. What time would suit you?

Lin: We think we will be in Guangzhou during April 16 ~ 18. We are expecting you any time during that period.

Wade: Good. Would 6:00 p.m., April 17 be all right with you?

Lin: OK. Let's make it 6:00 p.m., April 17 in your hotel lobby. Have you booked your hotel in Guangzhou?[3]

Wade: Not yet. Could you do us a favor and book a hotel for 12 days from April 14?

Lin: Yes, of course. How many rooms should we book for you? Any special requirements for the hotel?

Wade: Nothing special. My colleague Mr. Brandon will go with me. So please make reservations for two standard rooms for us.

Lin: We will make a reservation for you immediately.

Wade: Oh, please book the hotel with convenient transportation to the Fair, because we are not familiar with the city and we don't want to spend too much time on the way back and forth everyday.[4]

Lin: Please don't worry about it. We will try our best. I think Overseas Chinese Hotel is a nice option.[5] It is within walking distance to the fair. You don't have to take any taxi, shuttle or other vehicles.

Wade: It is very considerate of you to do so.

Lin: That's all right. What projects should we discuss this time?

Wade: We'd like to talk about BBQ Oven, Grill Steel and BBQ set. Please bring all the related samples if possible.

Lin: Sure. Anything else?

Wade: We will bring some samples of new items, such as cutlery, wine bottle openers, etc. As you know, we are dealing with all kinds of kitchenware and bathroom appliances. We hope the cooperation between us will be expanded step by step.

Lin: I'm glad to hear that. I'll call you again when the reservation is made.

Wade: Thank you for calling, Miss Lin. Bye!

Lin: Thank you! Bye.

Communicative Scene 2

Making Changes for the Appointment

(Mr. Wade is calling back to Miss Lin for the change of appointment.)

Wade: Hello! Miss Lin, this is Wade from Mexico City.

Lin: Hi! Mr. Wade. Nice to hear from you again.

Wade: I appreciated very much your effort for hotel reservation in Overseas Chinese Hotel. However, I'm terribly sorry to inform you that we have to cancel the reservation.

Lin: Is anything wrong? Are you going to cancel your trip to China?

Wade: No, no. <u>Our visiting itinerary remains the same.</u>[6] The delegation from our country will stay in Garden Hotel. We prefer to stay with all the members of our delegation.

Lin: Got it. It's no problem. I'll cancel your reservation.

Wade: <u>Thank you all the same and I'm very sorry for the inconvenience caused by us. I apologize for that.</u>[7]

Lin: Not at all. Shall we meet at 6:00 p.m., April 17 in the lobby of Garden Hotel as planned?

Wade: I am afraid I've to postpone our appointment because of something unexpected.

Lin: No worries. Let's say 7:30 p.m., all right?

Wade: <u>It's a date.</u>[8]

Lin: Why not have dinner together? We'd like to invite you to dinner in Garden Hotel. We can have a discussion while we are having dinner.

Wade: It's very kind of you. By the way, does your company have a display in Canton Fair?

Lin: <u>Naturally.</u>[9] You may see our new products during the fair.

Wade: Um, who is going to take care of the business and production of our orders while you are absent? <u>Please make sure our products are shipped without delay because they are strongly seasonal goods.</u>[10] Even a little delay will cause big trouble.

Lin: My colleagues will take care of the orders. I'll stay in Guangzhou for only 3 days. It is only a one-hour flight from Guangzhou to our city. I guarantee that your orders will be fulfilled in time for delivery.[11]

Wade: Thanks a lot. My mobile phone number is 555-753-9900. It is on 24 hours. You can call me when necessary.

Lin: Fine. My mobile phone number is 013905622789.

Wade: Let's meet in Guangzhou. Have a nice day.

Lin: Have a nice day. Bye.

Making Arrangements

(*Miss Xue is making arrangements for Mr. More.*)

More: Hello, Miss Xue. How are you?

Xue: I'm fine. Thank you! What can I do for you?

More: Yes, as you know, I'm going to visit Canton Fair next week. I'll stay there for more than two weeks. During the first and second sections, there is a break of 4 days. I may have nothing to do but stay in the hotel as I have been in Guangzhou many times.

Xue: Are you going to travel somewhere else?

More: Yes, you are right. I am planning to bring my wife with me this time.

Xue: Is this your wife's first trip to China?

More: Yes.

Xue: What kinds of places are you going to visit?

More: I don't have any idea as I always stay in Guangzhou for business though I have been to China so many times.

Xue: Oh. I understand the situation now. As you know, China is a large country and 4 days is not long enough for travel in China. If you and your wife would like to have a relaxing break, I suggest you to visit Hainan Island or Guilin City, where you will enjoy the beauty of nature.[12] If you are interested in historic sites, you can fly to Xi'an, I suppose.[13]

More: Could you tell me more about the island? We are from the inland country. We prefer to stay on the island during that time.[14]

Xue: OK. Hainan Island is the second largest island in China. Its tropical weather is mild and nice during April. You will enjoy the sunshine on the seashore and have fun there.[15]

More: It sounds marvelous. How can we get there?

Xue: You can get there by air. It is only about an hour's trip by air. If you agree, I can make the arrangement with a travel agent, which is the most convenient way to make your trip easy and comfortable.

More: It's really a good idea. Could you make a reservation for us? All the expenses will be on us.

Xue: No problem, it is my pleasure to help you. I'll send you an e-mail for the itinerary when it's fixed after I make the arrangement with the travel agency.

More: I can't thank you enough.

Xue: Please don't mention it. You are always welcome. Bye.

More: So long.

Words and Expressions

1. beforehand	adv.	预先	
2. lobby	n.	门厅，门廊	
3. shuttle	n.	短程穿梭运输工具	
		（如往返展览会和宾馆之间的大巴）	
4. convenient	adj.	便利的，方便的	
inconvenience	n.	不方便，麻烦	
5. option	n.	选择	
6. BBQ oven		烧烤炉	
7. grill steel		烧烤架	
8. BBQ set		烧烤用具	
9. cutlery	n.	（西餐的）刀叉餐具	
10. kitchenware	n.	厨房用品	
11. bathroom appliances		洁具	
12. itinerary	n.	旅程，旅行计划	
13. delegation	n.	代表团	
14. display stand		摊位	
15. guarantee	vt. & n.	保证，担保	
16. fulfill	vt.	完成，履行，满足	
17. release	vt. & n.	释放，解放，免除	
have a releasing break		有休闲的间隙	
18. island	n.	岛屿	
inland	n.	内陆，内地，国内	
	adj.	内陆的，国内的	
	adv.	向内地	
19. tropical	adj.	热带的	

Notes

1. I'm eager to meet you because we have a lot of things to discuss with you face to face.
   我迫切希望见到您，因为我们有许多事情要和您面谈。

face to face
▶ 面谈，直接交流

例句：

The manufacturers are talking face to face with the consumers.

厂家与消费者正在进行直接交流。

▶ 直接面对

例句：

Your financial investment option depends on whether you are face to face with a bullish or bearish market.

你的金融投资选择取决于你是直接面对牛市还是熊市。

2. Could you tell me the schedule of your visit so that we can make arrangement beforehand?

能否告知您的日程，以便我们预先做出安排？

make arrangement beforehand 预先做出安排

beforehand

▶ 预先

例句：

Here is a copy of itinerary we have worked out for you beforehand.

这是我们为你预先拟定的活动日程安排。

▶ 提前

例句：

The buyer have to be beforehand with his payment because he needs his goods urgently.

因为买主急需产品，不得已提前支付货款。

3. Have you booked your hotel in Guangzhou?

您在广州的宾馆预订了吗？

book the hotel 预订房间

例句：

Make a reservation for a room overlooking the sea, please.

请预订一间临海的房间。

He booked a standard room for business fair.

他为参加交易会预订了标准房。

4. Oh, please book the hotel with convenient transportation to the Fair, because we are not familiar with the city and we don't want to spend too much time on the way back and forth everyday.

噢，请订方便去交易会的宾馆，因为我们对广州不熟悉，不想每天在来回的路上花太多的时间。

① convenient 方便的，便利的

▶ convenient transportation 便捷的交通

▶ convenient food 方便食品

▶ convenient locations 便利地点

② back and forth *adv.* 来回地，前前后后地，来来去去地

同义短语： backward and forward, to and fro, from side to side

Chapter 4 Business Appointment and Arrangement

5. I think Overseas Chinese Hotel is a nice option. It is within walking distance to the fair.

   华侨饭店就是很好的选择，步行就可到达交易会。

   ① option 选项，选择权，买卖的特权

   例句：

   There are quite a lot of options open to me.

   我有很多选择。

   He has no option but to apply for a mortgage loan.

   他别无选择，只好申请抵押贷款。

   ② within walking distance 步行距离，步行能达到的地方，在……附近

   例句：

   China Council for the Promotion of International Trade is within walking distance.

   中国国际贸易促进委员会就在附近。

   within touch 在……能达到的地方，在……的附近，可以接近的

6. Our visiting itinerary remains the same.

   我们的访问日程不变。

   例句：

   As a special accommodation, our discount will remain unchanged for you.

   作为特殊照顾，我们给你的折价保持不变。

7. Thank you all the same and I'm very sorry for the inconvenience caused by us. I apologize for that.

   太感谢了，对此造成的不便深表歉意，我为此道歉。

   ① be terribly /very sorry for 深表歉意

   例句：

   I'm terribly sorry to inform you that we have to cancel the reservation.

   我非常抱歉地通知你，我们不得不取消这个预订。

   ② apologize 道歉

   例句：

   No reason to apologize.

   不必道歉。

8. It's a date.

   那就说定了。（非正式口语用法）

9. naturally adv. 必然地，自然地（表示肯定的用语）

   同义词：surely，certainly，of course，as expected

10. Please make sure our products are shipped without delay because they are strongly seasonal goods.

    请一定保证我们的货物按时发运，因为这些产品的季节性很强。

    ① without delay 立即

    同义词：at once，soon

    ② strongly seasonal goods 季节性很强的产品

11. I guarantee that your orders will be fulfilled in time for delivery.

    我保证你们的订单会按时完工并发送。

① guarantee *n. & vt.* 保证，担保

例句：

> He guaranteed that he would keep appointments unchanged.
> 他保证会守约。

② fulfill *vt.* 履行，执行

fulfill the orders 按时完成订单

fulfill the task 完成任务

fulfill the plan 完成计划

例句：

> China will fulfill its plan to finish building a moderately prosperous society in all respects and realize the first centenary goal.
> 中国将全面建成小康社会，实现第一个百年奋斗目标。

12. If you and your wife would like to have a relaxing break, I suggest you to visit Hainan Island or Guilin City, where you will enjoy the beauty of nature.

    如果您和夫人喜欢轻松休闲，我建议去海南岛或者桂林，在那儿，你们可以享受美丽的大自然。

    have a releasing break 有个休闲的间隙

13. If you are interested in historic sites, you can fly to Xi'an, I suppose.

    如果你们对历史名胜感兴趣，我想可以去西安。

    historic sites 历史古迹

    注意以下二词的用法有所不同：

    ① historic *adj.* 历史上著名的（指历史上有重要意义的）

    ② historical *adj.* 历史上的，有关历史的

14. We are from the inland country. We prefer to stay on the island that time.

    我们来自内陆国家，更愿意到岛上去。

    注意inland（内陆，内地，国内）和island（岛屿）的区别。

15. You will enjoy the sunshine on the seashore and have fun there.

    您可以在海边享受阳光，在那里玩得开心。

    ① have fun there 在那里玩得开心

    ② be fun 玩得开心

    例句：

    > Chinese historic sites are great fun. 中国历史古迹真好玩。
    > You are no fun. 你这人真没劲。

Part B Practical Key Sentences

1. making appointments

   make appointments with your clients 与客户约会

Chapter 4 Business Appointment and Arrangement

make arrangements for your clients 为客户作安排

替换表达：

We are having an appointment with our clients.

The client asked me to reserve a single room with a private bath.

They are making an arrangement for business visit.

2. finding suitable time

询问对方，找到双方合适的时间：

What time would suit you?

你们什么时间方便呢？

Would next Tuesday be convenient for you?

下周二您方便吗？

替换表达：

What is the most convenient time for you?

What time is good for you?

We are expecting you any time during that period.

Would 10:00 a.m., July 1 be all right with you?

Let's say 7:30 p.m., all right?

How about meeting at 12 o'clock this afternoon?

Will you be available this evening, say from 7 to 11?

3. expression of appreciation formally

It is very considerate of you to do so.

你这样做考虑得真周到。

That's most thoughtful of you.

你想得真周到。

替换表达：

That's very nice of you.

It's very kind of you.

That was extremely good of you.

That's very helpful of you to offer.

4. got it

Got it.

明白。（口语用法，可省略主语）

替换表达：

询问：You got it, didn't you?

　　　Do you take me?

　　　Do you understand?

　　　Are you there yet?

回答：I see.

　　　That's clear to me now.

I know.

5. something unexpected

something的修辞语放在something之后。

I am afraid I have to postpone our appointment because of something unexpected.

恐怕因未预料之事，我还得推迟约会。

替换表达：

The appointment has to be canceled for I have something important to do.

Something urgent has come up. It looks as if our arrangement has to be changed.

You still have something to do before we come to trade conclusion.

6. All the expenses will be on us.

The dinner is on me today.

今天这顿饭我请客。

I'll get the check.

我来付账。

替换表达：

Let me pay this time.

I'll pay the bill.

The boarding and lodging per day is on our boss.

Part C Integration of Theory and Practice

【知识点】现代国际商务活动特别崇尚效率，讲究时间观念，每日商务活动通常经过精心安排，无论商务洽谈还是社交活动都事先约定好，随意拜访必然会碰钉子。

1. making an appointment beforehand   预先约定

【知识点1】与客户或其他与业务有关的人之间进行的商务活动要预先约定，约定方式一般通过电话预约。预约时可开门见山，直奔主题，告诉约会的目的和计划，了解对方是否有兴趣见面。

【技能训练句型】

A: We are planning to visit the fair. We would appreciate it if you could meet us there.

我们打算参加这次广交会。如能在会上与你见面，我们将非常荣幸。

B: I'm eager to meet you because we'd like to exchange views with you about promoting sales face to face.

我也迫切希望见到您，因为我们想就推销事宜和您面谈，交换意见。

【知识点2】预约前常客气地征求意见，询问对方是否有空，找到双方合适的时间。

【技能训练句型】

Do you have any opening?

您是否有空？

Could you tell me the schedule of your visit so that we can make arrangement beforehand?

Chapter 4 Business Appointment and Arrangement

能告诉我您的日程安排，以便我们预先做出安排吗？
Will you be available this weekend?
您本周末有事吗？
Any time will suit me.
我随时有空。

【知识点3】若不愿意和对方见面，可婉言谢绝或告知原因。
【技能训练句型】
I am afraid all the appointments are filled.
恐怕全部预约时间都已排满。
I had a careful check with my secretary and suddenly realized I had another appointment beforehand.
我与秘书仔细核对了一下，发现我已有其他约会。

【知识点4】若对方表示忙，不能确定，可随后找时间再打电话预约，也许会有收获。
【技能训练句型】
A: I suppose you would be free tomorrow.
　　我想您明天有空吧？
B: Yes, I can manage to come then.
　　有，到时候我一定来。

【知识点5】当对方表示愿意时，接着用商量的口气，约定合适的时间。
【技能训练句型】
Could you arrange it for us?
您能帮我们安排一下吗？
We'll be in Guangzhou during the fair. We are expecting you any time during that period.
我们将参加广交会，在此期间随时都可以与你会面。
Would 8:00 p.m., Oct. 18 be all right with you?
那10月18日晚上8点如何？

【知识点6】双方同意见面后，定下约会的时间。
【技能训练句型】
OK. Let's make it 8:00 p.m., Oct. 18 in your hotel restaurant.
行，那就10月18日晚上8点在您下榻宾馆的餐厅见。
That's settled then.
就这么定了。
It's a date.
好的。

2. keeping an appointment　遵守约定

【知识点】预约后，要遵守约定，按时到达，因迟到让人久等是不礼貌的。当然，过早到达影响别人也不可取。
如果约会时隔太久，不妨赴约前再确认一次。
【技能训练句型】
A: I am calling to confirm my appointment with you at 9:00 tomorrow morning.

我想与您确认明天上午9点的约会。

B: I'll be expecting you.

明天上午我等您。

A: I hope you could come at 7:00.

希望你7点能到。

B: I'll be there right on time.

我会准时到达。

3. changing or canceling an appointment　更改约会或取消约会

【知识点】因特殊情况无法守约，应及时告诉对方，讲明失约的具体原因，表示道歉，请求谅解。征求是否更改约会时间或者取消约会。

【技能训练句型】

I am afraid I've to postpone our appointment because of something unexpected.

恐怕因未预料之事，我得推迟约会。

Sorry. I stood you up. I had something urgent so I had to cancel the appointment.

对不起，我失约了。我有紧急公务不得已取消约会。

A: I'm terribly sorry to inform you that we have to change the appointment. I am tied up recently.

十分抱歉，我们不得不更改约会时间，因为我最近抽不开身。

B: It doesn't matter.

没关系。

A: Can we make it another time?

其他时间行吗？

B: Let's say 7:30 p.m., all right?

那么，晚上7:30行吗？

A: It's a date. Sorry again for the inconvenience caused by us.

那就说定了。对此造成的不便再次深表歉意。

Part D　Practice

I. Complete the Following Dialogues

Fill in the blanks with the following expressions.

a releasing break	Got it	keep him long
have an appointment	be filled	do me a favor
be convenient for	have a try	look at his schedule
something urgent	be available	Let's make it
be very kind of	be afraid	for business activities

Chapter 4 Business Appointment and Arrangement

Lee: Good morning. I'd like to have a business discussion with Mr. White.
Secretary: Do you ___1___ with Mr. White?
Lee: No, I ___2___ not. I have ___3___ to talk with him.
Secretary: But all the appointments ___4___.
Lee: Could you ___5___ and arrange it for me?
Secretary: It is very important to make an appointment beforehand ___6___.
Lee: ___7___. But it is really something unexpected.
Secretary: I'll ___8___ and ___9___.
Lee: I guarantee that I won't ___10___.
Secretary: There is ___11___ at 11:30. I'll ask him if he ___12___ at the moment.
Lee: It ___13___ you to do so.
Secretary: Mr. White asks if the talking at 11:50 ___14___ you?
Lee: Fine. ___15___ at 11:50.

II. Interaction Activities

Task 1

Students role play and make a dialogue according to the situation.

Mr. Smith is going to pay a business visit to your company. Make a reservation for hotel and arrange everything well to make his visit comfortable.

Use the following expressions:

Role A	Role B
pay a business visit	book your hotel
make a hotel reservation	have your business schedule
be very considerate of	any special requirements
Just make a reservation for	Let's fix it.
visit natural wonders	strongly recommend
a nice option	have a lot of fun there

Task 2

You have to break an appointment with your client because you have pressing business to attend to. You are calling the client to say sorry for the changing of time and explain the reason.

Use all of the following expressions in your dialogue:

(1) I'm terribly sorry
(2) keep the appointment with you
(3) What's up
(4) I have pressing business
(5) put off the meeting
(6) make it another time
(7) How about...

(8) be tied up then

(9) When is the most convenient time for you?

(10) be expecting

(11) be settled

III. Actual Practice

Students make up a dialogue according to the following situation with partners.

Mr. James is an Australian trader of chemical fertilizer. He is going to attend China Technology and Projects Fair and makes an appointment beforehand to meet Mr. Tao, director of the factory. Mr. Tao wants to know the itinerary in order to make arrangement. They discuss the purpose of the meeting and the proper time to meet.

IV. Creative Discussion

The teacher divides the class into groups, and the students make discussions with their partners and share their opinions with other groups.

Topic:

Making appointments is very common in business activity. How should you make an appropriate appointment politely with the managing director of your client when he is very busy?

If the managing director tells you that he is tied up recently and suggests contacting him sometime later, how can you tell whether he is telling the real thing or declining your offer by an excuse? Please discuss the topic with the members in your group.

Chapter 5
Offer and Counter-offer

Learning Objectives
Upon completion of this chapter, you will be able to

- get familiar with the process of the offer and counter-offer.
- learn how to persuade clients to accept the offer.
- learn how to make a counter-offer.
- improve the communication skills.
- conduct the activities related to offer and counter-offer.
- understand promoting mutual benefit.[1]

---

1 理解促进互惠互利。

Making an Offer

(Mr. Smith is a purchaser from Italy. Miss Arenas is Mr. Smith's assistant. Jane is the sales manager of a garment manufacturing company. They are talking about the prices.)

Jane: Mr. Smith, did you have a good time yesterday?

Smith: Oh, yes. We climbed the Great Wall and had a great time up there.

Jane: Good! How about you, Miss Arenas? Have you enjoyed your first visit to China?

Arenas: Oh yes. I've enjoyed everything about it!

Jane: I'm glad to hear that. <u>Well, since you both have had a good time, maybe it's time to talk business now.</u>[1]

Smith: I think so.

Jane: Terrific. Now let's get down to business. Your e-mail of August 24 says you want to buy bathrobes from us.

Smith: That's correct. Here are the designs.

Jane: Thanks. <u>Fleece, 260 g/m^2, one size fits all. Quantity: 6,000 pcs.</u>[2]

Smith: <u>I was wondering if you would give us a response to our inquiry.</u>[3]

Jane: Certainly. We are pleased to offer you 6,000 pcs micro-fibre fleece bathrobe, 100% polyester at USD 5.90 each, FOB Shanghai.

Smith: Packing?

Jane: The bathrobes will be packed in plastic bags, each four dozen in a corrugated cardboard box.

Smith: How to make delivery?

Jane: Well, according to your requirement, the goods will be delivered in two consignments of 3,000 each, the first by September 30 and the second by October 15.

Smith: How about terms of payment?

Jane: The terms of payment will be the same as those in the previous contract, that is, sight letter of credit.

Smith: Thank you very much for your offer, and we'll give it serious consideration. As it'll take us some time to calculate, may I suggest we take a 20-minute break? Then we'll give you an answer.

Jane: Fine.

Chapter 5 Offer and Counter-offer

Communicative Scene 2

Counter-offer

(They are negotiating. Smith tries hard to buy at a lower price, but Jane persuades the opposite to accept their price by bargaining hard.)

Smith: Well, Jane. I've discussed your offer with Miss Arenas, and <u>I'm afraid we found it rather on the high side.</u>[4]

Jane: Why do you think so?

Smith: To tell you the truth, just before we left for China, we were approached by a Guangdong garments manufacturer. Their offer was USD 4.50 FOB Guangzhou each bathrobe, so we don't see why we should pay more for your bathrobe.

Jane: USD 4.50 each bathrobe? Really?

Smith: That's right, USD 4.50.

Jane: That's really cheap. <u>I guess you must have bought a lot from this manufacturer.</u>[5]

Smith: We bought 200 pieces.

Jane: Only 200?

Smith: Well, as we don't know much about that firm, we just placed a trial order.

Jane: Right, it takes time to find out whether a business partner is trustworthy.

Smith: This is why we sent our inquiry to you. <u>I believe you are not only trustworthy but also competitive in price.</u>[6]

Jane: <u>You bet.</u>[7]

Smith: <u>But your offer is obviously far from competitive.</u>[8]

Jane: Then what do you think a competitive price would be?

Smith: USD 4.50, the price we paid the Guangdong Manufacturer.

Jane: Oh, come on, our bathrobe certainly deserves more than that.

Smith: Oh, why?

Jane: It's true that our price is higher, but isn't it equally true that our quality is better? <u>Mr. Smith, you wouldn't disagree on that, would you?</u>[9]

Smith: <u>You may have a point there.</u>[10] But, how can you prove your bathrobe is better than the Guangdong ones?

Jane: Well, we have won a gold medal from the General Association of Textiles. Here is the certificate.

Smith: Oh, thank you.

Reaching an Agreement

(The final transaction has been concluded. Both parties have made some concession.)

Smith: All right, Jane. What about USD 5.00 each bathrobe? To be frank, I've increased it more by 11%.

Jane: I appreciate your effort toward reaching an agreement, but I'm afraid your concession is too moderate.

Smith: Oh come on, Jane. You'll drive us bankrupt if you raise the price any further.

Jane: You can't be serious, Mr. Smith. As an expert in garments business, you know our bathrobe is worth much more than your counter-offer.

Smith: Thanks for the compliment. But as an expert, I don't think your offer is in alignment with the prevailing price in the market.[11]

Jane: I'm afraid I can't go along with you on that.[12] However, to show our goodwill to an old friend, let me cut my offer by 40 cents and make it USD 5.50. What do you say to that?

Smith: Well, I have to say we still can't afford to pay at that price. Jane, I hate to say this, but I am already in a tight corner and can't move any more.

Jane: Well, it seems to be a real hard nut to crack.[13] Mmm, well, I've got an idea. I suggest that you increase your quantity to 10,000 pcs, and we'll manage to make it USD 5.00.

Smith: I'm afraid I'm not authorized to make such a compromise.[14] I'll have to contact my boss and see what he says.

Jane: OK, please go ahead.

(Mr. Smith calls his boss, then comes back to Jane twenty minutes later.)

Smith: Well, after communicating with my boss, we'll make it happen although it is a little bit out of our budget plan.

Jane: That's all right. Shall we discuss the details of your delivery?

Smith: Sure.

Words and Expressions

1. polyester	n.	涤纶
2. on the high side		价格偏高
3. gold medal		金牌
4. concession	n.	让步
5. moderate	adj.	适度的，轻微的
6. bankrupt	adj.	破产的

7. counter-offer		还盘
8. compliment	n.	称赞，恭维
9. in alignment with		与……一致
10. in a tight corner		处于困境
11. micro-fiber fleece		摇粒绒（一种布料）
12. consignment	n.	货物，运送
13. trustworthy	adj.	值得信赖的
14. deserve	vt.	值得，应得
15. prevail	vi.	流行
16. corrugated cardboard box		瓦楞纸板箱
17. sight letter of credit		即期信用证
18. quantity	n.	数量
19. 100% polyester		全涤
20. budget plan		预算计划

Notes

1. Well, since you both have had a good time, maybe it's time to talk business now.

    既然你们玩儿得很愉快，那么现在该谈生意了吧！

    It's time to do sth. 该做某事了

    例句：

    It's time for me to make an offer.

    我该报价了。

    It's time to have another meeting.

    该开另一场会议了。

2. Fleece, 260 g/m^2, one size fits all. Quantity: 6,000 pcs.

    摇粒绒，260克每平方米，单码，数量6,000件。

    ① fleece 摇粒绒（布料名称）

    ② 260g/m^2 指每平方米的质量为260克

    ③ one size fits all 单码（单一尺码）

3. I was wondering if you would give us a response to our inquiry.

    我想知道你是否可以对我们的询价给一个答复。

    例句：

    I wonder who he is.

    我想知道他是谁。

    I was wondering how to establish business relation with clients from abroad.

    我想知道如何与来自国外的客户建立业务关系。

4. I'm afraid we found it rather on the high side.

    恐怕你所报的价格太高。

on the high side 高价

例句：

  If the price is on the high side, it's hard to conclude the transaction.

  若价格太高，生意是很难成交的。

5. I guess you must have bought a lot from this manufacturer.

  我想您一定从此制造商买进大批的货品。

  must +现在完成时，表示对过去事情的推测。

  例句：

    You must have drunk a lot.

    你一定喝多了。

6. I believe you are not only trustworthy but also competitive in price.

  我相信你们不仅可靠，而且价格有竞争力。

  not only ... but also ... 不但……而且……

  例句：

    The bike is not only cheap but also attractive in its design.

    这款自行车不仅价格便宜，而且设计新颖。

7. You bet.

  请您放心。

8. But your offer is obviously far from competitive.

  不过，你们的报价可是明显没有竞争力啊。

  be far from 远非，完全不

  例句：

    Your work is far from satisfactory.

    你的工作一点也不令人满意。

    The newspaper accounts are far from being true.

    报纸的报道远非事实。

9. Mr. Smith, you wouldn't disagree on that, would you?

  史密斯先生，你对这点不会不同意吧？

  wouldn't ..., would you? （反意疑问句子）

10. You may have a point there.

  你说的也许有点道理。

11. But as an expert, I don't think your offer is in alignment with the prevailing price in the market.

  不过作为行家，我觉得你的报价与市场的主流价格不太相符。

  be in alignment with ... 与……相符

  例句：

    It is not in alignment with our company's regulations.

    它与我们公司的规定不相符。

12. I'm afraid I can't go along with you on that.

  恐怕在这一点上我不敢苟同。

13. Well, it seems to be a real hard nut to crack.

    这似乎真是个难题啊。

14. I'm afraid I'm not authorized to make such a compromise.

    恐怕我无权做出如此大的让步。

*15. qty.＝ quantity

 Part B Practical Key Sentences

1. light talk before formal negotiation

Did you have a good time yesterday?

昨天玩得开心吗?

正式谈话前，通常说一些轻松的话题，此时可用此类句子。

替换表达：

Did you have a pleasant flight?

Yes, the flight was smooth. The service was good, too.

How do you like the weather here? It's nice. It is really sunny.

What do you think of your hotel?

Do you like the food here?

2. starting the negotiation

Well, since you both have had a good time, maybe it's time to talk business now.

既然你们都过得愉快，那现在该谈生意了吧!

替换表达：

Well, shall we get down to business?

Well, I understand that you want to buy some leather shoulder bags from us.

OK, let's get down to our main point.

May I know what line of business you are in?

Could you give me a general picture of your company?

Well, the purpose of my visiting your company is to inquire about the possibility of establishing business relationships with you.

This is the outline of our proposal. Now, let's talk business.

I'm glad to hear that you've overcome jet-lag. Now let's talk business.

3. making an offer

We are pleased to make an offer to you ...

我们很高兴向您报……的价格。

替换表达：

As requested, we are pleased to make you a firm offer.

Our offer is a non-firm offer. It is subject to our final confirmation.

Could you make an offer on FOB basis?

We were thinking of making you an offer.

4. **counter-offer**

   I'm afraid we found it rather on the high side.

   我们觉得价格仍然偏高。

   替换表达：

   In reply, we regret to inform you that your price is out of line with the market level.

   I don't think your price is in alignment.

   We can not close negotiations at that price.

   Your price is too high for us to accept.

   Your quotation is beyond our reach.

   Yet on the other hand, your price is not as competitive as theirs.

   It's true that our price is higher, but isn't it equally true that our quality is better?

5. **making a concession**

   I suggest that you increase your quantity to 10,000 pcs, we'll manage to make USD 5.00.

   若您能将数量提高到1万件，我们就把价格定在每件5.00美元。

   替换表达：

   We are prepared to allow you a 5% discount if you can increase the quantity of your order to 2,000 dozen.

   May I suggest we go fifty-fifty and close the gap?

   I think we should fill the gap by compromise.

   Shall we meet half way? Each makes a further concession so that business can be done.

   We agree to grant you a 5% discount.

   With an eye to future business, we'll make an exception and allow you a 2% discount.

   In order to promote our business, we are prepared to give you a 3% discount.

   For the sake of encouraging future business, we may grant you a special discount of 1%.

   From a sincere desire to increase trade between us, we are going to reduce our price by 2%.

6. **sentence patterns for price negotiation**

   Business is closed at this price. 交易就按此价敲定。

   Your price is acceptable (unacceptable). 你方价格可接受（不可接受）。

   Your price is feasible (infeasible). 你方价格是可行（不可行）的。

   Your price is workable. 你方出价可行。

   Your price is realistic (unrealistic). 你方价格合乎实际（不现实）。

   Your price is reasonable (unreasonable). 你方价格合理（不合理）。

   The goods are (not) competitively priced. 此定价有（无）竞争力。

   The goods are priced too high. 定价太高。

   Your price is prohibitive. 你方价格高得令人望而却步。

   Your price is rather stiff. 你方价格相当高。

7. **expressions for rising and falling of price**

   Price is turning high (low). 价格上涨（下跌）。

Price is high (low). 价格高（低）。
Price is rising (falling). 价格上升（下降）。
Price is up (down). 价格上涨（下跌）。
Price is looking up. 价格看涨。
Price has skyrocketed. 价格猛涨。
Price has shot up. 价格飞涨。
Price has risen in a spiral. 价格螺旋上升。
Price has hiked. 价格急剧抬高。
Price has risen perpendicularly. 价格直线上升。
Price has advanced. 价格已上涨。
Price is leveling off. 价格趋平。

Part C Integration of Theory and Practice

1. offer   报盘

【知识点】在商务活动中，报盘也称报价，是一个重要的环节。通常卖方应买方询盘要求发出，也可主动报盘。报盘还可分为实盘和虚盘。实盘是指报盘人明确表示其签发实盘，一旦被受盘人所接受，报盘者必须承担严格依照发盘条件向对方供货的法律责任，是有约束力的报盘，因此报盘者应对盘中的每个细节给予重视。报盘通常用以下方式表达：

【技能训练句型】

We offer you our best price, at which we have done a lot of business with other customers.
我们向你们所报的是最优惠价，按此价我们已经与其他客户做了大量交易。

Can you make an offer, CFR London, at your earliest convenience?
您能尽快报一个伦敦港成本加运费价格吗？

Please make us a cable offer for 5 metric tons of walnut.
请电报5吨核桃仁的价格。

Our offer is USD 30 per set of tape-recorder, FOB Tianjin.
我们的报价是每台收录机30美元，天津离岸价。

We quote lowest lithium battery at USD 2500 per set CFR New York.
我们报锂电池最优惠的纽约成本加运费价每套2500美元。

All your prices are on CIF basis.
你们所有价格都是成本加保险费运费价格。

We'll let you have the official offer next Monday.
下星期一就向您正式报盘。

This offer is based on an expanding market and is competitive.
此报盘着眼于扩大销路，很有竞争性。

2. firm offer   实盘

【知识点】清晰而准确的实盘应包括以下诸点：

（1） a detailed description of the item 对货物的具体描述
（2） price, currency 价格，货币
（3） packaging 包装
（4） minimum or maximum quantity 最大或最小数量
（5） quality 质量
（6） shipping date, mode 装运日期，方式（指海运、空运或其他方式）
（7） terms of payment 付款方式
（8） a time frame during which your offer is available 发盘的有效期

3. indefinite offer / non-firm offer 虚盘

【知识点】虚盘是指报盘人未明确指出其接受意向的发盘。与实盘相比，虚盘对发盘人并无约束力，虚盘通常不一定像实盘那样，包括交易所需要的所有细节。虚盘常会有"subject to our final confirmation"（以我方最后确认为准），或"for reference only"（仅供参考）等说法，以示发盘者有所保留。

【技能训练句型】

发盘时常说：

We quote our best price, and we hope it will interest you.

我们提供最优惠的报价，希望你们有兴趣。

We can offer you a quotation based upon the international market.

我们可以按国际市场价格给您报价。

We are in a position to offer tea from stock.

我们现在可以报茶叶现货。

The offer is for your reference only, subject to our final confirmation.

此报盘仅供参考，以我方最后确认为准。

4. counter-offer 还盘

【知识点】当受盘人对报盘中的某些条款不满意时，可以提出一套新的条款或通过对报盘做些修改来有条件地接受报盘，这就是还盘。事实上，一个还盘就是一个取代原报盘的新的报盘，还盘一经提出，原来的受盘人就成了新的报盘人，而原来的报盘人就成了新的受盘人。新的受盘人可选择拒绝还盘、再次还盘或接受还盘。

【技能训练句型】

In reply, we regret to inform you that our buyers in Paris find the price you offered much too high.

我方很遗憾地通知贵方，我方巴黎买主觉得贵方的报价太高了。

Your offer is too high to be acceptable.

你方报价太高，不能接受。

Your price is out of line with the market here.

你方定价高出我方市场价。

I wish to point out that yours are about 9% higher than the quotation I have received from your competitors.

我方得指出你方的报价比从其他竞争商家收到的报价高约9%。

We can't accept your offer unless the price is reduced by 5%.

除非你们减价5%，否则我们无法接受报盘。

My offer was based on reasonable profit, not on wild speculations.
我方的报价以合理利润为依据，不是漫天要价。

Moreover, we've kept the price close to the costs of production.
再说，这已经把价格压到生产费用的边缘了。

5. strategy of making an offer　报价策略

【知识点】（1）报价时机：报价之前把商品的使用价值介绍清楚，待对方对其产品已有所了解之后，再提出价格。

（2）价格分割策略：报价时可利用对方的求廉心理，用较小的计价单位报价，造成需方心理上的便宜感。

（3）价格优惠策略：报价时可把价格和商品的优越性或优惠条件联系起来。

（4）价格比较策略：提出己方价格时，可联系另一种商品的价格进行比较，突出相同使用价值的不同价格，或突出相同价格的不同使用价值。

（5）价格差异策略：根据商品的流向、买方的需求急缓程度、购买次数、购买时间、付款方式的不同，可采取不同的价格。

6. tips of making concession while negotiating　谈判中的让步技巧

【知识点】（1）在让步的最后阶段，让出全部可让利益。

（2）等额地让出可让利益。

（3）让步先大后小，逐步提高。

（4）让步从大到小，然后微升。

（5）让步从大到小，渐次缩小。

（6）出让全部可让利益后赔利相让，然后再讨回赔利。

Part D Practice

I. Complete the Following Dialogues

(1)

Li: How are you, Mr. Morer? It's very ＿＿1＿＿ of you to see us in ＿＿2＿＿.

Morer: Hello. It's good to see you in person in the Canton Fair as we have a lot of written ＿＿3＿＿ in the ＿＿4＿＿ years.

Li: Yeah, and I think through your ＿＿5＿＿ we can settle the price for beach chair one way or ＿＿6＿＿. How I wish to point ＿＿7＿＿ that due ＿＿8＿＿ sharp increase of raw material we'll be ＿＿9＿＿ need to adjust our export prices before ＿＿10＿＿.

(2)

Li: I think it ＿＿1＿＿ for either of us to insist ＿＿2＿＿ his own price. How about meeting each other ＿＿3＿＿? I only ask you to make a ＿＿4＿＿ of 3% on your quotation. That's ＿＿5＿＿, isn't it?

Morer: To tell you the ＿＿6＿＿, the price we ＿＿7＿＿ you last is ＿＿8＿＿ the lowest and we cannot stand any cuts. Had it not been for an old ___9___, like you, we would not ___10___ made you such a low offer in the first place.

II. Role-plays

Task 1

Students work in pairs and make a dialogue based on the following situation.

Jack is going to import 5,000 pcs T-shirt from China to America. But he finds the price quoted by Miss Wang on the high side. He tries his best to persuade Miss Wang to reduce her price with good reasons. The words or phrases suggested below might give you a hand:

(1) Your price is beyond our reach / rather out of line.

(2) Our price is most moderate / favorable in line with the prevailing market.

(3) This price has been reduced to the limit from 5% to 6% lower than others.

(4) If you insist on your price, we can hardly come to terms.
(Hang on the previous quotation, business is impossible.)

(5) With an eye to future business, for the sake of encouraging future business.

(6) We agree to grant you a 2% discount, if you increase your quantity from 5,000 pcs to 10,000 pcs.

Task 2

Short conversations.

(1) Suppose you bargain with your client.

(2) Describe your offer.

III. Guided Talking

Students work in pairs.

Talk about offers in details. The following information can be used for reference:

(1) soccer money box

(2) size (15 cm / diameter)

(3) logo (2 color / 1 position, 3 colors / 1 position)

(4) material: polyresin (树脂)

(5) quantity: 50,000 pcs

IV. Creative Discussion

The teacher divides the class into groups and asks them to discuss one of the following topics, then choose a representative form each group to present their discussion. The student who expresses well will be the winner.

Topic:

What are a firm offer and a non-firm offer?

What are the main differences between firm offer and non-firm offer?

Chapter 6

At China Import and Export Fair

Learning Objectives
Upon completion of this chapter, you will be able to

- know the words and expressions related to business fairs.
- describe your products in detail.
- establish business relations with customers.
- know how to promote sales in the fair.
- understand building global partnerships.[1]

---

[1] 理解建立全球伙伴关系。

At China Import and Export Fair

(Helen, a representative of a Greek company, is now in the bag booth of Canton Fair. Jack is the salesman who works for JOY Bag Company.)

Jack: Good morning. <u>Welcome to our booth.</u>[1]

Helen: Good morning. Nice to meet you. I'm Helen from Greece. Here is my card. We are one of the leading importers at our end. <u>I wish to have a discussion with you about those backpacks on display.</u>[2]

Jack: Thank you. Here is my card. <u>It's a pleasure to have a chance to talk business with you personally.</u>[3] We appreciate your interest. I have some catalogues, and I'd like you to have a look at them.

Helen: Thanks! <u>Do these cover all products displayed on your booth?</u>[4]

Jack: Yes, of course.

Helen: Well, we are managing to import some satchels for the coming season. Would you recommend some for our reference?

Jack: Well. How about these? Item number YX-01 to YX-10. The series of satchels are specially designed for pupils. We use transferring printing to make the logo with vivid cartoon figures which will be popular among pupils.

Helen: Could you tell us the material of those satchels?

Jack: Some of them are 600D × 600D polyester, some are micro fibre.

Helen: Could you give me more details about them?

Jack: <u>Well, here are the specifications for the satchels: 16″ length × 10″ width, and 5″ depth; backing PVC sheet lining; U shaped main compartment entry; removable and adjustable shoulder strap.</u>[5]

Helen: All right. What's the minimum quantity of each item?

Jack: Usually the minimum quantity of each item is 1,000 pcs.

Helen: MOQ?

Jack: 3,000 pcs.

Helen: May I have your price-list ?

Jack: Here you are.

Helen: Oh, it's very considerate of you. If you excuse me, I'll go over your price-list first, then come back again.

Jack: Take your time. Hope to see you.

Talking about Products

(Miss Lin, Manager of Sales Department. Mr. Brown is a client from abroad.)

Lin: Good afternoon! My name is Lin, Manager of Sales Department.

Brown: Nice to see you, Miss Lin.

Lin: Nice to see you too, Mr. Brown. Please have a seat. What would you like, tea or coffee?

Brown: I'd prefer coffee if you don't mind.

Lin: Not in the least. What do you think of the Fair?

Brown: Well, there is a great change about the Fair. I have attended three of your fairs, but I find the business scope this time has been broadened, and there are more businessmen than ever before.

Lin: Really. Did you find anything interesting?

Brown: Yes, quite a few. We have special interest in your products, particularly in your kid's shoes. These shoes are fashionable and suit our market. <u>If they are of high quality and the prices are reasonable, we'll purchase large quantities of them.</u>[6]

Lin: Our shoes are in various colors and sizes. All products have to go through five checks in the whole process. <u>They are not only superior in quality but also attractive in designs as well.</u>[7] They are well-received overseas and are always in great demand.

Brown: That sounds nice.

Lin: Well, for your information, there is an upward tendency on the world market and our prices are likely to rise at any moment. <u>We have specially made out a price-list which covers the most saleable on your market.</u>[8] Here is our price sheet and catalogues.

Brown: Oh, that's nice. By the way, how long will your offer hold good?

Lin: 15 days. Our prices compare most favorably with quotations you can get from other manufacturers. You'll see that from our price sheet. The prices are subject to our confirmation.

Brown: Well, I sincerely hope to establish good business relationship with you and I'd like to have a further discussion with you.

Lin: Me too.

Making Acquaintance with a Business Customer

(*Nancy is a purchaser from America. Park is a salesman of an electronic household corporation.*)

Park: Good morning. May I help you?

Nancy: I wonder if you can give me more information about this refrigerator model you're showing.

Park: I'd be glad to help. Would you like a packet of our promotional literature?

Nancy: Thank you. We've been thinking of placing an order if they are of the types we want and their prices are reasonable.⁹

Park: We also take special orders. That is to say, we can make refrigerators according to samples and specifications.¹⁰

Nancy: These models seem to be quite small.

Park: Yes, one of the problems that we were trying to solve when working on this model was to do away with the freezer. This refrigerator is only USD 50. Its appearance has been designed in the shapes of animals, such as pandas, bears, and so on.

Nancy: Remarkable! There's nothing quite like seeing a problem and solving it to create a good product. Are all the components made here in Shanghai?

Park: Yes, we do some subcontracting, but only in Shanghai. These are made here. May I ask what company you work for?

Nancy: I represent Electronic Supply Company from the United States.

Park: Would you like to tour our factory and perhaps even one or two of our subcontractors?

Nancy: Yes, if it wouldn't take too long to arrange. I'm due to fly back to the States on Friday.¹¹

Park: I'm sure we can arrange it before then. How about meeting the founder of our company? Would you be interested in talking with him about our ideas for upcoming models?

Nancy: That's a good idea. To tell you the truth, we're looking for ways to outperform our competitors. In the past few months, we've been considering the possibility of transferring some of our manufacturing to China as a way to reduce production cost. Our marketing people have done some studies, but their data is mostly second hand.

Park: I guess this is why you came to this fair.

Nancy: You're right. I'd like to have face-to-face contact with people like you.

Park: I see. Why not contact the founder of our company right away?

Nancy: Yes, I think that would be useful. Thank you for your help.

Words and Expressions

1. booth	n.	展摊
2. leading importer		主要进口商

Chapter 6 At China Import and Export Fair

3. at our end		在我方市场
4. logo	n.	标识语
5. polyester	n.	涤纶面料，聚酯纤维
6. micro fibre		超细纤维
7. MOQ =Minimum Order Quantity		最小订购量
8. satchel	n.	书包
9. compartment	n.	分隔的口袋
10. transferring printing		热移印（一种印花技术名称）
11. sales department		销售部
12. superior in quality		质量上乘
13. subcontracting	n.	转包合同
14. specification	n.	规格
15. freezer	n.	冷冻室（冰箱）
16. component	n.	成分
17. outperform	vt.	胜过
18. face-to-face contact		面对面接触

Notes

1. Welcome to our booth.
   欢迎参观我们的展摊。

2. I wish to have a discussion with you about those backpacks on display.
   我想同您谈谈所展出的背包。

3. It's a pleasure to have a chance to talk business with you personally.
   我很高兴有机会与你面谈。
   to have a chance to do sth. 有机会做某事
   例句：

   I'm glad to have a chance to cooperate with you.
   我很高兴有机会与您合作。

   I'm glad to have the chance to call on you.
   我很高兴有机会拜访您。

4. Do these cover all of your products displayed on your booth?
   您展摊上展出的产品都在目录上吗？
   ① displayed on your booth 过去分词短语作定语，修饰products。
   ② on display 展出
   例句：

   A great variety of new products are on display at the fair, which offers a variety of attractions.
   交易会上陈列着多种新产品，很有吸引力。

5. Well, here are the specifications for the satchels: 16″ length × 10″ width, and 5″ depth; backing

PVC sheet lining; U shaped main compartment entry; removable and adjustable shoulder strap.

书包的规格： 长度16英寸，宽度10英寸，厚度是5英寸，PVC背胶，U形口袋，可调整肩带。

specification 规格

例句：

Shall we talk about the specification of the products?

我们能否谈谈产品的规格？

6. If they are of high quality and the prices are reasonable ...

如果质量好，价格合理……

① Our price is most favorable.

我们的价格是最优惠的。

② both reasonable and practical 既合理又可行

③ closely calculated 经过仔细核算

7. They are not only superior in quality but also attractive in designs as well.

它们不仅质量上乘而且设计新颖。

not only ... but also 不但……而且……

例句：

It's not only durable but also competitive in price.

此产品不仅经久耐用，而且价格上很有竞争力。

8. We have specially made out a price-list which covers the most saleable on your market.

我们专门做了一个报价表，上面的产品都是你方市场上畅销的。

saleable 畅销的

例句：

I'm sure the goods will be readily saleable on your market at this price.

我相信此价格在贵方市场上是很好销的。

9. We've been thinking of placing an order if they are of the types we want and their prices are reasonable.

如果是我们要的类型，价格又合理的话，我们会考虑下订单。

we want 是定语从句，修饰types。

They are of the types = they are the types

10. We also take special orders. That is to say, we can make refrigerators according to samples and specifications.

我们还接特殊订单。也就是说，我们可以根据客户的样品及规格生产冰箱。

11. I'm due to fly back to the States on Friday.

我定于星期五飞回美国。

① be due to 将要做

例句：

China International Import Expo is due to show a civilized, open and inclusive China to the rest of the world.

中国国际进口博览会，将向世界展示一个文明、开放、包容的中国。

② in the due time 在规定的时间

③ due to bad weather 由于坏天气

Part B Practical Key Sentences

1. **talking about the products on display**

   I wish to have a discussion with you about those backpacks on display.

   我想同您谈谈展出的背包。

   替换表达：

   I'd like to have a further discussion on the import of hardware with you.

   Is there any way of ensuring we'll have enough time for our talks about the aquatic products business?

   We'd have to compare notes on what we've discussed on the products displayed on your booth during the day.

2. **I'd like to know whether you manufacture ...**

   I'd like to know whether you have photocopier XXC830?

   贵公司是否经营XXC830复印机？

   替换表达：

   Do you have digital answering phones?

   I'm thinking of purchasing /ordering / buying trays.

   I'd go for projectors which are mainly used in conferences.

3. **I have some catalogues ...**

   I have some catalogues and I'd like you to have a look at them.

   我有一些产品目录，请您看一看。

   替换表达：

   Here is a copy of the itinerary we have worked out for you and your friends. Would you please have a look at it?

   Could I have a set of catalogues of all your products?

   Here is my business card and some of the catalogues of our products.

   These drawings on the wall are process sheets and they describe how each process goes on to the next.

4. **Our company specializes in ...**

   Our company specializes in manufacturing office furniture.

   我们公司主要生产办公家具。

   替换表达：

   We are in the line of stationery. We are a state-owned corporation.

   Their line of business is light industrial products.

Our company is one of the leading exporters of MP4.

5. Which appeals to you more ...

Which appeals to you more, the type of NN1 or the type of NN2?

您想要哪种型号，NN1型还是NN2型？

替换表达：

These photo supplies may interest a lot of foreign traders.

You may find packing machinery interesting /of interest.

Which type would you prefer?

6. introduce the characteristics of the dealings

First of all, I will outline the characteristics of our sales.

首先，我将简略说明我们销售经营的特性。

We have adopted much more flexible methods in our dealings.

我们在经营的具体做法上灵活多了。

替换表达：

We have adopted some usual international practices in our trade.

We represent Electronic Products Company and our trade policy has always been based on equality and mutual benefit and exchange of needed goods.

Part C Integration of Theory and Practice

1. attending the fair   参展

【知识点1】参展是企业与客户建立和保持业务联系的最有效的方式之一。与前来展台的客户进行交谈绝非易事，如同在参展前准备样品、布置展摊一样，这种交谈需要一定的技巧。某些客户可能成为企业产品的未来买主，企业代表在展台对他们的接待将决定着参展的成功与否。

【知识点2】与客户接洽的第一步是鼓励他们在你处展台驻足，要表现得热忱，让人感到你们乐意与他们交谈。

【技能训练句型】

Have you seen our latest innovation?

你们见过我们最近的新产品吗？

Do you import products from China?

您从中国进口产品吗？

【知识点3】取得客户的资料，这对企业日后与客户保持联系是很重要的。

【技能训练句型】

May I have your business card, please?

您能否给一张名片？

【知识点4】呈上自己的名片（上面须有详细的资料，如公司名称、姓名、电话号码、手机号和e-mail，有的背面还注明了企业的经营范围及企业网址）。名片要设计新颖，以吸引客户。

【技能训练句型】

Hello, I'm Bill. Here is my card.

您好，我是Bill，这是我的名片。

【知识点5】保留交谈记录，以便日后与参观者进一步联系，增加谈成业务的可能性；记录内容为客户名片、经营范围、对哪些产品感兴趣、产品的资料。

【知识点6】同时要注意以下三点：① 要自信。② 要熟悉自己的产品。因为买家可能非常专业，这就要求我们也要专业。③ 要注意礼节，因为各个国家的习俗是不一样的。

2. introduction of products 产品介绍

【知识点】企业参展的目的是推销自己的产品，产品介绍得成功与否直接影响交易的成败。

【技能训练句型】

通常我们可以这样介绍产品：

Let me tell you about its special features. It's made of leather/wood/steel/aluminium. It weighs just 2.3 kilos. It comes in a wide range of colors.

让我来介绍一下产品的特色之处吧。它是用真皮/木头/钢材/铝制成的，重量只有2.3千克，有多种颜色可供选择。

It has several special features. The most useful feature is the energy-saving design. Another advantage is its very small size.

它有几个特点，最有用的是它的节能设计，另一个长处是它的体积非常小。

Yet on the other hand, our products are hundred percent natural.

不过，我们的产品可是100%全天然的。

This new type of electromobile car can drive 200 kilometers per hour with a built-in air-conditioner.

这种新款电动汽车每小时可行驶200公里，自带空调。

The electric fan needs no lubrication and will not heat up if left on around clock.

这种电扇不用润滑，全天运行也不会发热。

Try this notebook computer. It features a dictionary with 60,000 entries and can store 12,000 addresses.

试一下这种笔记本电脑。它带一部60,000个条目的词典，并能存储12,000个地址。

3. make acquaintance with business customers 接触和认识客户

【知识点】中国进出口商品交易会是中国规模最大，到会国外客户最多，成交效果最好的综合性国际贸易盛会。来自全世界的客商云集，洽谈业务，增进友谊，这是认识客户、建立贸易关系的好机会。

参加展会的重要任务是接触和认识客户，确定贸易对象，发展客户关系，包括巩固与现有客户的关系和发展潜在客户，尤其是后者。潜在客户往往意味着公司的未来发展希望，但是由于展会时间短、客户多，展会接待工作大多是尽可能多地接触和认识客户。展会期间的客户工作应重数量，而展会之后的客户工作则应重质量。要加深与客户的相互了解，建立相互信任关系，使之发展成伙伴关系和买卖关系。

在整个展会中，如何同客人打招呼是很重要的，当客人走到你的展位前停留时，有两种情况：一种是感兴趣的，一种只是随便看看的。一定要注意观察客人的视线停留在哪一类型的产品上，并主动上前同客人打招呼。简单地说"Hi""Morning"或"Hello"，有时甚至一个眼神就可以了，只要引起客人的注意，让他知道你在关注他！

真正的客户，他们一般都会主动和你打招呼的。这时，你就可以开始介绍你公司的产品了。对于无礼的或者傲慢的客人，一定要不卑不亢。

【技能训练句型】

Perhaps you've heard our product's name. Would you like to know more about it?

也许您已听说过我们的产品。您想进一步了解吗？

The purpose of my coming here is to inquire about possibilities of establishing trade relations with your company.

我此行的目的正是想探询与贵公司建立贸易关系的可能性。

If you are interested, I will prepare a list of them.

如果您感兴趣的话，我可以列表让您参考。

I'd like to introduce you to our company. Is there anything in particular you'd like to know?

我将向您介绍我们的公司，您有什么特别想了解的吗？

I'd like to know something about the current investment environment in your country.

我想了解一下贵国的投资环境。

Part D Practice

I. Complete the Following Dialogues

(1)

A: Hello, my ___1___ is Jimmy. Here is my card. Yesterday, I took ___2___ in your demo and found myself particularly ___3___ in your drapery system.

B: Thank you. Here is my ___4___ card and some of the ___5___ of our products.

A: I'm a leading ___6___ at our end. We found your ___7___ are salable in our ___8___.

B: Good. Our drapery system is patented ___9___ its unique design.

A: By the way, are you licensed to ___10___?

B: Yes, of course. We have a licensed exporter since 1989.

(2)

A: Good afternoon, ladies and gentlemen, welcome to Y&X mobile phone booth. Today, I take ___1___ in presenting to you one of our ___2___ developed mobile phone, YX192. The new ___3___ incorporates multiple functions.

B: My name is John Smith. I'm the sales manager of G&X Company. Could you ___4___ your products' multiple functions?

A: The remote control can control ___5___ functions individually. It is a unique design. The timer can preset times open/close with 24 hours.

B: Could I ____6____ a set of catalogue of all your products?
A: Yes, of course. Could you ____7____ me your ____8____ card, please?
B: OK.

II. Role-plays

Task 1

Question and answer.

At the Q&A session, some visitors ask a lot of questions, such as: Could you specify the function of your unique design? Could I have a set of catalogues of all your products?

Students work in pairs to give as many questions as possible. Then the teacher chooses two members to be the chairpersons of the Q&A session and others work as visitors questioning the chairpersons.

Task 2

Short conversation.

Suppose you are a stationery purchaser from Australia. You visit Canton Fair. You go to talk with the sales promoters of the stationary booths. Make 3 dialogues according to the following topics:

(1) establishing a business relationship
(2) asking for the product catalogue
(3) inquiring about the price

III. Guided Talking

Students work in pairs.
Topic: At the show
Use the following to practice with your partner:
(1) Establish or consolidate business relationship
(2) Solve specific problems
(3) Find a new market
(4) Appoint agents /seek principals
(5) Discuss specific terms /conditions
(6) Seek the latest products
(7) Obtain new technical knowledge
(8) Discuss business needs in a neutral environment

IV. Creative Discussion

The teacher divides the class into groups and asks them to discuss and choose a representative of each group after discussion. The student who expresses well will be the winner.

Topic:

1. Have you ever attended any show? What are your reasons for attending it?

2. What is your impression at China Import and Export Fair?

Chapter 7
Business Visit

Learning Objectives
Upon completion of this chapter, you will be able to

- ☑ get to know the process of welcoming visitors.
- ☑ learn how to introduce your company or factory.
- ☑ conduct the activities related to being a host.
- ☑ discuss more details with clients at working site.
- ☑ understand drawing on each other's strengths.[1]

---

1 懂得优势互补。

Part A Situational Dialogue

Communicative Scene 1

Visiting the Factory

(Mrs. Elizabeth Gage, General Manager of Union Supplies Company from the United States of America, is paying a visit to Mr. Huang's factory for the first time.)

Huang: I am so happy to meet you again in our factory, Mrs. Gage. How are things going with you and your family?

Gage: Fine, just fine. Thank you. Since we are old friends, please call me Lisa. May I call you "Huang"?

Huang: Sure, Lisa. How is your lovely boy, Tom? He must have grown up a lot since I saw him last time in the States.

Gage: Yes, he is now a high school student. I should say he is a handsome man.

Huang: Good! How is Mr. Gage? Why didn't he come this time?

Gage: Fine, just fine. Thank you. He is fully occupied by his work.

Huang: It's a pity. <u>Please extend my sincere wishes to him.</u>[1]

Gage: I will. In fact, I am fully responsible for the business between our two companies now.

Huang: I'm very happy to work with you. I believe the cooperation between us will be more delightful and fruitful.

Gage: Me too.

Huang: May I give you a tour of the factory?

Gage: Sounds great.

Huang: <u>As you may know, it is now the peak season for nanometer antibacterial shoes, so our factory is working at full capacity.</u>[2] We have a production capacity of 10 thousand pairs of shoes per day.

Gage: Good. One of our purposes to visit is to see how well our order is carrying out. The quality of the products is always the most important matter and the delivery time is also a vital point, especially for the seasonal products.

(<u>While talking, they are approaching the production line where the products for Union Supplies Company are under processing.</u>)[3]

Huang: I fully agree with you. I'm sure that our products will meet the standards specified in our contract and your requirement. According to our working schedule, your order will be completed in time for delivery. Don't worry about it.

Gage: Could you complete all the orders from other customers at the same time besides our company?

Huang: Basically yes, our workers will work overtime 2 hours every day in peak season, though we have to pay double overtime payment.

Gage: How do you control the quality?

Huang: Here is the Quality Inspection Section. All shoes are made under an extremely tight quality control.

Gage: I am very interested in learning more about it.

Huang: The finished products will flow to this section before they continue their trip to the packing area. The products are 100% checked here and defective ones will be thrown out to these boxes for <u>the head of the workshop and technicians to analyze what the problems are and find out the ways to prevent the occurrence again.</u>[4]

Gage: Is that your Design Department?

Huang: Yes, look at our revolutionary new nanometer products. We always make great efforts to keep the novelty of products. What's your overall impression of our factory?

Gage: Wow, excellent! Seeing is believing. Mr. Gage told me a lot about what he had seen in your factory. Now I have seen with my own eyes. I will report everything I saw here and I believe our orders will be placed immediately after the delivery of this batch.

Huang: Thanks a lot!

Meeting in the Showroom

(Miss Jin, Sales Manager of Broad Arts & Crafts Company accompanies Mr. Brian from a Canadian company to look around the showroom of the company.)

Brian: How nice your showroom is!

Jin: Thank you! Please feel free to look around our showroom, which is fully opened to you.

Brian: I'm glad to hear you say so. As I introduced to you last night in my hotel room, our company is one of the major dealers of arts and crafts in Canada. We are handling various kinds of art products. The variety of numbers is up to 1 500. Most of them are imported from China because the Chinese arts and crafts are well appreciated by our customers.

Jin: What particular products are you looking for?

Brian: I'm seeking arts porcelain, ornaments for display, imitation antique porcelain, and so on.

Jin: You have found the right place because our main products are ceramic arts and crafts. With rich raw materials, the workmanship, up-to-date patterns and <u>featuring great varieties,</u>[5] our products enjoy a good reputation at home and abroad.

Brian: Great!

Jin: Let's look around all the display of arts and crafts first. Then sit down and have a detailed talk on quality, quantity, price and other issues.

Brian: OK. Can you provide us with some samples?

Jin: Sure. Are you going to take them with you? If so, I'll pack them now.

Brian: No, they are heavy and I'll travel to some other places. Could you send them back to my office directly?

Jin: No problem. However, you may have to pay for the postage. I'll send them by postage due.

Brian: That will be fine. Thank you for your kind help. Here is a new design from our company. Can you make a counter sample for us? I hope I'll take this one back with me.

Jin: We'll make the counter sample in about ten days. When are you leaving?

Brian: Saturday. I don't think there is enough time before I leave. Will you send it together with your samples? We hope your counter sample can meet all the requirements indicated in this description sheet.

Jin: You can rest assured. I believe that <u>well begun is half done</u>.[6] I hope the counter sample is a satisfactory beginning of the new business between us.

Brian: I hope so, too.

Communicative Scene 3

Discussion on Investment

(Mr. Dong is discussing an investment proposal with Mr. Watt, CEO of a foreign company.)

Dong: Mr. Watt, to our regret, we are unable to supply the bearing you are asking since it is the busiest season and our factory has been operating in three shifts. We are totally booked up until next March.

Watt: Sorry to hear that. However, I'm coming not only to push you to make the best arrangement of our order, but also to discuss the possibility of our investment on a new machine line to produce bearing for us.

Dong: We appreciate your timely help. But you know to build up a new production line takes a long time. How can we have our production capacity doubled overnight?

Watt: We had a manufacturing line in Korea before. As the labor cost got higher and higher, the products manufactured there lost their competitive ability. If we ship the existing line here, it won't take too much time. <u>The new production capacity will come into being in two or three months</u>.[7]

Dong: It is an interesting proposal. Do you have a more detailed plan to carry out your proposal?

Watt: Sure. It takes about two weeks to disassemble and pack the line. Another two or three weeks are needed to ship the goods and one more week for customs declaration. If we lose no time, we can reassemble and adjust the machine line in three weeks. And then the line can be put into production by the end of this year, which means we can save more than two months than just waiting for the present production lines.

Dong: Are you sure the line can be rebuilt up and put into use in such a short time?

Watt: I'm quite confident because we can bring the engineers and workers who had worked in this factory before. They knew the line very well just as their own children.

Dong: How are you going to charge for this line?

Watt: We don't want to have additional charge for the line itself. We request the line must be used for our orders only. The cost of daily maintenance of the machine line should be covered by your side.

Dong: Please let me think it over.

Watt: Our company won't pay any down payment for our orders, because we'll have deposited our machines in your factory.[8] Of course, we will pay full amount when the orders are completed. It is your responsibility to keep the machines in good condition. During the period while our line is used in your factory, we will possess the complete right to dispose our properties.

Dong: It sounds very reasonable. We will provide necessary assistances for customs declaration, local transportation, and assembly in our workshop. We will give you a final reply in two days after our board meeting tomorrow. In my personal opinion, I am certain that our board meeting will approve this "win-win" proposal.[9]

Watt: I'm glad to hear that and looking forward to having your positive decision.

Words and Expressions

1. simplify		vt.	使简单，简化
2. delightful		adj.	令人高兴的，使人快乐的
3. fruitful		adj.	多产的，富有成效的
4. nanometer antibacterial shoes			纳米抗菌鞋
5. vital		adj.	极其重要的；必不可少的；致命的
6. peak		adj.	最高的，高峰的
7. approach		vt.	接近，靠近
8. overtime		adj.	超时的；加班的
9. defective		adj.	有缺陷的
10. occurrence		n.	发生，出现
11. novelty		n.	新颖，新奇，新鲜
12. batch		n.	批，次
13. accompany		vt.	陪，伴
14. arts and crafts		n.	工艺品
15. arts porcelain			美术陶瓷
16. ornaments for display			陈设（陶瓷）
17. imitation antique porcelain			仿古陶瓷

18. bearing	n.	轴承
19. shift	n.	轮班；转变
20. overnight	adv.	一夜间，一下子，突然
	adj.	一夜间的，突然的
21. disassemble	vt.	拆卸，分解
22. maintenance	n.	维修；保养；维持，保持
23. responsibility	n.	责任，职责；责任心；任务
24. possess	vt.	拥有，占有
25. dispose	vt.	处理；布置；安排
26. property	n.	财产，资产；性质，特征
27. assistance	n.	帮助，援助
28. transportation	n.	运输，运送
29. workshop	n.	车间
30. positive	adj.	正面的；积极的；肯定的；明确的

Notes

1. Please extend my sincere wishes to him.
   请代我向他转达我的衷心祝福。
   extend *v.* 给予，提供；延伸，伸展；扩张
   例句：
   We extend a warm welcome to Chairman of Chamber of Commerce.
   我们给予商会会长热烈的欢迎。
   Our factory intends to extend our production line.
   我们打算扩大生产线。

2. As you may know, it is now the peak season for nanometer antibacterial shoes, so our factory is working at full capacity.
   你可能了解，现在是纳米抗菌鞋的生产高峰期，我们的工厂正在满负载生产。
   ① peak season 高峰期，比busy season的程度更强，表示最繁忙。
   ② at peak periods 在最繁忙的时刻，在高峰期
   ③ at off-peak producing period 在低谷生产期
   ④ the peak output 最高产量
   ⑤ at full capacity 满负载，以全部力量，满功率

3. While talking, they are approaching the production line where the products for Union Supplies Company are under processing.
   谈话间，他们来到正在生产联合供应公司产品的生产线。
   ① under processing 正在加工中
   under 在……中（表示过程）

Chapter 7 Business Visit

例句：
The products quotation is under way.
产品的报价正在进行中。
The trade showroom of the factory is under construction.
工厂的展室正在建设之中。

② While talking...
本句中while 是连词，引导状语从句。while从句中要用延续性动词。
▶ while 当……的时候
例句：
While (I am) making a business appointment, my secretary gets ready for taking notes.
当我正在联系商务约会的时候，我的秘书做好准备记录。
▶ while 虽然，但是
例句：
While you have a point there, I can't agree with you.
虽然你说得有道理，但我还是不同意。

4. The head of the workshop and technicians analyze what the problems are and find out the ways to prevent them from occurring again.
车间主任和技术员分析问题原因，并找出防止再度发生的办法。
① find out 指通过观察和探索而发现真相，发现秘密和调查出原因。
例句：
The bank has helped us to find out the potential customer's credit standing.
银行已帮助我们调查潜在客户的资信状况。
② find 常指偶然发现，碰到。当表示了解、打听的意思时，与find out同义。
例句：
You'll find the right products in our factory.
你在我们工厂能找到想要的产品。
③ find与looking for, discover 的区别：find强调找到的结果，而looking for强调寻找的过程，discover强调发现客观事物的存在。

5. featuring great varieties 种类繁多
feature vt. & n. 以……为特色；特征，特色
例句：
The automated production features largely in the factory.
自动化生产是这家工厂的一大特色。

6. Well begun is half done.
（谚语）良好的开端是成功的一半。

7. The new production capacity will come into being in two or three months.
可在两三个月内形成新的生产能力。
come into being 产生，形成，成立
例句：
Before fax came into being, telex was a popular means of communication.

在传真还没出现以前，电传是流行的通信工具。

8. Our company won't pay any down payment for our orders, because we'll have deposited our machines in your factory.

我们公司将不再支付我方订单的预付款，因为我们的机器已经抵押在贵厂了。

① down payment 预付定金

② deposit *vt.* & *n.* 储蓄，寄存；定金，押金

9. In my personal opinion, I am certain that our board meeting will approve this "win-win" proposal.

但我个人认为我们的董事会定会批准这项"双赢"的建议。

① win-win 是指双方都有赢利，达到双赢。

例句：

Fair trade is a win-win situation because both producers and consumers benefit.

公平贸易达到双赢，生产者和消费者都有利可图。

② no-win 指在没有结果的情况下，各方皆有损失。

*10. by postage collect 采用邮费到付

freight collect 运费到付

collect call 受话方付费电话

Part B Practical Key Sentences

1. **asking after somebody**

见面询问家庭情况时的常用语：

How are things going with you and your family?

家里一切都好吗？

转达问候的常用语：

Please extend my best wishes to him.

请代我向他转达我的衷心祝福。

Please give my kind regards to him.

请向他转达我的问候。

替换表达：

How is everything with you and your family?

How is everything at home?

Please remember me to your husband.

Say hello to your colleagues for us.

2. **showing around the factory**

May I give you a tour of the factory?

我可以带您参观工厂吗？

Let me show you around the factory.

我带您参观一下工厂。

替换表达：
　　Let me take you to have a look of the production line.
　　Shall we go to the showroom?

3. be fully occupied

The producers are totally booked up until next March from now.
从现在到明年三月份的订单已经满了。
He employed himself in the design of up-to-date patterns.
他正忙着设计最新的款式。
He is fully occupied by his work.
他正忙着工作。

替换表达：
　　He occupied himself with touring a factory.
　　The manufacturers busied themselves preparing counter-samples.
　　The president is engaged. Can you call him an hour later?

4. be fully responsible for

I am fully responsible for the business between our two companies now.
我现在全权负责我们之间的业务。
take full responsibility　全权负责，对……负完全责任
例句：
　　General manager took full responsibility for the company affairs.
　　总经理负责公司的全部事务。

替换表达：
　　The inspectors are in charge of product inspection.
　　The manufacturer has an obligation to deliver the goods as required.
　　It is our duty to make good quality goods.

5. make great efforts

We always make great efforts to keep the novelty of products.
我们总是竭尽全力保持产品的新颖性。
The designers do their utmost to make the color of products more attractive.
设计师们全力以赴让产品的色彩更引人注目。

替换表达：
　　Our company goes all out to develop overseas market.
　　The manufacturers do their best to improve the quality of products.

Part C Integration of Theory and Practice

1. enhancing close relationship　　加深友情

　　【知识点】拜访或接待客户时，先说些轻松的话题，拉拉家常，可增强彼此的亲切感。

【技能训练句型】

Since we are old friends, please call me Lisa. To be simplified, I'll call you "Huang", is it OK?

既然我们是老朋友了，请叫我丽莎。我可以简单点叫你小黄吗？

Sure, Lisa. How is your lovely boy, Tom? He must have grown up a lot since I saw him last time in the States.

当然可以，丽莎。您那可爱的儿子汤姆好吗？自从我上次在美国见到他以来，他一定长大了许多。

2. visiting the guest most concern section　考察客户最关心的环节

【知识点1】如果来访的客户想了解产品生产过程、生产工艺、质量检验环节等，则应妥善安排，让客户一饱眼福，眼见为实。

【技能训练句型】

One of our purposes to visit is to see how well our order is carrying out. The quality of the products is always the most important matter and the delivery time is also a vital point, especially for the seasonal products.

我此行的目的之一就是想了解我们订单的执行情况。产品质量永远是最重要的，而交货期也是一个关键因素，尤其对于季节性产品来说。

【知识点2】以本文的客户为例，当了解客人来访的目的后，可带他们到工厂看看，并针对来访目的多考察客户最关心的环节。

【技能训练句型】

They are approaching the production line where the products for Union Supplies Company are under processing.

他们来到正在生产联合供应公司纳米抗菌鞋产品的生产线。

Here is Quality Inspection Section. All shoes are made under an extremely tight quality control.

这里是质量检验区，所有的产品都经过极其严格的质量检测。

I'll show you around our Design Department.

我带你看看我们的设计部门。

3. introducing with specific detail　具体详细的介绍

【知识点1】向客人介绍工厂或公司情况时，要重点介绍自己的特色。

【技能训练句型】

You have found the right place because our main products are ceramic arts and crafts. With rich raw materials, fine workmanship, up-to-date patterns and featuring great varieties, our products enjoy good reputation at home and abroad.

您算找对地方了，因为我们的主要产品就是工艺瓷器。由于资源丰富、工艺精湛、款式新颖和种类繁多，我们的产品在国内外市场上享有盛誉。

【知识点2】向客人介绍工厂或公司情况时，要实事求是，不可过分拔高公司。

【技能训练句型】

We are the leading porcelain enterprise in China.

我们是中国陶瓷的龙头企业。

【知识点3】我们对客户作业务介绍时，常用上述的句子，但如果未达到龙头企业水准，就不要任意添油加醋。应该作具体详细的介绍，多用实际数字说话。

【技能训练句型】

We have a production capacity of 30 thousand pairs of shoes per day.

我们工厂的生产能力达到每天3万双鞋。

We are handling various kinds of art products. The total article numbers are up to 2,000.

我们经营着品种繁多的工艺产品，总数可达2,000种。

4. feeling satisfactory at the visit   让客户感到满意

【知识点1】让客户对最关心的产品标准、按期交货、产品种类和款式新颖等感到满意。

【技能训练句型】

I'm sure that our products will meet the standards specified in our contract and your requirement. According to our working schedule, your order will be completed in time for delivery.

我确信我们的产品会符合合同规定的标准和您的要求。根据我们的工作日程安排，贵方的订单将按期完工交货。

Look at our revolutionary new nanometer products. We always make great efforts to keep the novelty of products.

请看我们的创新纳米产品。我们总是尽力保持产品的新颖性。

【知识点2】考察结束后，要及时询问客户的感觉，激起客户购买的欲望。如有不妥的地方，则应进一步完善。

【技能训练句型】

What's your overall impression of our company?

您对本公司的总印象如何？

Seeing is believing. Mr. Gage told me a lot about what he had seen in your factory. Now I have seen with my own eyes. I will report everything I saw here and I believe our orders will be placed immediately after the delivery of this batch.

真是眼见为实啊。盖治先生曾多次告诉我他在贵厂的所见所闻，现在是我亲眼所见。我将向公司报告我的所见所闻，我相信在这批产品发货后，后续订单会接踵而来。

5. please think it over   请考虑考虑

【知识点】与客户商谈时，若遇到重大事情切不可急急忙忙地做出决定。守信是商务活动的基本原则，答应的事情如反悔改变，会产生不良后果。因此，碰到重大决策时要认真思考，请客户给点时间考虑。

【技能训练句型】

Please let me think it over.

请让我考虑考虑。

I am not in a position to give you a decision now. I have to discuss it with my colleagues.

我无法现在就给你做决定，我不得不与同事共同商议。

Part D Practice

I. Complete the Following Dialogues

(1)

Ye: Hello, nice to see you again, Mr. Bill.

Bill: Hi, long time no see. To be ___1___, just call me Bill.

Ye: OK, Bill. Let me give you a ___2___ of the factory.

Bill: That's exactly what I want to do. There is nothing like ___3___ things with my own eyes.

Ye: What do you like to see in ___4___?

Bill: I'd like to see your production ___5___ first.

Ye: Come on. Please ___6___ me to the workshop.

Bill: I appreciate the engineers and workers do their ___7___ to make the high quality products.

Ye: Thank you.

Bill: I see that the automated production ___8___ largely in the factory.

Ye: Some machines are designed by our engineers.

Bill: Great. It is really a large factory. I think I have found the right ___9___ for my future orders.

Ye: I think you'll have a better idea about our factory now. I am ___10___ your order.

(2)

Yang: Martin, shall I give you a general ___1___ of the company?

Martin: Certainly. I couldn't ___2___ more.

Yang: Ours is a large washing machine company in the province. We have a good ___3___ in this field.

Martin: What is your production ___4___?

Yang: We have a production capacity of 80 thousand washing machines ___5___ month.

Martin: When is your ___6___ season?

Yang: Oh, we are fully ___7___ until next December from now.

Martin: My purpose to visit is to see how well our order is ___8___ out.

Yang: Don't worry. We ___9___ ourselves to meet the standards specified in our contract and your requirement.

Martin: I am glad to hear it.

Yang: Look! Your washing machines are ___10___ processing there.

II. Interaction Activities

Task 1

Ask students to work in pairs and make a dialogue according to the situation.

A and B talk about the new products.

Use the following expressions:

(1) design department
(2) revolutionary new nanometer products
(3) up-to-date patterns
(4) make great efforts
(5) have a new face
(6) upgrade products
(7) overall impression
(8) Seeing is believing.

Task 2

Talking about joint investment.
Use the following expressions in your dialogue:
(1) after looking around the plant
(2) While ... the production capacity is not large enough.
(3) enlarge the production scale
(4) double overnight
(5) be kidding
(6) prevent sb. from expansion
(7) out of funds
(8) joint investment
(9) in detail
(10) provide the existing line
(11) It's not incredible that ...
(12) come into being

III. Actual Practice

Make up a conversation and role-play the following practical situation.
1. Mr. Tang, director of the factory, is showing Mr. Watt around the factory.
2. Mr. Watt is seeking for arts porcelain, ornaments for display, imitation antique porcelain.
3. Mr. Tang believes his products will meet the client's demand.
4. The showroom displays a great variety of porcelain.
5. Mr. Tang introduces the features of the ceramic arts and crafts.
6. Mr. Watt wants to see everything with his own eyes instead of telling story by Mr. Tang.
7. After the visit, Mr. Watt considers to place an initial order soon.

IV. Creative Discussion

The teacher divides the class into groups and asks students to discuss. Then each group takes turns presenting its conclusions.

Topic:

1. What are the important aspects to show the visiting clients?

2. How should you make an appropriate introduction of the factory?

3. How should you make clients feel satisfied at the visit so as to induce them to place more orders?

Chapter 8

Innovative and Power Brand Strategy

Learning Objectives
Upon completion of this chapter, you will be able to

- learn the importance of innovative strategy and own brands.
- improve your communication skills on technical discussions.
- discuss more specifically technical issues with your clients.
- avoid disputes on technical issues when you deal with a business transaction.
- make yourself more knowledgeable in more fields.
- move with the tide of the times.[1]

1　顺应时代发展潮流。

Part A Situational Dialogue

Communicative Scene 1

Discussion on Innovative Commodity

(Mr.Nixon is visiting Miss Zhao's company and they are discussing the innovative products and own power brands.)

Zhao: Hello, Mr. Nixon. It's so nice to meet you again.

Nixon: Hello, Miss Zhao. Have you received our fax regarding the issues of commodity innovation that we want to talk with you? To promote the sales in our market, our company wants to improve and modernize the design, quality and some other matters.

Zhao: Oh, yes. Shall we begin our discussion now?

Nixon: Sure, let's start from the design. As your products have been sold in the market for some time, there have been some copies from other manufacturers and importers. <u>To lead the market, we'd like to show our customers some new faces of tools.</u>[1] Do you have any good ideas for that?

Zhao: Yes. That is what we are worrying about. We have paid special attention to it for some time. Our company is adopting an innovative strategy. We'll try our best to create our own power brands.

Nixon: Great!

Zhao: <u>Only through innovation and creation of our own power brands can our company hold market share in this intensified market competition.</u>[2]

Nixon: Absolutely.

Zhao: Our designers have developed some new designs for you to choose from. We may start with one or two of them to see the response from the customers while we are selling the old items.

Nixon: That's a good idea. They all look very nice. I believe they will meet with great favor in our market. Also, <u>to make our products look more fancy, our company is going to adopt a new series of color sleeves</u>.[3]

Zhao: Printing these new sleeves is not a problem. We'll use brighter paper to print the sleeves to make them look brighter.

Nixon: I'm anxiously looking forward to seeing innovative products with the new series packing on the store shelves of our supermarkets. We have still received some complaints from our customers, though the quality of your tools are basically acceptable. We'd like to mention it again, because we don't want to lose our market and customers due to small quality problems.

Zhao: We certainly appreciate your reminding us of quality. As a matter of fact, the quality is always a key point in our mind. For your information, our company has just passed ISO 9000 and our products are applying for a CE Certificate now. With CE Certificate, our products will stand higher in European market, which will specially benefit your company.

Nixon: I'm so glad to hear the good news. Last but not least, we request that all the tools should be heat-treated.⁴

Zhao: That will not be a problem from technical point of view. However, the overall price, due to production cost, will be some 20% higher than the present one in the case all the tools are heat-treated.

Nixon: I understand, but I'm sorry to say it is a must.⁵ Meanwhile we don't like to force our customers to pay higher prices.

Zhao: In this case, may I suggest a compromise? Let us make easily worn-out screwdriver bits heat-treated instead of all the tools, so that we can increase the rank of our tools and keep the prices steady.

Nixon: Personally speaking, I accept your proposal. However, I'm not entitled to the decision in this matter.⁶ I'll have to call my headquarter office to get their approval. Anyway, I'm very pleased to see everything being settled so smoothly. I appreciate your kind cooperation on almost every field.

Zhao: You are always welcome.

Communicative Scene 2

Specific Technical Negotiation

(*Technical negotiation between Mr. Chen and Mr. Marks is going on.*)

Chen: Mr. Marks, we have carefully studied your prototype and related drawings of the ladder hooks. We are very interested in developing this new patent product with you.

Marks: I'm glad to hear that. What can I do for you now?

Chen: First of all, we'd like to discuss some technical issues with you. We tested your prototype and found that the plastic clip part bends easily, even breaks if the screw is tightened too much. To solve this problem, we suggest using metal parts to replace the plastic ones.

Marks: It is technically OK, but commercially not, because the metal part does not look as good as the plastic one.

Chen: Got it. We may have to make the plastic part thicker than the original design to strengthen the weak point.

Marks: That is what we want.

Chen: Before starting work on it, we'd like to see if we can find a ready market for ladder hooks.

101

Marks: I don't know for sure.

Chen: Do you have any idea how many pieces you are going to order for the first time?

Marks: Does that matter?

Chen: Yes. It certainly does. As you know, to produce the plastic portion for this product, we must build three injection molds. Each one will cost USD 1,000. Moreover, we need 5 dies and USD 200 for each. We shall invest at least USD 4,000 at the very beginning. If the order quantity were too small, the unit price for each product would be very high.

Marks: Is there a better way out?[7]

Chen: You may have to pay for the moulds and dies first. We'll pay you back the cost for moulds and dies by deducting from the unit price when your future orders accumulate up to 100,000 pieces.[8]

Marks: That means I'll have to take the risk of USD 4,000 investment until I can sell 100,000 pieces. Is there any way to minimize my risk?

Chen: Let me think...OK, let's share the risk by half and half. Our company will pay USD 2,000 and you'll pay the rest.

Marks: That's very kind of you. Thank you so much.

Chen: But, please note since we share the risk with you, we'll be unable to pay you back your portion no matter what quantity of products you are going to order in the future. Do you agree?

Marks: Sure, you are quite right. We will write it down in our contract.

Chen: Good! Let's move forward.

Communicative Scene 3

Trademark and Patent

(Mr. Zhang and Mr. Brown are discussing an electronic product sales contract.)

Brown: What a relief after 3 days of tough negotiation on this contract! I'm so happy we have finally come to a successful conclusion.

Zhang: As a Chinese saying goes, "The road to happiness is always strewn with setbacks."[9] Before celebrating victory, we still have two more points to discuss with you.

Brown: Two more "setbacks"? My goodness!

Zhang: Please don't worry. We believe they can be settled without any difficulties.

Brown: Really? What are they?

Zhang: As you mentioned in articles 11 and 12, your high-tech product is a US patented product and we should sell your products with your trademark.

Brown: Is there any problem?

Chapter 8 Innovative and Power Brand Strategy

Zhang: No, not at all. At first, we need you to provide us with copies of your patent certificate and trademark registration to show you are the owner of the patent and trademark.[10] We also want to see that your patent and trademark are still valid.

Brown: OK. That is no problem. We will attach the copies to this contract as the appendixes.

Zhang: At the same time, we strongly recommend you to apply for the trademark in China to protect yourself from offences.[11] In case the trademark is registered by someone else, it'll be a headache.

Brown: You are absolutely right. Thank you for reminding me. We will register our trademark in China without any delay. By the way, as we are not familiar with related Chinese laws and regulations, could you help me to do this in someway?

Zhang: Certainly. To do this, we need an authorized letter from your company before we start.

Brown: Thank you ever so much.

Zhang: Now we can cheer for the conclusion of our business.

Words and Expressions

1. fancy	adj.	花哨的；奇特的；异样的
2. modernize	v.	使现代化
3. adopt	vt.	采用，采纳，采取；收养
4. innovative strategy		创新战略
5. intensify	vi. & vt.	加强，增强
6. sleeve	n.	套管，color sleeve 彩套
7. shelf	n.	货架
8. complaint	n.	抱怨；投诉
9. as a matter of fact		实际上，其实
10. for your information		供参考
11. ISO	abbr.	International Organization for Standardization 国际标准化机构
12. compromise	n., vi. & vt.	套管；折中，让步
13. worn-out		用坏的，穿旧的
14. screwdriver bits		螺丝刀头
15. entitle	vt.	给权力，有资格
16. prototype	n.	原型；模型；样板
17. ladder hook		梯用挂钩
18. clip	n.	夹子，回形针
19. bend	vt.	夹住；修剪
	vi.	弯曲；屈服
20. injection	n.	注射；喷射；注塑
21. mould	n.	注塑模，压铸模
22. die	n.	冲压模

23. accumulate	*vt. & vi.*	积累，积聚
24. portion	*n.*	部分
25. tough	*adj.*	坚韧的，强硬的，严峻的
26. strew	*vt.*	撒，播；铺盖
27. setback	*n.*	挫折；失败；逆流；旋涡
28. appendix	*n.*	附件，附录
29. high-tech		高科技
30. patent	*n.*	专利权
31. offend	*vt.*	冒犯；伤害
offense (Chiefly America)	*n.*	冒犯；伤害
offence (Chiefly British)	*n.*	冒犯；伤害
32. regulation	*n.*	规则，规章；调节
33. authorized letter		授权书

Notes

1. To lead the market, we'd like to show our customers some new faces of tools.

   为了引领市场，我们想让客户看到新面孔的工具产品。

   ① to lead the market 为了引领市场

   同义词： to direct the market, to guide the market

   ② show *n.,v* 指示；出示；引导；显示；说明；展出

   非正式用语，使用范围广，所表示的"显示"可以是有意的，也可以是无意的，或由于疏忽而暴露。而display是强调摆给别人看，特别把要给人家看的东西精心陈列出来，如精心陈列展品，以期收到良好的展示效果。

2. Only through innovation and creation of our own power brands can our company hold market share in this intensified market competition.

   只有通过产品创新和创立名牌，我们公司才能在激烈的市场竞争中占一席之地。

   ① 本句为倒装句，重点强调产品创新和创立名牌。Only在句子开头，can随其后，倒装句型提醒读者后边是一个条件句，起强调作用。

   例句：

       Only through the introduction of competition can we cut down the prices.

       只有引入竞争机制，才能把价格降下。

   ② power brand 品牌

   ③ brand power strategy / brand strategies 品牌战略

3. To make our products look more fancy, our company is going to adopt new series of color sleeves.

   为了让我们的产品看上去更有花样，我们公司准备采用新系列的彩套。

   ① fancy

   ▶ fancy *adj.* 超过的，不合理的

   例句：

Chapter 8 Innovative and Power Brand Strategy

    Mr. Smith paid a fancy price for a computer.
    史密斯先生以过高的价格买下一部电脑。

► fancy *vt.* 设想，认为，爱好，自负 *n.* 爱好，迷恋，想象力
例句：
    Fancy meeting you here in the exhibition!
    想不到在展览馆见面！

► take / catch the fancy of 使……喜欢；吸引
例句：
    The Commodity Fair catches the fancy of thousands of businessmen.
    商品交易会吸引了数以千计的商人。

► take a fancy to 喜欢上……

② adopt

► adopt *vt.* 采用，采纳，采取；收养
例句：
    Our company is adopting an innovative strategy.
    我们公司正推行产品创新战略。
    adopt new series of color sleeves 采用新系列的彩套

注意 adopt 与 adapt，adept 的区别：

► adapt *v.* 使适应，改编
例句：
    The manufacturers should adapt themselves to the market requirements.
    生产厂家应使自己适应新的市场要求。

    adept *n.* 内行；有很高技巧的人，专家

4. Last but not least, we request that all the tools should be heat-treated.
最后，很重要的一点是要求将所有工具进行热处理。
Last but not least 是插入语，位于句首，起加强语气和承上启下的作用。翻译时注意不要照字面译成"最后，但并非不重要的一点"，而应译为"最后，很重要的一点"。
例句：
    Last but not least, I'll have to make a report to the general manager to get the approval.
    最后，很重要的一点是我不得不向总经理汇报以便得到批准。

5. I'm sorry to say it is a must.
我很抱歉，必须这么做。
be a must 必须做
例句：
    A good command of English is a must in foreign trade.
    从事外贸，掌握好英语是必须的。

6. Personally speaking, I accept your proposal. However, I'm not entitled to the decision in this matter.
我个人可以接受你的建议。但在这个问题上，我无权决定。

① be entitled to 有权，给……权利，给……资格

② entitle sb. to do sth. 给某人做某事的权利

例句：

  The seller is entitled to the payment on presenting documents.

  卖方有权在递交单证后得到支付。

7. Is there a better way out?

  有什么解决的办法？

  Please find a way out.

  请找出路。

8. We'll pay you back the cost for moulds and dies by deducting from the unit price when your future orders accumulate up to 100,000 pieces.

  当你的订货数量累计达到10万件时，我们将从单价中扣还模具的费用。

  ① deduct *v.* 扣除

  ② accumulate *v.* 积累

  accumulate使用范围较广，强调经过一段较长的时间由少积多的积累，可以表示数量方面的积累增长。

  ③ up to 多至……；一直到；等于

9. As a Chinese saying goes, "The road to happiness is always strewn with setbacks."

  正如中国话所说的，"好事多磨"。

  ① strew *vt.* 播，撒．

  例句：

    Export documents were strewn all over the floor.

    出口单证撒满了一地板。

  同义词：distribute，spread，scatter

  ② setback *n.* 挫折

10. At first, we need you to provide us with copies of your patent certificate and trademark registration to show you are the owner of the patent and trademark.

  首先我方需要贵公司提供专利证书和商标注册的复印件，以表明贵公司是这项专利和商标的所有权人。

  trademark registration 注册商标

  同义词组：registered trademark，have trademark registered，apply for the registration

11. We strongly recommend you to apply for the trademark in China to protect yourself from offenses.

  我们竭力建议贵公司在中国申请此商标以保护自己免受侵犯。

  ① recommend sb. to do sth. 建议……做……

  例句：

    The lawyer strongly recommended to prepare a lot of documents for trademark registration, and many of them must be notarized.

    为了申请注册商标，律师强烈忠告要准备就绪大量凭证，许多凭证还要公证。

② recommend 后接从句结构时，要用虚拟语气

例句：

The manager strongly recommended that you notice the trademark to be limited by region.

经理强烈建议要注意商标受地域的限制。

*12. However, it is greatly related with the matter of production cost.

然而，它与生产成本有很大关系。

① be greatly related with ... 与……有很大关系

② relate with / to 使联系

例句：

CFR prices relate the cost with freight.

成本加运费价涉及成本与运费。

Part B Practical Key Sentences

1. expressing the idea of good sale

Our newly designed artificial intelligence have met with great favor home and abroad.

我们新设计的人工智能产品在国内外很受欢迎。

find a ready market 畅销，好销路

find a market 找到销路

be popular 畅销，流行

be welcome 受欢迎

替换表达：

China's power brands are the best sellers all over the world.

The new style will be welcomed by our customers.

I believe they will find a ready market in our area.

There is a good market for our hand tools.

You'll find a promising market for our new products.

2. for your information

顺便告知，仅供参考

For your information, our company has just passed ISO 9000 and our products are applying for CE Certificate now.

顺便告诉你，我们公司已经通过了ISO 9000的认证，我们的产品也正在申请CE认证。

国际商务业务中常用此句型，婉转地传达有关信息。又如：

for your perusal 供你方斟酌，供你方细读

for you to study 供你方研究

替换表达：

For your information, computer sales have increased rapidly and will keep on rising in the years to come.

For your perusal, the price list gives reference prices for all our export products.

For you to study, we have sent you catalogues and samples.

3. **replace sth. with sth.**

   replace是指代替他人或他物的相等物或替换物。

   To solve this problem, we suggest using metal parts to replace the plastic ones.

   为了解决这个问题，我们建议用金属部件来代替塑料部件。

   替换表达：

       instead of 代替，而不是

       instead *adv.* 代替，顶替

       Let us make the easily worn-out screwdriver bits heat-treated instead of all the tools.

       substitute *n.* 用人或事来取代，替代品

       The oil prices keep rising so people are trying to find substitute for petroleum.

       take the place of another 用……替代

       Moral power will take the place of physical force.

4. **minimize the risk**

   They try to minimize the risk of their investment to zero.

   他们试图把投资降到零风险。

   He took out a patent in order to minimize the risk of innovation.

   为了降低创新的风险，他申请获得了专利。

   试用下列含risk的短语造句：

   minimize the risk 把风险降到最低

   share the risk by half and half 承担一半的风险

   at risk 处境危险

   at the risk of one's life 冒着生命危险

   at all / any risks 无论冒什么危险

   do business at one's own risk 自负盈亏

   take / run a risk 冒险

5. **saying you are not sure**

   I don't know for sure.

   我没把握。

   I am not quite sure about the exchange rate today.

   我对今日外汇汇率不清楚。

   替换表达：

       I can't make out why you are making a compromise suggestion.

       I am in two minds about ...

       It is not certain that ...

       It is hard to say.

6. **be valid**

   We also want to see that your patent and trademark are still valid.

我们还需要有关证据来表明你们的专利和商标仍然有效。

be good 有效

remain valid 有效

The lawyer strongly recommended that you apply for a renewal within 6 months before expiry. Each renewal is good for 10 years.

律师竭力建议你在期满之前6个月内申请继续注册，每次继续注册有效期为10年。

替换表达：

The duration of patent right remains valid for at least 15 years.

How long will the registered trademark be valid?

Our firm offer is good for 10 days.

Part C Integration of Theory and Practice

1. apply for CE Certificate   申请"CE"标志

【知识点】"CE"标志是一种安全认证标志，被视为制造商打开并进入欧洲市场的护照。凡是贴有"CE"标志的产品就可在欧盟各成员国内销售，无须符合每个成员国的要求，从而实现了商品在欧盟成员国范围内的自由流通。

在欧盟市场，"CE"标志属于强制性认证标志，不论是欧盟内部企业生产的产品，还是其他国家生产的产品，要想在欧盟市场上自由流通，就必须加贴"CE"标志，以表明产品符合欧盟《技术协调与标准化新方法》指令的基本要求。这是欧盟法律对产品提出的一种强制性要求。

过去，欧共体国家对进口和销售的产品要求各异，根据某一国标准制造的商品到别国，也许不能上市，作为消除贸易壁垒之努力的一部分，CE应运而生，代表欧洲统一。事实上，CE还是欧共体许多国家语种中的"欧共体"这一词组的缩写，原来用英语词组EUROPEAN COMMUNITY的缩写EC，后因"欧共体"的法文是COMMUNATE EUROPEIA，意大利文为COMUNITA EUROPEA，葡萄牙文为COMUNIDADE EUROPEIA，西班牙文为COMUNIDADE EUROPE等，故改EC为CE。

欧（洲）共（同）体后来演变成了欧洲联盟（简称欧盟）。近年来，在欧洲经济区（欧洲联盟、欧洲自由贸易协会成员国，瑞士除外）市场上销售的商品中，"CE"标志的使用越来越多，商品加贴"CE"标志，表示其符合安全、卫生、环保和消费者保护等一系列欧洲指令所要表达的要求。

我国企业生产的产品若要成功进军欧盟市场，就要特别注意申请"CE"标志（CE Certificate）。

2. strategy of power brands   自主品牌战略

【知识点】在商务交易中，商品是买卖双方首先需要明确和洽谈的事宜。

塑造自主品牌和技术创新，构建核心竞争力是当今我国出口商品的重要战略决策。企业要善于技术创新，提高产品质量和经营方式，促进产品升级换代，创立自主商品名牌，增加出口商品的国际竞争力。

企业积极申报，争取通过质量认证体系和质量标准，这等于获得了进军海外市场的许可证，对占领细分市场份额十分有利。

本章出现不少有关品牌战略的句型，可实践操练：

【技能训练句型】

Our company is adopting innovative strategy. We'll try our best to have our own power brands.

我们公司正推行产品创新战略，力争创自主品牌。

Only through innovation and creation of our own power brands can our company hold market share in intensified market competition.

只有通过技术创新和创立名牌，我们公司才能在激烈的市场竞争中占一席之地。

Our company has just passed ISO 9000 and our products are applying for CE Certificate now. With CE Certificate, our products will stand higher in European market, which will specially benefit your company.

我们公司已经通过了ISO 9000的认证，我们的产品也正在申请CE认证。有了CE认证，我们的产品将以更高的身价进入欧洲市场，这对贵公司尤为有利。

3. trademark and patent　　商标和专利

【知识点1】商标由品牌名称、符号、数字、图案和颜色等标志组成。一旦商标注册登记成功，生产商便在此商标上具有垄断权。商品名称和商标是商品不可分割的部分，名牌产品因其良好的质量深受消费者欢迎。

【技能训练句型】

Trademarks ensure the quality of products and encourage its improvement and it also enable the consumers to choose what is dependable in quality and reasonable in price to meet their demand.

商标确保产品质量并促进改善创新。商标促使消费者挑选质量可靠、价格合理的商品来满足他们的需要。

【知识点2】为确保产品在国外市场畅销，尤其是大宗重要出口产品，最好也在国外注册商标，维护商标持有者的正当权利。按照中国与申请国关于商标互惠的双边协议，外国商标也允许在中国注册，受到保护。

【技能训练句型】

As you mentioned in articles 11 and 12, your product is a US patented product and we should sell your products with your trademark.

正如您在条款11和12中提到的那样，你们的产品在美国享有专利，我们销售时必须使用你们的商标。

At the same time, we strongly recommend you to apply the trademark in China to protect yourself to be offended. In case the trademark registered by someone else, it will be a headache.

同时，我们竭力建议贵公司在中国申请此商标以保护自己免受侵犯。如果商标被别人注册，那将是很头疼的事。

We will register our trademark in China without any delay. By the way, as we are not familiar with related Chinese laws and regulations, could you help me to do this in someway?

我们将立即在中国注册我们的商标。请问，您能帮帮忙吗？因为我们对中国的法律法规不

Chapter 8　Innovative and Power Brand Strategy

熟悉。

【知识点3】专利法（patent law）给予发明者使用以及授予他人使用其发明的独占性和排他性的权利。要使专利得到保护，除了要在本国注册专利外，还需在国外注册。

【技能训练句型】

The aim of our patent law is to encourage invention, advance science and technology and promote technical exchanges with other countries.

我国专利法目的是鼓励发明创造和先进的科学技术，促进与各国之间的技术交流。

At first, we need you to provide us with copies of your patent certificate and trademark registration to show you are the owner of the patent and trademark.

首先我方需要贵公司提供专利证书和商标注册的复印件，以表明贵公司是这项专利和商标的所有权人。

We also want to have the evidence to see your patent and trademark are still valid.

我们还需要有关证据来表明你们的专利和商标仍然有效。

To do this, we need an authorized letter from your company before we start.

办理此事之前，我们需要贵公司的授权书。

Part D　Practice

I. Complete the Following Dialogues

(1)

Marks: Mr. Wang, the ___1___ is going on well. We have already ___2___ on many points. What shall we talk ___3___ this time?

Wang: First of all, we'd like to discuss some technical issues ___4___ you. This is the first time your products will be ___5___ in our market, they must be attractive and helpful to the sales. Do you have any good ideas for that?

Marks: That is what we ___6___ about. In order to ___7___ customers, our designers have ___8___ some new designs for your choice.

Wang: That is what we want to hear. Very nice looking! I believe they will be ___9___ by our ___10___.

(2)

Fill in the blanks with the following expressions:

be entitled to	do sb. a favor	promote technical exchanges
don't know for sure	be a must	enjoy the exclusive right
The aim of	authorized letter	so far as rights are concerned
take out		

111

A: I am going to ___1___ a patent on my new invention. But I ___2___ about Patent Law. Could you ___3___ ?

B: Certainly. ___4___ our patent law is to encourage invention, advance science and technology and ___5___ with other countries.

A: Got it.

B: Well, ___6___, the one who owns the patent rights ___7___ to exploit them. Nobody else ___8___ the invention without the owner's written ___9___.

A: Yes. I think it ___10___.

II. Interaction Activities

Task 1

Work in pairs and make a dialogue according to the situation.

A and B discuss the design and color of stationery.

Use the following expressions:

(1) it's high time

(2) to lead the market

(3) look more fancy

(4) pay special attention to

(5) looking forward to

Task 2

Talk about trademarks.

Use following expressions in your dialogue:

(1) strongly recommend that

(2) protect yourself to be offended

(3) have ... registered

(4) better way out

(5) for your information

(6) contact the Trademark Office

(7) go through the formality

(8) no opposition to

(9) be valid

(10) don't know for sure

III. Actual Practice

Practise with your partner and role-play the conversation.

Talk about the issues of commodity innovation. The conversation should be well organized with the following items you have learnt in the text:

1. introduce the development of innovative products

Chapter 8 Innovative and Power Brand Strategy

2. adopt innovative strategy
3. have own power brands
4. develop some new designs
5. hold market share in the world market
6. obtain CE Certificate
7. find a ready market

IV. Creative Discussion

Debate

Students choose one topic for debate.

Topics:

1. Chinese enterprises should adopt innovative strategy in order to be more competitive in the world market.

2. Do you think it is necessary to apply for trademarks and patents?

The class is divided into several groups. The affirmative side is supposed to develop as many affirmative statements while the negative side is supposed to develop as many negative statements as possible. Give the arguments reasonable support.

Chapter 9

Packing and Quality Inspection

Learning Objectives
Upon completion of this chapter, you will be able to

- understand that quality is a key to business door.
- know the importance of packing in foreign trade.
- learn how to introduce the quality of your products.
- improve your communication skills on packing and quality-related issues.
- perform the right role in quality inspection.
- focus on openness and inclusiveness.[1]

---

1 聚焦开放包容。

Quality Control

(*Mr. Zhou, Manager of QC Department of Jin Xin Loudspeaker Company, is introducing his company to Mrs. Carl, a quality inspection representative.*)

Zhou: Mrs. Carl, welcome to our company.

Carl: Hello, Mr. Zhou. It is my pleasure to visit your company. My boss, Mr. Albert Gordon sent me here for quality inspection.

Zhou: Oh, Mr. Gordon is an old friend of our company. I believe he must have told you something about our company.

Carl: He did. I'll appreciate it if you can tell me more about your company before starting quality inspection on the products under our Contract #5406.

Zhou: To let you know more about us, I'd like to introduce our company, our products as well as our inspection department briefly.

Carl: Go ahead, please.

Zhou: Our company is one of the main manufacturers of loudspeakers in China with hundreds of different kinds of loudspeakers, which are mainly exported to over 30 foreign countries and regions. We employ about 500 workers and staff. Among them, 150 members are engineers and technicians.[1] The annual export is about 80 million US dollars.

Carl: Real cool![2]

Zhou: Our quality control department, directly under the general manager, is in charge of all quality control related matters.[3]

Carl: It's essential that your boss attach importance to the quality.[4] How many people are there in your department?

Zhou: 25 people, plus 15 inspectors in every workshop.

Carl: What is their responsibility? Or what is their daily job?

Zhou: They spread out to every corner of the workshops. They check the products from the production lines, test and record the technical parameters of our products, put forward the ideas on how to improve the quality and minimize the defects and others.

Carl: Do you think their inspection in the first line is effective and workable?

Zhou: Strictly speaking, yes. Very effective and workable. They do form the first line of our quality control. Few defective products in the warehouse are checked out. According to statistics, the average rate is less than 0.015%.⁵

Carl: Thank you for your introduction. Should we go and meet these quality controllers and inspect the products?

Zhou: It's my pleasure. Let's go to the workshops.

Packing

(After showing Mrs. Carl around the workshops, Mr. Zhou is talking about packing with her.)

Carl: Your efficient inspection work left a favorable impression on me. Generally speaking, our order is being carried out in a good manner. My boss will be satisfied with your products after reading my inspection report.

Zhou: Thanks a lot. I'm so delighted to hear your positive comments on our job. I always believe that quality is a key to business.

Carl: Absolutely! I don't have anything more to say for the loudspeaker itself, except for the matters I mentioned while we were walking around the production lines. But I'd like to emphasize the importance of packing to the general aspect of quality.

Zhou: Please don't hesitate to let us know the weak points of our packing.⁶ We'll do our best to improve it.

Carl: All right. First, the poly-bag for wrapping up each loudspeaker could be a little thicker. I don't think it would cost more because the poly-bags seem too thin. Loudspeakers may scratch the thin poly-bay during the transportation and handling. The poly-bag is the final packing when our products reach the hands of our consumers, though its cost is very subtle compared with other parts of the entire products.⁷

Zhou: You're right. The bags with double thickness will be used for your order.

Carl: Good. We request the plastic recycle mark should be printed on the backside corner of the poly-bag. It is a necessity of environmental protection.

Zhou: We'll do it.

Carl: The next issue is the inner box. The size of the inner box should be unified. Being too tight or too loose may damage the inner box that is the outlook of our products on the shelves of the stores.

Zhou: We'll pay special attention to that point.

Carl: The last point is the master carton. Please do not use iron staples and plastic belts that are commonly used for outside packing.

Zhou: I believe that's also better for environment protection.

Carl: Correct. That's all for today.

Zhou: Thanks. Your kind and timely suggestions are very precious for us to improve the quality not only of your goods, but also of other products supplied to all our customers. We'll keep them in mind.

Commodity Inspection

(Mr. Zhou and Mrs. Carl are going on talking about commodity inspection.)

Carl: Mr. Zhou, we won't be able to send anyone else to your company before the goods are shipped. For this reason, we request the commodity inspection should be conducted for our order.

Zhou: No problem. Our export inspections are mainly made by Entry-Exit Inspection and Quarantine Bureau. It enjoys high international reputation all over the world.

Carl: I've heard about it.

Zhou: The inspection will be carried out within 5 days before delivery. The Bureau has branch offices in all port cities, such as ours, so it's very convenient to carry out the inspection.

Carl: What standards are they using?

Zhou: The Chinese national standards will be applied, if the commodity is a compulsory inspected item.[8] If not, the standards can be ones stipulated in applicant's commercial contract.

Carl: Since the certificate of quality and quantity issued by the Bureau will be an important document for L/C negotiation, can they issue the certificate in German?

Zhou: I don't think so. As a rule, the inspection certificates are made in the form of Chinese and English.[9]

Carl: All right. A copy in English would also be acceptable. Can we make re-inspection at the port of destination when the goods arrive?

Zhou: Theoretically yes, but I don't think it is necessary, because it may cause disputes. If you prefer an inspection agency other than Entry-Exit Inspection and Quarantine Bureau, it will be fine for us, as we are confident with our products. However, the expenses for inspection will be covered by your company.

Carl: OK. I hope there is no occasion for any disagreeable things to happen. An eye finds more truth than two ears.[10] I think I have completed all my tasks for this trip.

Zhou: Why not take a trip to look around our city to relax?[11]

Carl: Thank you. That sounds nice.

Words and Expressions

1. loudspeaker	n.	扬声器，喇叭
2. annual	adj.	每年的，一年一次的

Chapter 9 Packing and Quality Inspection

3. spread out		分布；展开
4. put forward		提出（意见、建议）；推举出
5. parameter	n.	参数
6. statistics	n.	统计
7. warehouse	n.	仓库
8. emphasize	vt.	强调，着重
9. poly-bag		塑料包装袋
10. wrap	v.	包装，卷，裹
	n.	包装纸；披肩；外套，大衣
11. scratch	vt. & vi.	抓破，划伤
12. subtle	adj.	微小的，细微的
13. recycle	vt.	再循环
14. environmental	adj.	环境的
15. uniform	adj.	（与其他）一样的，统一的；一致的
16. tight	adj.	紧的
17. staple	n.	订书钉，U形钉
18. plastic belt		塑料打包带
19. precious	adj.	珍贵的，宝贵的
20. Entry-Exit Inspection and Quarantine Bureau		进出口检验检疫局
21. compulsory	adj.	强迫的；强制的；义务的
22. re-inspection		复检
23. theoretically	adv.	理论上
24. dispute	n.	争论；争议；辩论
25. cover	vt.	支付，偿付
26. disagreeable	adj.	不合意的；不愉快的

Notes

1. We employ about 500 workers and staffs. Among them, 150 members are engineers and technicians.
   我们拥有员工500人，其中包括150名工程师和技术员。
   表示拥有员工，用employ最贴切，不用possess。
   possess *v.* 拥有，占有，possess后一般不跟随人。
   例句：
   　　Our company possessed valuable technical know-how.
   　　本公司拥有宝贵的技术诀窍。

2. Real cool !
   好极了，了不起。（俚语）

3. Our quality control department, directly under the general manager, is in charge of all the quality

control related matters.

质量控制部由总经理直接领导，负责所有质量控制有关的事宜。

directly under general manager 插入语

4. It's essential that your boss (should) attach importance to the quality.

贵方老板重视产品质量至关重要。

It's essential that ... 至关重要的，紧要的

主语从句中的虚拟语气。一些表示important（重要的）、imperative（迫切的）、urgent（紧迫的）、necessary（必要的）、requested（要求）、proposed（建议）等意思的形容词和过去分词，在主语从句中，谓语动词用should加动词原形或仅用动词原形，表示虚拟。

例句：

It's appropriate that the factory upgrade the products every year.

工厂的产品每年升级换代很有必要。

It is vital that this tax be abolished.

废除这项税收是非常重要的。

5. They do form the first line of our quality control. Few defective products in the warehouse are checked out. According to statistics, the average rate is less than 0.015%.

他们的确形成我们质量控制的第一道防线。从库房中检出的次品非常少。据统计，次品平均比率不到万分之一点五。

① check out 检验，检测；合格；结账

例句：

Our products are made under reliable quality control and they are checked out seriously.

我们的产品经过认真检验，在严格的质量管理下生产。

② average adj. 平均

例句：

Frankly speaking, the quality of that kind of refrigerator is below average.

坦率地说，那种电冰箱的质量在一般水平之下。

6. Please don't hesitate to let us know the weak points of our packing.

请不必顾虑地告诉我们包装方面的缺点。

don't hesitate to 不必顾虑

例句：

Please don't hesitate to tell me if you need help.

如果你需要帮助，请告诉我。

Don't hesitate about pointing out the mistakes I made when calculating the prices.

若我计算价格有误，请大胆指出。

7. The poly-bag is the final packing when our products reach the hands of our consumers, though its cost is very subtle compared with other parts of the entire products.

虽然与整个产品的其他部分相比，塑料袋的成本是微不足道的，但却是我们的产品到达顾客手中时的最终包装物。

compare with 与……相比

Chapter 9 Packing and Quality Inspection

例句：
> Your quotation seems a little too high compared with the offers from other similar companies.
> 与其他同类公司的报盘相比，贵方的报价似乎有点偏高。

8. The Chinese national standards will be applied, if the commodity is a compulsory inspected item.
   如果是法定商检产品，将采用中国国家标准。
   ① apply to 适用于；运用于；关系到；把……运用于
   例句：
   > We should apply the economic theory that we learned in the classroom to practice.
   > 我们应当把课堂所学的经济学理论应用于实践。

   ② apply oneself to 致力于，集中精力做某事
   ③ apply one's mind to 专心于

9. As a rule, the inspection certificates are made in the form of Chinese and English.
   通常，证书是用中文和英文的。
   ① in the form of 以……的形式，呈……状态
   ② form *n.* 形式
   例句：
   > The right of cargo is presented in the form of Bill of Lading.
   > 货物所有权以提单的形式体现。

   ③ shape 强调 "外形" "形状"
   ④ figure 强调 "外形" "轮廓"

10. An eye finds more truth than two ears.
    百闻不如一见。

11. Why not take a trip to look around our city to relax?
    为何不到我们市转一转，放松一下？
    ① Why +not +动词原形，表示提出建议。
    ② Why +动词原形，表示所做的动作不必要做或毫无意义。
    例句：
    > Why not look around Quality Control Center with our inspectors?
    > 为什么不和我们的检验员一起到质量管理中心看看？
    > Why spend so much time negotiating for the increase of price? There is no way to persuade him to accept your offer.
    > 为什么花这么多的时间洽谈提价？根本就无法劝说他接受你方的报盘。

Part B Practical Key Sentences

1. strictly speaking
   副词＋speaking 形成的副词短语，位于句首。
   Strictly speaking, yes. Very effective and workable.

严格说来，是的。行之有效。
Frankly speaking, our company only accepts L/C.
坦率地说，我公司仅仅接受信用证付款。
替换表达：

  Properly speaking, your prices are on the high side.

  Generally speaking, we are fully confident about the quality of our air conditioners.

  Roughly speaking, our factory produces more than 5,000 shoes everyday.

  Briefly speaking, our prices are in line with the prevailing market.

  Broadly speaking, your products are in standard quality.

2. attach importance to

Our manager attached importance to the development of new products.
我们的经理重视产品创新。
emphasize the importance of 重视
lay emphasis on 强调，突出重点
The director of the factory laid particular emphasis on quality control.
厂长特别强调质量管理的重要性。
替换表达：

  The workers emphasized the importance of packing.

  The workers think much of quality inspection.

  The buyer puts emphasis on terms of payment.

3. according to statistics

According to statistics, the rate is less than 0.015% on average.
据统计，次品平均比率不到万分之一点五。
By estimate, our orders will exceed a total amount of USD 100,000 this month.
据估计，本月我们的订单将超过十万美元。
替换表达：

  By statistics, Mr. William's account was overdrawn USD 200 this week.

  At a rough estimate, your commission for trade will be 1,000 Pounds or over.

  It is estimated that the effective work will reduce cost by 20%.

4. give sb. a favorable impression

Your efficient inspection work gave me a favorable impression.
你们有效的检验工作给我留下美好的印象。
The tight quality control of your factory made a deep impression on us.
贵工厂严格的质量管理给我们留下深刻的影响。
替换表达：

  Your excellent packing method impressed me a great deal.

  The attractive advertisement left a good impression on all customers.

  Your idea of environmental protection made an impression on the manufacturers.

5. conduct the inspection

We request the commodity inspection should be conducted for our order.

我们要求对我们订单项下的货物实施商品检验。

conduct *v.* 进行；开展；实施；处理

We are conducting an advertising campaign to make ourselves known by TV ads.

我们大力开展广告宣传，让外界通过电视广告了解我们。

替换表达：

The production of ordered goods will be made as soon as the L/C is opened.

The packing of products is carried out before shipment.

The inspection should be done by Entry-Exit Inspection and Quarantine Bureau.

Part C Integration of Theory and Practice

1. packing　商品包装

【知识点】科学、美观、适销和牢固的商品包装能保护商品，方便运输和增加商品价值。商品包装分为销售包装（内包装inner packing）和运输包装（外包装outside packing）。现代包装的发展日新月异，随着超市的发展，销售包装造型更美观大方，印刷条形码，讲究包装装潢，突出商标品牌，吸引顾客，提高有形商品的内外在质量。

【技能训练句型】

The size of the inner box should be unified. Too tight or too loose may damage the inner box that is the outlook of our products on the shelves of the stores.

内盒的尺寸必须一致，太松或太紧都可能损坏内盒。内盒是我们的产品在货架上的形象展示。

Your kind and timely suggestions are very precious for us to improve the quality not only of your goods, but also of other products supplied to all our customers.

您中肯、及时的建议有利于我们产品质量的提高，这不仅有益于你们，也有益于其他客户。

2. environmental protection consciousness　环境保护意识

【知识点】现代商品包装充分体现了环境保护意识，使用环保材料，印制环保标志，实现绿色包装。

【技能训练句型】

Please do not use iron staples and plastic belts that are commonly used for outside packing.

请不要使用通常用于外包装的订书钉和塑料打包带。

We request the plastic recycle mark should be printed on the backside corner of the poly-bag, which is a necessity of environmental protection.

我们要求在塑料袋背面的角落上印上可循环塑料的标志，这是环境保护的要求。

3. quality control　质量管理

【知识点】良好的产品质量是商品畅销的重要保证，生产企业一定要花大气力，严格把好质量关。出口商品要尽量采用国际标准,提升竞争能力。质量赢得市场,诚信铸就品牌。创立名牌,以质取胜。

【技能训练句型】

Our export commodity are all quality goods. The aim of our company is "Quality and Customers first".

我们的出口商品全是一级品,公司的宗旨是"质量第一,用户第一"。

All products are made under an extremely tight quality control.

所有的产品都经过极度严格的质量检测。

4. quality of goods 商品品质

【知识点】商品品质是合同首先要明确规定的交易条件,国际贸易中常见对商品品质的要求。

(1) 凭样品买卖 (Sales by sample)。例如:

凭卖方样品买卖 Quality as per Seller's Sample

凭买方样品买卖 Quality as per Buyer's Sample

对等样品买卖 Quality as per Counter Sample

样品指从一批商品中抽出来,足以反映和代表整批商品品质的少量实物。

(2) 凭规格、等级、标准买卖。例如:

凭规格买卖 Sale by Specification

凭等级买卖 Sale by Grade

凭标准买卖 Sale by Standard

(3) 凭品牌或商标买卖 Sale by Brand Name or Trade Mark

(4) 凭产地买卖 Sale by Name of Origin

(5) 凭说明书和图样买卖 Sale by Descriptions and Illustrations

制定品质条款的诀窍:

(1) 要根据生产实际,恰如其分,不可定得太高,否则导致无法履约。而定得太低,则影响声誉和价格。

(2) 正确运用各种表示品质的方法,采用何种表示品质的方法,应视商品特性而定。凡能用科学的指标说明其质量的商品,适合凭规格、等级或标准买卖;有些难以规格化和标准化的商品,则适于凭样品买卖;名优产品,适于凭商标或品牌买卖;某些性能复杂的机器、电器和仪表,则适于凭说明书和图样买卖;凡具有地方风味和特色的产品,则可凭产地名称买卖。

(3) 品质条件的规定应明确具体,不用"大约""左右"之类的含糊字眼,以免在交货品质上引起麻烦。

5. quality inspection 商品检验

【知识点】商品检验是外贸的重要环节之一,商品的品质关系重大,买方担心实际交货是否与样品保持一致。有些进口商为了确保产品质量,专门派人或委托专业检测部门来了解和验货,卖方可向他们详细介绍本企业提高产品质量和质量检测的措施。

【技能训练句型】

The inspectors check the products from the production lines, test and record the technical

Chapter 9 Packing and Quality Inspection

parameters of our products, put forward the ideas on how to improve the quality and minimize the defects and others.

检验员检查生产线下来的产品，测试和记录产品参数，提出改进质量和减少次品的建议等。

The products are 100% checked here and defective ones will be thrown out to these boxes for the head of the workshop and technicians to analyze what the problems are and find out the ways to prevent future occurrence.

百分之百的产品都经这里检验，次品被扔到这些箱子里，由车间主任和技术员分析存在的问题，并找出防止再度发生的办法。

6. compulsory inspected item 法定商检

【知识点】列入国家质检总局颁布的实施出口质量许可、出口食品卫生注册登记"两证"管理目录的产品生产企业，必须获得"两证"，方可出口。国家法定商检项目，出口前须进行商检。商检部门对进出口商品的品质、数量、重量和包装等实施检验，根据需要出具检验证书（Inspection Certificate）。非法定商检产品的检验标准由买卖双方自行商定。

【技能训练句型】

The Chinese national standards will be applied to, if the commodity is a compulsory inspected item. If not, the standards can be ones stipulated in applicant's commercial contract.

如果是法定商检产品，将采用中国国家标准；若非法定商检产品，可采用申请人的商业合同中指定的标准。

Part D Practice

I. Complete the Following Dialogues

(1)

Fill in the blanks with proper words.

A: I understand packing is a ____1____ to business door.

B: That's why we always ____2____ importance to packing.

A: Proper ____3____ can protect the goods from ____4____ during transportation.

B: How many kinds of packing?

A: There are mainly two kinds of ____5____, inner and outside packing.

B: Could you tell me more about them?

A: Outside packing prevents the goods from damage of shipment. ____6____ packing is the final packing to reach the ____7____ of customers.

B: I think inner packing should be not only strong but also ____8____ to attract customers.

A: Quite right. The novel packing will help promote ____9____. We also take environmental protection into ____10____ when choosing the packing materials nowadays.

B: Thank you. I have learned a lot from you today.

(2)

Complete the following dialogue with expressions or sentences.

A: Why not ___1___ packing now, Mr. White?

B: Yes. ___2___ the usual way to pack Qingdao Beer?

A: Sure. We always lay ___3___ packing because the bottles of beer are easily broken.

B: I agree.

A: Master cartons are used for ___4___ and nylon straps are used to strengthen them.

B: ___5___ they are not strong enough.

A: ___6___ use wooden cases?

B: Our master cartons are strong enough ___7___, but wooden cases ___8___ trans portation and they will cost more.

A: Do you use warning marks for handling?

B: Yes. ___9___, we print "Handle With Care" in the outside cartons.

A: Great! I can ___10___ about it now.

II. Interaction Activities

Task 1

Mr. Zhu, from an inspection bureau, goes to the factory to inspect the export goods before shipment.

Students make conversations by using the following expressions.

(1) be ready for
(2) look round
(3) quality inspection
(4) attach importance to
(5) under strict quality control
(6) it's essential that
(7) form the first line
(8) spread out
(9) effective and workable
(10) checking out
(11) it's time to
(12) select a few goods at random
(13) don't hesitate to
(14) give sb. a favorable impression

Task 2

Students make up a conversation between Mr. Green and the manager of an export company.

Mr. Green is sent to inspect the quality of porcelain goods by his company. After inspection, he finds some problems for packing:

1. outside packing for improvement
2. poly-bag of inner packing
3. the outlook of box

Please find the solution to the problems, including timely suggestions made by Mr. Green and promise for improvement made by the manager.

III. Actual Practice

Students work in groups and try to give advice for the following business situations:

1. What standards of quality will he choose if Sam is going to import a large quantity of sugar from China? Give the reasons.

2. What standards of quality will she choose if Cindy is going to import some arts porcelain and imitation antique porcelain? Give the reasons.

3. What standards of quality will he choose if David is going to import Haier Washing Machine? Give the reasons.

4. What standards of quality will he choose if Mark is going to import local specialities? Give the reasons.

IV. Creative Discussion

It's known to all of us that there are heated competitions in the international market.

In order to dominate the market, Company A adopts the strategy of lowering prices by sacrificing the quality.

In order to dominate the market, Company B adopts the strategy of improving quality but keeping the prices on the high side compared with other companies.

The class is divided into several groups to discuss which strategy is better according to the situation in different countries. Every student gives his own idea about the propositions with reasonable supporting points.

Each group provides a summary to present in the class.

Chapter 10
Acceptance and Orders

Learning Objectives
Upon completion of this chapter, you will be able to

- acquire knowledge of skills of price negotiation.
- learn how to accept the orders from the clients.
- open the mind to differentiated marketing.
- improve the communication skills for business talks.
- conclude business transaction.
- understand building a community of shared interests, shared responsibility and shared future.[1]

---

1 理解打造利益共同体、责任共同体、命运共同体。

Part A Situational Dialogue

Communicative Scene 1

Showing an Interest in the Products

(Ms. Liu, General Manager of Hope Tool Enterprise, is attending an international fair in Poznan, Poland. Mr. Mason, an import manager from a European company, comes up to Liu's booth, looking at samples at the show.)

Liu: Good afternoon! Can I help you?

Mason: Yes. I am interested in 100 pc tool kits. Can you show me more samples?

Liu: Sure. Here are some samples of different kinds of 100 pc tool sets.[1] They contain different tools for different purposes.

Mason: They look wonderful.

Liu: This is for professional use, because the materials used for each individual tool are high quality steel and they are all heat-treated. The 5-year warranty is granted.[2]

Mason: What about this one?

Liu: These two items are for family use. They will be nice gifts for Father's Day.

Mason: Perfect. Oh, I guess this must be for Mother's Day.

Liu: Yes, you are right. We specially designed it for lady use. Look, the box and all plastic handles are light and clear pink. It is lady's color, don't you think so?

Mason: Yep, it is very thoughtful. I like it very much. What's the cost?

Liu: It is USD 2.49 per set FOB China port, and this price is based on the FCL.[3]

Mason: I don't think we can order so many for the first time. We have never dealt with the tools for ladies. It is a brand new idea for the market, too. Well, let me see. Maybe we can combine some other tool kits, such as professional tools and family items in one container.[4]

Liu: That's all right. However, as you may know, the production costs and handling fee for assorted goods will be much higher than just a single product.

Mason: That's understandable, but ...

Liu: OK. To establish business relations with your esteemed company, we'll consider making you a concession. Now, we offer you USD 2.59 per set FOB China port on condition that the minimum order quantity should reach 500 sets.

Mason: Thank you for your kindness. I will come back later.

Liu: Here is my business card with my mobile phone number and our booth number on it. You are always welcome to come back again. So long!

Mason: So long!

Detailed Business Bargain

(Ms. Liu is negotiating with Mr. Mason on prices at the fair.)

Liu: Nice to see you again, Mr. Mason. How are you doing?

Mason: Fine, thank you.

Liu: It has been two days since we met each other for the first time. Have you made up your mind?

Mason: Not really. Your tool kits look nice, but comparing them with others, they seem a bit overpriced. Could you reduce the price a little further? Let's say, USD 2.29 per set.

Liu: Frankly speaking, yes, our price is a little higher than others. However, if the new styles and features open up markets, aren't they worth the money? Moreover, our quality is superior to other manufacturers'. [5]

Mason: Sounds reasonable. Shall we come to the price again later on after we finish with the other terms and conditions? Firstly, please let me know the leadtime for 500 sets.

Liu: It will be about 30 days after your order confirmation and receipt of your down payment.

Mason: Could it be a little faster, say 20 days? You see, it will be midseason.

Liu: No problem.

Mason: Wow, you're a lot of help. What about the terms of payment?

Liu: We usually accept payment by L/C. That is our usual practice.

Mason: L/C payment requires a high fee and slows down our capital flow. We prefer T/T payment.

Liu: For T/T payment, we request a 30% down payment upon your order confirmation and the balance payment will be paid before shipment.

Mason: How about after shipment?

Liu: I'm afraid not.

Mason: Oh, there is one more important matter. Please tell me about the packing.

Liu: Every individual tool will be put in the pink box as the sample you saw two days ago. Each box will be covered by a 4-colour printed sleeve and then wrapped by shrinkage film. Five boxes are packed to one export carton. You can print your company's logo and description in different languages on the color sleeve. [6]

Mason: Everything sounds great aside from the price. [7]

Liu: To conclude the business and show our sincerity, we agree to cut 10 cents for each set.

Mason: USD 2.29/set?

Liu: Should we meet each other half way? USD 2.49 is already our bottom price.

Mason: Let's close a deal.

Liu: Thank you very much. I'll prepare the contract in a few minutes. Would you please wait here or walk around and come back in 20 minutes?

Mason: I prefer to wait here as I have stepped over to every corner of the exhibition hall.

Communicative Scene 3

Repeat Orders[10]

(*Mr. Mason will place repeat orders with Ms. Liu.*)

Mason: How are you doing, Ms. Liu?

Liu: Fine, thank you. And you?

Mason: I'm fine, too. Thanks. I'm very happy to inform you that your goods are selling remarkably well in our market. Your new concept has been warmly welcome by our consumers. To meet the heavy demand from all the supermarkets where we are selling your tool kits, we'd like to place a new order with you immediately.

Liu: I'm glad to hear the good news. We'll do our best to meet your requirements.

Mason: To meet the rapidly growing demand, our quantity of order will be more than triple of the last one. Please give us your best offer based on the quantity of 2,000 sets.

Liu: That will be USD 2.48 / set FOB China port.

Mason: It is almost the same price as we had last time.

Liu: You are right. However, it actually is much cheaper than last time.

Mason: Why do you say that? Could you give me some more explanation?

Liu: The situation has changed a lot since your first order. We are facing pressures from at least two aspects. As you may know, the US dollar has been devaluing against Chinese currency since then. For this reason only, we have already lost 3%.

Mason: I'm sorry to hear that.

Liu: Worse still, affected by oil prices in the international market, steel and plastic prices in Chinese domestic market have increased tremendously. You see, steel and plastics are our main materials. Under such circumstances, we still offer you the same price, even a little lower. It means we are giving you a special favor on the price.

Mason: Understand. We'll not insist on our position anymore. We accept your price. In case the international oil price falls, we request our prices follow automatically.

Liu: Fully agreeable. We hope the situation will get better in the near future.

Words and Expressions

1. acquire knowledge of		获得知识
2. kit	*n.*	成套工具，工具箱
tool kit		成套工具，工具箱

3. warranty	n.	保证；理由；证书
4. professional	adj.	专业的
5. grant	vt. & n.	同意，准予，授予
6. Father's Day		父亲节（六月份的第三个星期日）
7. Mother's Day		母亲节（五月份的第二个星期日）
8. yep	adv.	是（俚语）
9. thoughtful	adj.	考虑周到的；体贴的；思考的
10. FCL abbr. Full Container Load		整集装箱货
11. assorted	adj.	各式各样的，混杂的
12. understandable	adj.	可理解的
13. on condition that ...		条件是……
14. esteemed	adj.	尊敬的；尊贵的
15. bargain	v.	讨价还价
	n.	（通过讨价还价）成交的商品；便宜货
16. make up (one's) mind		决定，下决心
17. feature	n.	特色，特征
18. lead time		交货期
19. midseason	n.	旺季
20. capital flow		资本流动
21. down payment		订金，预付款
22. balance payment		余款
23. T/T abbr. telegraphic transfer		电汇
24. sleeve	n.	袖子；外套；体壳
25. shrinkage	n.	收缩；缩水
26. conclude the business		成交
27. bottom price		底价
28. triple	n.	三倍
29. pressure	n.	压力
30. devalue	vt.	贬值
31. tremendously	adv.	极大地；惊人地

Notes

1. Here are some samples of different kinds of 100 pc tool sets.
   请看这些不同款式的100件组合工具。
   ① 100 pc tool sets 表示包含100件不同用途的各种工具。
   ② tool kits / tool sets 成套工具；工具箱

2. The 5-year warranty is granted.
   保质期五年。

grant *v.* 准许，同意

例句：

  Warranty is granted for household appliances made by our factory.

  我们生产的家电有保修。

  The manager granted the salesman permission to cut the price by 5%.

  经理允许推销员降价5%。

3. This price is based on the FCL.

   这价格是基于整货柜的订量。

   根据集装箱货物装箱数量和方式，集装箱可分为整箱和拼箱两种。

   ① FCL 整箱（Full Container Load）

   指出口商自行将货物装满整个集装箱以后，以箱为单位托运的集装箱。一般在货主有充足货源装载一个或多个整箱时采用。

   ② LCL 拼箱（Less than Container Load）

   指承运人接受出口商托运的数量不满整箱的货物后，根据货物运输的目的地和商品的特性进行分类整理。把运往相同目的地的货物，集中到足够数量，拼装入集装箱。一个集装箱内有不同货主的货拼装在一起，称为拼箱。

4. Maybe we can combine some other tool kits, such as professional tools and family items in one container.

   也许我们可以和其他组合工具拼柜，比如专业工具和家用工具拼柜。

   ① combine *v.* 使结合，合并

   指与其他组合工具拼柜，用的是拼箱的方法装入集装箱。

   ② combine with ... 把……与……相结合

   例句：

     We must combine international economy theory with trade practice.

     我们把国际经济学理论与贸易实践相结合。

5. Moreover, our quality is superior to other manufacturers'.

   而且，我们的质量比其他厂家更优越。

   be superior to 优良的，优越的，上等的，胜过……的(to, in)

   例句：

     The function of this kind of aerator is superior to that one made in Korea.

     这种增氧机的功能在很多方面比韩国造的好。

6. Every individual tool will be put in the pink box as the sample you saw two days ago. Each box will be covered by a 4-colour printed sleeve and then wrapped by shrinkage film. Five boxes are packed to one export carton. You can print your company's logo and description in different languages on the color sleeve.

   正如你两天前见到的样品那样，所有工具都放在粉红色工具盒里。每盒套上四色印刷的彩套，然后包上收缩膜。五盒装一个外纸箱。贵公司可在彩套上印上公司标志和不同语言的说明文字等。

包装的表示方法：

① be packed in 用某种包装物包装

例句：

    We require live clam be packed in strong gunny bags.

    我们要求活文蛤用结实的麻袋包装。

② be packed to 装入某种包装物

例句：

    Toys are packed 2 pieces to a box and 10 boxes to a carton.

    每2件玩具装一盒，10盒装一纸箱。

③ each containing ... 每包装物内装……

例句：

    Straw mushrooms are in polythene bag, each containing 500g.

    草菇装聚乙烯袋，每袋装500克。

④ be packed in ... of ... each 用某种包装物包装，每包装物内装……

例句：

    Women's blouses are packed in a carton of 12 dozen each.

    女式衬衫使用纸箱包装，每箱装一打。

7. Everything sounds great aside from the price.

各项都很好，就剩下价格问题了。

aside from *prep./adv.* 除……以外

例句：

    I think we have discussed all details of the trade aside from claims.

    除索赔外，我们已经讨论了交易的各个细节。

*8. OK与That's OK 的区别

众所周知OK是"好的"，但如果认为That's OK也是相同意思，则是有误。当别人问是否要做时，回答OK是"要"做，而回答That's OK却是"不要"。回答身体状况时，That's OK表示"我很好，不用操心"。That's OK意思是"没关系，无所谓"。

*9. Now we understood more about your situation. We are not going to insist on our position anymore. We accept your price.

现在我们明白了你的处境，就不再坚持自己的立场。我们接受你们的报价。

insist on 坚持，主张（常与on、that连用）

例句：

    If you insist that the payment be paid by D/A, I am afraid that we can't make a deal.

    如果你坚持承兑交单支付，恐怕我们无法成交。

    It is unwise of you to insist on maintaining your uncompetitive price.

    坚持毫无竞争性的价格是不明智的。

*10. repeat orders 续订的订单（与上一订单商品一样，但有些条款不同）

    duplicate orders 重复订单（与上一订单数量等条款相同）

Part B Practical Key Sentences

1. be worth doing + *n*.

worth *adj.* 值……的，相等于……的价值

用作表语，后接名词或动名词作宾语。

How much is this antique of handicraft worth?

这件手工艺品古董值多少钱？

It is worth at least USD 6 million for its special value of age.

它因其年代悠久而具有特殊价值，至少值六百万美元。

It's worth buying, don't you think so?

你不认为值得买吗？

替换表达：

It's worth attending business fair.

The older its age, the more it's worth.

It is worth while to visit the factory.

It is worthwhile negotiating price before signing the contract.

2. keep one's mind on ... though something reasonable

That is understandable, but ... 这可以理解，但……

That is understandable that you are short of workforce, but the products we need are seasonable. We can't miss it.

你方缺乏劳力可以理解，但我们要的产品是季节性的，不可错过。

替换表达：

It is a brand new concept, but it should be tested by the market.

While I appreciate your effort, I have to point out the problems of your quality.

Much as we are pleased to get your quotation, we are regretful that we still think your prices are not competitive enough.

3. let's say

Your prices seem a bit overpriced. Could you please reduce the price a little more? Let's say, USD 2.29 per set.

贵公司的定价偏高了些。能优惠一些，再降点价吗？比如每套2.29美元。

Considering your cooperation, we decide to cut the price by USD 10, i.e. to USD 190 per set.

考虑到你方的友好合作，我们决定降价10美元，即每台190美元。

替换表达：

To encourage business, we'll give you the reduction of price by 5%, that is, USD 6.00 per kg.

It's better for you to decrease the price, say HKD 5 per set.

4. buyers' reasons avoid using L/C

L/C payment requires high fee and slows down our capital flow. We prefer T/T payment.

信用证付款的费用挺高，并减缓资金周转。我们更赞成电汇付款。

Chapter 10 Acceptance and Orders

替换表达：

An opening of L/C will add some extra cost to us.

The payment by letter of credit will cause both of us some inconvenience.

Our money will be tied up if you insist on L/C payment.

5. accept only L/C or other terms

Our company only accepts terms of payment by confirmed, irrevocable letter of credit. It assures the safe payment.

本公司只接受保兑的、不可撤销的信用证付款方式。它保证卖方收支安全。

但卖方若一直坚持信用证付款方式，可能会失去订单，不妨采取一些灵活但不影响收汇安全的方式。

For T/T payment, 30% down payment upon your order confirmation and balance payment will be paid before shipment.

采用电汇付款，合同确定后预付30%，发货前付清余款。

替换表达：

Only L/C is acceptable to us. That is our usual practice.

We agree to make an exception by accepting D/P at sight.

6. make no more price reduction

Let's meet each other half way. USD 2.49 is already our bottom price.

我们各让一半。2.49美元已是我们的底线。

We can't make further reduction because this is our floor price.

我们无法进一步减价，因为它是我们的地板价了。

替换表达：

We can't accept your counter offer for it is our rock-bottom quotation.

It is hard for us to decrease the price. We have lowered the price to the limit.

7. large quantity affects prices

Our quantity of order will be more than triple of the last one. Please give us your best offer based on the quantity of 2,000 sets.

我们的订量将是上次的三倍以上。请按2,000套的数量报个最优惠价格。

替换表达：

Now we quote you USD 5.00 per piece CFR Sydney on condition that the minimum order quantity should reach 10,000 pieces.

Further discount is possible if you place a large order.

We grant you a special discount if you increase the quantity by 10%.

Part C Integration of Theory and Practice

1. product warranty 产品保修

【知识点】产品出口必须使顾客感到放心。敢于承诺保修，表明产品质量可靠，如有损坏，卖主在一定期限内和一定条件下将免费维修或更换损坏的部分。良好的售后服务有利于交易。

对于出口产品，加强售后服务不可掉以轻心，尤其是机电产品，若无产品保修，客户和消费者容易产生抱怨或不满，使一些潜在客户和消费者对企业的产品望而却步。

现在出口电器等产品到欧美等地，须签订保修合同。欧美等国加紧了对电器产品质量的控制，对机电产品质量标准和保修要求更加严格。

当然，中国产品出口，因为远离本国，考虑到维修的不便，售后服务还要量力而行。非机电产品出口则大部分不保修。

让客户对最关心的产品标准、产品质量、按期交货、产品种类和款式新颖等方面感到满意。

【技能训练句型】

The 3-year warranty is granted for our electronic appliances.
我方的电器保修期3年。

The machine warranty assures customers of the reliability of the products.
机器保修确保了产品的可靠性。

Product warranty gives a guarantee to the quality of products. It will be helpful for product promotion.
产品保修使产品的质量有了保证，这有助于产品的促销。

2. marketing strategy　市场营销策略

【知识点】由于消费者的需求存在差异，哪家企业能够领先发现新的消费群体需求，根据市场细分对其产品进行开发和差异化营销（differentiated marketing），谁就能获得不菲的回报。

市场细分就是把一个看似完整的市场，划分成为多个存在内在逻辑关系的、相对独立的、更小的市场。科学的市场细分能充分发挥市场营销的效率，从而更有效地占领目标市场。

企业可根据自己的产品特性，寻找不同的消费群体，开发不同的市场，并针对不同的市场进行不同的市场营销策划，使产品适销对路，提高经济效益。同时实施品牌战略，增强企业核心竞争力。例如，工具市场是一个完整的市场。公司可以根据自己的产品特点，按不同的用途和功能来细分为专业工具、家用工具、电动和手动工具等。按消费对象来细分为男式工具和女式工具等。这样可充分满足消费者多层次的需求。

【技能训练句型】

We specially designed the tools for lady use. Look, the box and all plastic handles are light and clear pink. It's lady's color, don't you think so?
我们是专为女性设计的。瞧，外盒及工具的手柄都用鲜艳亮丽的粉红色。那是女性专用的颜色，不是吗？

These two items are for family use. They will be nice gifts for Father's Day.
这两款是家用的，是父亲节的上好礼品。

3. acceptance　接受

【知识点】构成有效的接受（法律上称作承诺）要具备以下条件。

（1）交易的一方在接到对方的报盘或还盘后，以声明或行为向对方表示同意。接受一定

Chapter 10 Acceptance and Orders

要由受盘人做出表示同意。

（2）受盘人表示接受时，要采取口头或书面的声明向报盘人明确表示出来。

（3）应该是无条件的接受，接受的内容要与报盘的内容相符。如果对报盘的内容作了增加、限制或修改，则称为有条件的接受，不能成为有效的接受，而属于还盘。

【技能训练句型】

Let's close a deal. We'll accept your offer by sending fax soon.

成交！我们通过传真接受贵方的报价。

（4）接受的通知要在报盘的有效期内送达报盘人才能生效。接受不可更改和撤销。

4. skills of price negotiation 洽谈价格技巧

洽谈价格时，客户经常用同类价格比较的方法压低价格，可尝试以下技巧。

【知识点1】如果买方称价格太高，卖方可重点谈产品质量好，谈卖方产品和销售优势的方面，谈影响价格的不利因素，生产条件良好的话可带客户参观企业，增加价格的砝码。

【技能训练句型】

A: Compared with others, your TV sets seem a bit overpriced. Could you give us more favor to reduce the price a little further?

与其他公司相比，贵方的电视机定价有些偏高。您能给我们一些优惠，再降一点价吗？

B: The new styles and features to open markets are worth the money, aren't they? Moreover, our quality of TV sets is superior to other manufacturers'.

开辟市场的新时尚和新特色就值得这价格，不是吗？而且，我们的电视机质量比其他厂家更优越。

【知识点2】不要和客户纠缠自己的价格和同类价格比较。为了避免这种比较，可岔开话题。

【技能训练句型】

Shall we come to the price again later on after we finish other terms and conditions?

那么我们先谈其他条款，回头再谈价格问题好吗？

【知识点3】当卖方降了价，而买方仍不满意，或在交易会上想货比三家时，买方可婉转表示过一会儿再来。

【技能训练句型】

Thank you for making a more competitive quotation. I'll look around and come back later.

谢谢报更优惠的价格。我想到周围转转，过一会儿再来。

【知识点4】价格是谈判中双方最敏感的主要问题。但国际贸易涉及方方面面，许多其他条件和方式也很重要。在谈判桌上多涉及几个问题，双方互相让步，找到交换条件，使双方均有利可图，便于成交，达成双赢。

当买方要求T/T支付时，卖方采取灵活的方式，不坚持非信用证不可，在支付条件上先作了让步。

当回到最敏感的价格问题时，价格分歧较大，为了成交，卖方作了让步。卖方告知已是底价，几乎无利可图了，这样容易打动买方，双方各让一步，买方欣然表示接受。

【技能训练句型】

We usually accept payment by L/C. That is our usual practice.

我们一般接受信用证付款，这是我们的惯例。

For T/T payment, 30% down payment upon your order confirmation and balance payment will be paid before shipment.

采用电汇付款，合同确定后预付30%，发货前付清余款。

To conclude the business and show our sincerity, we agree to cut 10 cents for each set.

为了促成生意，表示我方的诚意，我们同意每套降10美分。

Should we meet each other half way? USD 2.49 is already our bottom price.

我们各让一半好吗？2.49美元已是我们的底线了。

Part D Practice

I. Complete the Following Dialogues

(1)

Fill in the blanks with the proper prepositions.

A: We have talked about all terms aside ___1___ packing.

B: Well, I am eager to know the packing of vase as improper packing will result ___2___ the breakage of vase.

A: Each vase is packed ___3___ a plastic bag and 2 pairs ___4___ a box.

B: I see.

A: All vases are packed ___5___ cartons ___6___ 12 boxes each.

B: I worry ___7___ whether the cartons are strong enough.

A: We have taken ___8___ consideration and choose double cardboard to protect the goods.

B: Do you use warning mark ___9___ the cartons?

A: Sure. Warning mark ___10___ "Fragile" are painted outside the cartons.

B: Fine. We'll place an order ___11___ vases ___12___ you right now.

(2)

Fill in the blanks with the proper forms of the following expressions.

assure sb. of	close a deal	place a duplicate order	push the sale
be superior to	insist on	tell something about	on condition that
It is understandable but		be inconvenient for	

A: Mr. Wu, could you ___1___ warranty of electronic toys?

B: I am afraid not. Our quality ___2___ other manufacturers'.

A: ___3___ product warranty gives a guarantee to the quality of products.

B: You are right.

Chapter 10 Acceptance and Orders

A: Warranty ___4___ the reliability of the products.
B: But it ___5___ us to repair the electronic toys far away in your country.
A: Our customers ___6___ having product warranty before choosing the toys.
B: Well, I have an idea. Warranty is granted ___7___ you place a repeat order so that we can put additional toys for replacement.
A: OK. I am going to ___8___ each month.
B: Oh, you mean exactly the same orders every time?
A: Yes, you see, warranty will be helpful for us to ___9___ .
B: Great! It's worth trying.
A: OK. Let ___10___ .

II. Interaction Activities

Task 1

A foreign buyer is discussing prices for stainless wares with the seller. They can't reach the agreement on prices. At last, the seller agrees to meet each other half way on condition that the buyer increases the quantity of order.

Divide students into pairs. Make short dialogues and role-play them. The following expressions should be included in your dialogue.

(1) on the high side
(2) ask for a discount of 4%
(3) bad situation
(4) devaluation of the US dollar
(5) the increase of steel and plastic prices
(6) discount impossible
(7) seeking discount by large quantity
(8) more than triple, that is 3 FCL

Task 2

Imagine you are an importer. Try to persuade the seller to accept payment by T/T. Compose a conversation with your partner. Your conversation should cover the expressions below.

(1) terms of payment
(2) accept confirmed, irrevocable letter of credit at sight
(3) tied up capital flow
(4) cause some inconvenience
(5) protection of the banker's guarantee
(6) only a trial order
(7) It's not worth...
(8) costs less
(9) make an exception

(10) remit the payment before shipment

III. Actual Practice

Mr. John is having a negotiation with Mr. Xiao on the business of importing MP4.

Work in pairs and role-play the conversation.

Use the following background information:

(1) comparison with other suppliers

(2) prices on the high side

(3) superior quality

(4) beyond reach

(5) suggestion to discuss other terms and conditions first

(6) same thinking

(7) terms of payment

(8) suggestion to pay by D/A

(9) usual practice by L/C

(10) insist on payment by D/P

(11) In order to encourage business...

(12) make an exception

(13) ask for more reasonable prices

(14) carefully calculated

(15) rock-bottom prices

(16) no further reduction

(17) close a deal

IV. Creative Discussion

Divide the class into groups. Discuss the issue with your partners and share your opinions with other groups.

Topic:

Suppose you are running a large shoes company. You are planning to design a marketing strategy to occupy target markets. Make a market research first and find out what is the consumers' demand.

Then, according to the features of shoes, you fractionize the shoes markets to meet the demand of different consumers. How will you do to carry out the differentiated marketing?

Please discuss the issue with the members in your group.

Chapter 11
Business Telephone Calls

Learning Objectives
Upon completion of this chapter, you will be able to

- acquire some techniques of telephone conversation.
- get acquainted with the etiquette on the phone.
- acquire telephone communication skills.
- conduct the activities related to telephone communication.
- understand carrying out people-to-people exchanges.[1]

---

1 理解开展人文交流。

Part A Situational Dialogue

Communicative Scene 1

Hard to Reach Somebody

(*Mr. Sun met Miss Lin last week on an exhibition. He is trying to get her on the phone now. He dials the number, and <u>the telephone rings.</u>[1])*

Switchboard (answering machine): "Thanks for calling ABC Corporation. If you know your party's last name or extension, press 1. If you want to receive information of the corporation, press 2. If you want to talk to the operator, press pound sign or remain on the line."

(*Mr. Sun presses the button, and the music fades in ... The operator answers the call.*)

Operator: Hello? Thank you for waiting, what can I do for you?

  Sun: Can I speak to Miss Lin, please?

Operator: Would you like to tell me which department she works in? We have a couple of Miss Lins here.

  Sun: Er... I suppose it's in Purchasing Department.

Operator: Purchasing Department. Hold on please, I'll put you through.

(<u>*The extension is engaged.*</u>[2] *There comes the voice: the line is busy, hold on please... In a few seconds, Mr. Sun is through.*)

  Lin: Hello, Purchasing Department, who's speaking?

  Sun: Oh, hello, um...I'm an agent of shoes materials. May I speak to Miss Lin?

  Lin: This is she.

  Sun: Oh, good. Glad to hear you. This is Mr. Sun from Qing Shun Trading Company.

  Lin: Mr. Sun?

  Sun: Um...we met last week at the exhibition of shoes materials.

  Lin: (*Silence*)

  Sun: Er... You were quite interested in our synthetic and genuine leather and asked me to contact you later.

  Lin: Exhibition? No...no, I haven't been there. You've probably made a mistake.

  Sun: What? Sorry, er... maybe I got a wrong department.

  Lin: I think so. The Technology Department of our company is in charge of affirming the materials for new products. You probably want Miss Lin in the Technology Department.

  Sun: Oh, um...well...anyway, thank you, and <u>could you connect me back through the switchboard,</u>

Chapter 11 Business Telephone Calls

please?³

Lin: Well, let me try…

Taking a Message

(*Miss Liu is making an international long-distance call to inform the relevant issues about the visiting delegation.*)

Telephonist: Good afternoon, China Tiger Beverage Company.

Liu: Oh, good afternoon, this is Miss Liu calling from Malaysia. Could I speak to Mr. Zhang, chief manager of your company?

Telephonist: Certainly, Miss Liu, putting you through.

Secretary: Hello, Mr. Zhang's office.

Liu: Good morning, this is Miss Liu, I'm phoning from Malaysia, head office of the company. Is Mr. Zhang there?

Secretary: Sorry, he's in a conference now.⁴ This is his secretary Wang Li. Can I help you?

Liu: Hello, Wang Li, it's about the visiting delegation to your plant. Would you please take a message for me?

Secretary: Sure, with pleasure.

Liu: The delegation from Malaysia is supposed to arrive in your city on Wednesday afternoon, but I'm sorry to inform that the schedule of the delegation has to be changed due to the temporary cancellation of this flight to your city.⁵ The journey will be put off. They won't be arriving until this Saturday afternoon. And I want to make sure whether you are able to make adjustment accordingly.

Secretary: Right.

Liu: And I would also like to inform you that the members of the group have been trimmed down.⁶ Five of them are otherwise engaged.⁷

Secretary: OK, let me double-check. The delegation will come on Saturday afternoon instead of Wednesday afternoon, and the size of the group will be smaller…by the way…can I have the exact number, please?

Liu: Um…a group of 11 in total.

Secretary: 11…in total, right?

Liu: Yes, wonderful, thanks. Could you please ask Mr. Zhang to fax or send me an e-mail to confirm that he is ready for the change?

Secretary: All Right, I'll take the message and inform Mr. Zhang when he's back. He'll be in touch with you.⁸

Liu: Thank you very much.

145

Communicative Scene 3

Something to Complain

(Mr. Ma phones the Ads department to complain about the slip of broadcasting their commercials.)

Secretary: Good morning. Advertisement Department of Channel 9.

Ma: Good morning, lady. I'd like to speak to Mr. Wang, deputy chief of your department.

Secretary: Whom am I speaking with, please?

Ma: Mr. Ma of Qinqin Foodstuff Company.

Secretary: One moment, please. (To Mr. Wang) Mr. Ma of Qinqin Foodstuff Company wants to speak to you.

Wang: Hello, Mr. Ma. This is Mr. Wang.

Ma: Good morning, Mr. Wang. I'm calling about our commercials. Yesterday evening we didn't see our ads film during the commercial break of the TV series.[9]

Wang: I'm very sorry. I'm thinking to call you about this. We'll claim responsibility for this. Probably we could make up our slips by giving you another two times 30-second release free of charge. Do you agree?

Ma: Um... Well... What about the time?

Wang: The golden time, right after the news on the evening of Mar. 20 and 21.

Ma: Are you sure?

Wang: Sure, no problem.

Ma: OK, thank you. Goodbye.

Wang: Bye-bye.

Words and Expressions

1. etiquette	n.	礼节，礼仪
2. nuisance	n.	麻烦事
3. switchboard	n.	接线总机
4. answering machine	n.	电话答录机
5. pound sign	n.	#号键
6. fade in		（使）淡入；渐显
7. extension	n.	分机
8. engaged	adj.	使用中的，（电话）占线的
9. synthetic	adj.	合成的
10. genuine leather		真皮
11. delegation	n.	代表团

Chapter 11 Business Telephone Calls

12. accordingly	adv.	从而
13. trim down		裁减
14. double-check		仔细检查
15. deputy chief		副总经理
16. foodstuff	n.	食品
17. commercial break		（电视）广告时间
18. claim	vt.	认领；（根据权利）要求
19. release	vt.	发行；发布

Notes

1. The telephone rings.
   电话铃响了。
   ring 在此处指电话铃响。ring 还可以指打电话，ring在表示打电话时，多用于英式英语，美式英语中则用call来表示。比如：
   Ring me up. 给我打电话。
   Ring me back. 给我回电话。

2. The extension is engaged.
   分机占线。
   be engaged 指电话占线，多用于英式英语，而美式英语则多用busy，如：The line is busy.
   engaged line / number 占线　　line in use 占线（美式英语）
   engaged tone 忙音　　　　　　busy signal 忙音（美式英语）
   The line is free / open now. 现在不占线了。

3. Could you connect me back through the switchboard, please?
   请帮我转回总机好么？

4. Sorry, he is in a conference now.
   很抱歉，他在开会。
   ① hold a conference 举行会议
   ② attend a conference 参加会议
   ③ press conference 新闻发布会

5. I'm sorry to inform that the schedule of the delegation has to be changed due to the temporary cancellation of this flight to your city.
   我很抱歉通知您由于飞往贵城的航班临时取消，我们只好改变了访问团的日程安排。
   ① schedule 日程/行程安排
   ② tight schedule 安排得很满的日程
   ③ ahead of schedule 提前于原定日程
   ④ due to / because of 因为，例如：We canceled the travel due to the bad weather.

6. And I would also like to inform you that the members of the group have been trimmed down.
   还要通知您，代表团的人数减少了。

① trim one's hair 修剪头发

② trim the budget 削减预算

7. Five of them are otherwise engaged.

其中有五个人另有安排（不能去了）。

be otherwise engaged 另有安排

8. He'll be in touch with you.

（就此事）他会和你联系的。

be in touch (with) 多用于电话用语，也可用get in touch (with)替代，指就某事和某人在电话上联系。但 keep in touch (with) 则一般指两人经常没见面要保持联系。

9. Yesterday evening we didn't see our ads film during the commercial break of the TV series.

昨晚我们没看到电视剧中间播放我们的广告片。

① commercial break （电视节目中间的）广告时间

② ads film 广告片

Part B Practical Key Sentences

1. **This is ...** 我是……

   Good morning. This is Miss Smith.

   早上好，我是史密斯小姐。

   替换表达：

   This is Miss Smith, calling from the United States.

   This is Miss Smith.

   This is John speaking.

   Peter speaking.

   Speaking.

   This is she / he.

   当你正是电话那头要找的人，一般会回答：speaking或this is she / he，意即：我就是（你要找的人），后者多用于美式英语，使用时更要注意语气，否则会给人以唐突的感觉。

2. **One moment, please.** 请稍候

   这句话是话务员为来电者接入分机之前请来电者稍候的惯用语，或为来电者找人时使用。

   替换表达：

   One moment, please.

   Just a second, please.

   Could you hold a little longer?

   Hold the line, please.

   Hold on, please.

3. **Connect me with...** 请帮我接通……

   Can you connect me with Quality Control Department?

Chapter 11 Business Telephone Calls

请帮我接质检部好吗?

这句话是打电话需要总机转某个分机时的惯用语。

替换表达:

  Could you put me through to Public Relations Department?

  Could you connect me with the extension 3336?

  Extension 5096, please.

4. take a message or leave a message　带口信或留口信

Can I take a message for you?

能给您带个口信么?

She's out for lunch. Can I take a message for you?

她外出吃午饭,能给您带个口信吗?

Can I leave a message with you?

能帮我带个口信么?

替换表达:

  May I take a message?

  Do you want him to call you back?

  Any message for him?

  Would you like to leave a message?

5. put you through　为您接通电话

I'll put you through.

我给您转接过去。

替换表达:

  You're through.

  I'll connect you immediately.

  I'll get the extension for you.

  I'm transferring your call.

  I'm redirecting your call.

  I'll put her on the phone. Just a second.

6. Could I speak to...　找某人接电话

Could I speak to Dr. Henderson?

亨德森博士在吗?

替换表达:

  I'd like to speak to Ms. Chi.

  Could I have a word with Jenny?

  Is that Miss Chen?

  Is Miss Hu there?

  Is Mr. Watson available, please?

  May I speak to Customer Service director?

  I'm trying to get a hold of Miss Lin.

7. Contact me, please. 请和我联系。

You can reach me at this number.
拨这个号码能找到我。

替换表达：

  I'm at 83517303.

  My phone number is 87350510.

  Contact me by telephone.

8. You are wanted on the phone. 有人找您。

Our manager would like to talk to you on the phone.
我们经理想与您电话交谈。

And you are...?
在给职位较高的人打电话时，负责转接电话的秘书可能会问：And you are...?（您是……？）这是一个很实用的句子。

替换表达：

  You have a call from Mr. White.

  Whom am I speaking with, please?

Part C Integration of Theory and Practice

1. 用清晰而愉快的语调打电话。

  【知识点】国际商务运作离不开电话这一便捷的通信工具，而在打电话时你的声音是交流的唯一介质，因此充分体现语调的魅力至关重要。用清晰而愉快的语调接电话能显示出说话人的职业风度和可亲的性格。虽然对方无法看到你的面容，但你的喜悦或烦躁仍会通过语调流露出来。打电话时语调应平稳、柔和，这时如能面带微笑地与对方交谈，可使你的声音听起来更为友好热情。千万不要边打电话边嚼口香糖或吃东西。

2. 接电话时应注意得体的问答。

  【知识点1】接商务电话时通常应先报公司的名字，然后再说："May I help you?"（我能帮您什么忙？）如果更客气一点的话，则可以说："How can I help you?"（我该怎么帮您？）因为这样的问法表示我"该"怎么帮您，而非我"需不需要帮您"。

  【知识点2】接电话时，不要让铃声响得太久，应尽快接电话。若因为有急事或正在接另一部电话而耽搁时，应表示歉意。

  【技能训练句型】

  Thank you for waiting, John speaking.

  此处用Thank you for waiting 表示歉意，而不用Sorry for waiting.

  或用：I am sorry you had to wait, John speaking. 久等了，我是约翰。

  【知识点3】热情问候并报出公司或部门名称。如果对方打错电话，不要责备对方，知情时还应告诉对方正确的号码。

Chapter 11 Business Telephone Calls

【技能训练句型】

A: **Good morning,** QC Department. 早上好，这里是质检部。

B: Sorry, I must have dialed the wrong number. I wanted to reach the Sales Department. 对不起，我拨错号码了。我本想拨销售部的。

A: Take it easy. Their extension is 9143. 没关系。销售部的分机是9143。

【知识点4】打电话前应准备好电话号码，考虑好说话内容、措辞和语气语调。如有必要，可以做一个书面的提纲，让谈话的内容更全面、更有条理。

【知识点5】如果对方不在，可请代接电话者转告；或向代接电话者询问对方的去处和联系方式；或把自己的联系方式留下，让对方回来后回电话。

【技能训练句型】

I'm anxious to talk to him, could you give me his home number?

我有急事找他，您能告诉我他家的电话么？

Could you have him call me back? My name is Chen Ji. My phone number is 87546203.

您能让他给我回个电话么？我叫陈济。我的电话是87546203。

【知识点6】如果来电找的同事正在接电话，就告诉对方他所找的人正在接电话，并主动询问对方是留言还是等一会儿。如果留言，则记录对方的留言、单位、姓名和联系方式；如果只是等一会儿，则将电话筒轻轻放下，通知被找的人接电话；如果被叫人正在接一个重要电话，一时难以结束，则请对方过一会儿再来电话，或是留下回电号码。切忌让对方莫名久等。

【技能训练句型】

He is on the phone. Would you like to hold on for a moment or can I take a message?

他在打电话。您能稍候么？要不有事我帮您转告一下。

Hold on please, he will be available in a few seconds.

请稍等，他马上就来。

He is busy with another call. Would you like to try again later?

他忙着讲电话。您稍后打来好么？

3. 不能及时回电话时的处理。

【知识点】在商业投诉中，不能及时回电话的情况较为常见。为了不丧失每一次成交的机会，有的公司甚至做出对电话留言须在一小时之内答复的规定。一般应在24小时之内对电话留言给予答复，如果回电话时恰遇对方不在，也要留言，表明你已经回过电话了。如果自己确实无法亲自回电，应托付他人代办。

4. 拨打国际商务电话时应注意时差。

【知识点】打电话前要弄清楚地区时差以及各国工作时间的差异，不要在休息日打电话谈生意，以免影响他人休息，除非你了解对方的生活习惯。一般不要在早上8时以前或晚上9时以后给对方打电话，中午也要注意对方的休息。即使客户已将家中的电话号码告诉你，也尽量不要往家中打电话。

5. 恰当地使用电话。

【知识点】在美国你可以通过电话向一个素不相识的人推销商品，而在欧洲、拉美和亚洲国家，电话促销或在电话中长时间地谈生意就难以让人接受。发展良好商务关系的最佳途径是与客户面对面地商谈，而电话主要用来安排会见。当然一旦双方见过面，再通过电话沟通就方便多了。

6. 打国际长途电话时的注意事项。

【知识点】打国际长途电话，特别是电话费用较高的地区，不要随便要求对方主动打过来，可以问清时间后打过去。

7. 用手机打电话时的注意事项。

【知识点】在会场、医院、剧院、电影院等场所，均不宜使用手机；在飞机上禁止使用手机，在公共汽车、电车上使用手机也不合适；在餐厅用餐时，若必须接听电话，必须离开桌子到餐厅的角落接听。在双向收费的情况下，说话更要简洁明了，以节约话费；优先拨打客户的固定电话，打固定电话找不到对方时再拨打其手机；在嘈杂环境中，听不清楚对方声音时要说明，并让对方过一会儿再打过来，或你打过去；若必须在公共场合打手机，说话声不要太大，以免影响他人。

Part D Practice

I. Complete the Following Dialogues

(1)

Secretary: Good morning, Brain Time.

Ling: Good morning. May I ____1____ to Ms. Jones?

Secretary: ____2____ Ms. Jones is that? We have several.

Ling: Edna Jones.

Secretary: I'm ____3____ she isn't ____4____. May I take a ____5____ for you?

Ling: Yes. I wanted to talk to her ____6____ ordering some computers. My name is Ling Lihua.

Secretary: ____7____ is your number?

Ling: 2245109.

Secretary: OK, I'll tell her as soon ____8____ she comes in.

Ling: Thank you. Good-bye.

Secretary: Good-bye.

(2)

Operator: May I ____1____ you?

Cao: I'd like to ____2____ a collect, person-to-person call to Mr. Huang Hongwei please.

Operator: What's the name of the ____3____ calling?

Cao: That's Cao Yong.

Operator: ____4____ a moment please.

(Cao hears the operator say: "I have a ____5____, person-to-person call for Mr. Huang Hongwei from Mr. Cao Yong. Will you accept the ____6____?" He hears someone at the other end say: "Just a moment, please. I'll ____7____ you with his ____8____." He hears the phone ring.)

Huang: Hello.

Chapter 11 Business Telephone Calls

Operator: Is this Mr. Huang Hongwei?

Huang: Yes.

Operator: Will you ___9___ a collect call from Mr. Cao Yong in New York City?

Huang: Yes, I will.

Operator: (*To Cao*) Go ___10___, please.

(*Huang and Cao begin to talk.*)

II. Role-plays

Task 1

Students work in groups. Each student makes a business phone call to anther student. Design the situation by yourself and move to another student when you finish. Try to talk to as many people as possible.

Task 2

Work in pairs.

Make up your own dialogue according to the given situation.

This evening, you made a supper date with your girlfriend, Nicole Kidman. However, your boss asked you to make a counter-offer to the trade company and to work late, so you telephoned Nicole to make the date on another day. You called twice, yet she was either on a conference or out. You had to leave a message to her.

Here are some useful expressions:

(1) Hello, this is ... speaking.

(2) Hello, I'd like to speak to ...

(3) I'm afraid ... is not available right now.

(4) May I know who is calling?

(5) Can I leave a message?

(6) Would you like to leave a message?

(7) Please tell her ...

(8) Hold on ...

III. Guided Talking

Student A is the receptionist at a large record company. She answers the phone for three busy executives. Below are their schedules for this afternoon.

NAME	1:00 p.m.	2:00 p.m.	3:00 p.m.	4:00 p.m.
Liu Yifei	lunch with the music fans	on a long-distance call to Paris	audition new bands	party at Shangrila Hotel
Wang An	out to lunch	visit the recording studio	in a press conference	meetings with clients
Zhao Mingmin	lunch with Luther Martin	back at 2:30	meetings with lawyers	out of the office

(1)

Student B is a clerk in City Bank. She calls and wants to speak to Wang An. The message is that since the overdraft of his credit card has exceeded the permitted amount, he had better pay the due money, and he'd better go there as soon as possible. Use your own name and phone number.

The time of her call is 3:20 p.m.

(2)

Student C is an accountant. He calls to speak to Liu Yifei. The message is that he has to cancel his appointment on Friday. He would like Liu Yifei to call him so that he can arrange a new time. Use your own name and phone number.

The time of his call is 2:00 p.m.

(3)

Student D is an executive of another record company. He calls and wants to speak to Zhao Mingmin. The message is that he wants to ask about a new band.

The time of his call is 4:00 p.m.

IV. Creative Discussion

The teacher divides the class into groups for discussion. Each group chooses a representative after discussion. The student who expresses well will be the winner.

Topic:

Imagine that all telephones in your city suddenly stop working. What effect would it have on people's daily life? Can you do well without telephone?

Chapter 12

Terms of Payment

Learning Objectives
Upon completion of this chapter, you will be able to

- get familiar with different terms of payment.
- know how to use different kinds of payment.
- know how to open and arrange payment by L/C.
- acquire the skills of communication.
- conduct the activities related to payment.
- understand following the principles of extensive consultation, joint contribution and shared benefits.[1]

---

1 理解秉持共商共建共享原则。

Part A Situational Dialogue

Communicative Scene 1

Demanding Payment by L/C

(Mr. Smith, a businessman from Canada, is talking about the terms of payment with Miss Chen, who is working at Fujian Hope Import & Export Corporation. Finally, both of them agree the goods are paid by L/C and then arrange the details of payment.)

Smith: We've settled a lot of things such as price, packing and shipment. Now, there's one question left to discuss, that is, terms of payment: <u>We recommend the goods be paid by D/A.</u>[1] What do you think of the terms of payment?

Chen: To tell you the truth, D/A is impossible. Because you're our new customer, our company would take a great risk if we accepted your terms. Perhaps after more business between us, we would consider payment made by collection. <u>Now, to be on the safe side, we only accept payment by irrevocable letter of credit payable against shipping documents.</u>[2]

Smith: Well, you know our order this time is very large. When I open the letter of credit with the bank, I have to pay a deposit and the bank charges. <u>To open an L/C for such a large amount is costly, which will add to the cost of our imports.</u>[3]

Chen: You can consult your bank and see if they can reduce some deposit and charges.

Smith: However, it also usually takes a couple of months from the time we open the credit until our buyers pay us, <u>our funds will be tied up.</u>[4] It may cause us a great deal of troubles in view of the current difficult economic climate. Could you be a little more flexible and make some changes? I wonder if you could accept other kinds of payment such as D/P?

Chen: I'm afraid not. We regret to say that we cannot accept your proposal for changing in payment. Our usual practice is to accept payment by L/C only. An irrevocable L/C gives our exports the protection of a banker's guarantee and we'll get the right amount of money.

Smith: <u>I'm sorry that you adhere to payment by L/C. For you, payment by L/C is the safest method, but for us, the point is that to open an L/C with a bank does mean additional expense.</u>[5]

Chen: In fact, L/C is fair and beneficial to both the seller and the buyer. However, to help you get rid of difficulty, I would like to suggest that you reduce the order by half. Then you can go on placing the rest of the order.

Smith: Well, I'll consider it. (*After calculating on the computer and thinking about for some time*) All right, I'll reduce the order by half. <u>However, let's make a compromise about the terms of payment.</u>[6] Do you think you could accept a time L/C and allow us to delay payment, say, 60 days after sight?

Chen: We usually demand payment by L/C available by draft at sight. Payment by sight L/C is quite usual in international trade. But to make a successful deal for this time and encourage more orders for the future, we'll consider your request.

Smith: Thank you. You are of great help.

Chen: Then let's arrange the details of payment. Could you send the L/C 30 days before shipment?

Smith: No problem. I'll arrange for the L/C to be opened in your favor as soon as I return. When will the goods be ready and the shipment made?

Chen: According to the manufacturer, the goods will be ready by the end of May.

Smith: Since we are in urgent need of the goods and have to give our clients a specific delivery date, is it possible to persuade your manufacturer for an earlier delivery, say, at the beginning of May?[7]

Chen: We wish to satisfy every request of our customers, especially a new one like you. But our manufacturer has a heavy backlog on hand.[8]

Smith: Well, then I hope that the goods can be dispatched promptly after you receive my L/C. The time between May and June is our busy season, therefore, we would very appreciate it if you'd ship the goods as soon as possible.

Chen: You can rest assured of that.[9] We'll make the necessary preparations and effect the shipment in the prescribed time after we get the L/C.

Smith: That'll be great. By the way, what about the term of validity?

Chen: The L/C should be valid for 15 days after the date of shipment.

Smith: Could you tell me what other documents will be provided?

Chen: Besides the draft, we'll send you a full set of bills of lading, and an invoice, and an insurance policy, a certificate of origin and a certificate of inspection.

Smith: Thanks. I appreciate your cooperation.

L/C Amendment

(Miss Chen has received the relevant L/C, but she finds there are some differences between the L/C and Sales Contract No. 2345. So she calls Mr. Smith for the L/C amendment.)

Chen: Hello, Mr. Smith. This is Chen from Fujian Hope Import & Export Corporation.

Smith: Hi, Miss Chen.

Chen: I received your letter of credit on 8th of April. I'm afraid there are some differences between your L/C and Sales Contract No. 2345.

Smith: Go ahead.

Chen: First, goods should be insured for 110% of the invoice value, not 150%. Since all the terms in the L/C should be in full agreement with the contract, you should open the credit according to the clauses in the contract.

Smith: Really? It may be an oversight on my part. I'll check it up and inform you. Anything else?

Chen: Please insert the word "about" between "quantity" and "150M/T". What's more, the expiry date should be the 15th of June rather than the 5th of June.

Smith: I'm sorry for these mistakes caused by our carelessness. I'll approach the opening bank to amend the L/C immediately and I'll adopt some measures to avoid similar mistakes in the future.

Chen: Thank you for your cooperation. There is another thing I'd like to talk over with you. For some reason, there is only two vessels sailing for your port during May / June and it leaves here in the second half of a month. Shipping space for May is not available now. So we have to face two alternatives. It depends on you to extend the credit or allow transshipment.

Smith: Extension of credit will cause us a lot of troubles. I'll delete the clause "by direct steamer" and amend the credit to allow transshipment.

Chen: Thank you for understanding our situation and let us have your amendment notice as soon as possible so that we can effect shipment of the goods.

Communicative Scene 3

Demanding Other Modes of Payment

(*Mr. Smith and Miss. Chen are discussing about terms of payment of another order.*)

Smith: Miss. Chen, I'm glad that we have concluded a successful transaction, although your prices are on the slightly high sides compared with those in Malaysia. Considering the superior quality and attractive design of your products, I would like to make another order, but the quantity depends on the terms of payment. If you could offer us easier terms of payment, it would possibly lead to an increase in business. Could you give more favorable terms?

Chen: Thank you for another order. Our regular practice concerning terms of payment is by L/C. What about your proposal?

Smith: As everyone knows, L/C involves many additional expenses for us, which leaves us few profit margins. Could you please accept payment by D/A?

Chen: I'm afraid that it's very difficult for us to accept your suggestion. This mode of payment might cause sellers some troubles. As you know, the international monetary market is very unstable, and the devaluation of dollars and its impact on other currencies have raised serious uncertainties in the world market.

Smith: Then, I wonder if you will accept D/P?

Chen: Well, with an eye to future transactions and trust established through the last business, I think we can make an exception for you at this time. <u>To meet you half way, what do you say 50% by D/P and the rest by L/C?</u>[10]

Smith: <u>All right, thanks for your accommodation,</u>[11] I'll increase my order.

Chen: Thank you for your order again. I should mention that we can't regard it as setting a precedent for all our future transactions. You'd better establish the relative L/C in the prescribed time. When the goods are dispatched, we'll issue a sight draft against you. We trust you will honor it on presentation.

Smith: Certainly we'll follow the usual procedure. Our negotiation has been very pleasant and fruitful. I sincerely hope that the trade between us will grow in the future.

Words and Expressions

1. collection		n.	托收
2. deposit		n.	保证金，押金；存款
3. costly		adj.	昂贵的
4. be tied up			占压（资金）
5. compromise		v.	妥协
6. draft		n.	汇票
available by draft at sight			见票即付
7. backlog		n.	（一般用单数）积压未办之事
8. on hand			手头，现有
9. rest assure of			尽管放心
10. validity		n.	有效
11. bill of lading (B/L)			提单
12. an insurance policy			保险单
13. Certificate of Origin			产地证书
14. Certificate of Inspection			检验证书
15. regular practice			惯常做法，惯例
16. profit margin		n.	利润率，盈利率
17. devaluation		n.	贬值
18. uncertainty		n.	不稳定；不确定
19. accommodation		n.	通融
20. prescribed		adj.	规定的
21. honor the draft on presentation			见票即付
22. make exception			例外
23. precedent		n.	先例
24. procedure		n.	（正确的或通常做事的）步骤；手续

Notes

1. We recommend the goods be paid by D/A.

   我们建议用承兑交单的付款方式。

   ① recommend *v.* 建议，推荐（后可跟名词、动名词或从句，跟从句时须用虚拟语气）

   例句：

   The manager recommended that he (should) investigate the local market.

   经理建议他调查当地市场。

   Your firm has been recommended to us by the Chamber of Commerce in Beijing.

   北京商会把贵公司推荐给我们。

   ② recommendation *n.* 建议，推荐

   例句：

   We made a recommendation to the board.

   我们向董事会提出建议。

2. Now, to be on the safe side, we only accept payment by irrevocable letter of credit payable against shipping documents.

   目前为保险起见，通常我们采用不可撤销的信用证，凭装船单据付款。

   ① payable *adj.* 应付的（常用作后置定语）

   注意以下词组：

   bills payable 应付票据

   amount payable 应付金额

   account payable 应付账款

   a check payable at sight 见票即付的支票

   ② shipping 装运，运输

   注意和shipping有关的术语：

   shipping documents 装运单据

   shipping mark 装运标志

   shipping agent 货运代理人

   shipping instruction 装运须知

   shipping advice 装运通知

   shipping container 船运集装箱

   shipping order 装货单

   shipping space 舱位

   shipping date 装船日期

3. To open an L/C for such a large amount is costly, which will add to the cost of our imports.

   开立这么大金额的信用证费用太大，会增加我们的进口成本。

   ① open an L/C 开立信用证

   类似词组：

   establish an L/C

issue an L/C

② amount *n.& v.* 数额，金额，总额；（金额）合计，达到

注意与amount有关的词组：

the amount of 金额计

to the amount of 金额计

for the amount of 金额计

to amount to ... 金额达到……

to come to an amount of 金额达到……

4. Our funds will be tied up.

我们的资金就要被占用。

tie up

① （资金）被占用，不能动用

例句：

My money is all tied up in shares.

我的钱全套在股票上了。

② （交通）阻塞，塞车

例句：

The accident tied up the traffic for many hours.

那起事故使交通阻塞好几个小时。

③ 忙得脱不开身

例句：

I'm tied up at the draft contract all day.

我一整天忙着做合同草案，脱不开身。

5. I'm sorry that you adhere to payment by L/C. For you, payment by L/C is the safest method, but for us, the point is that to open an L/C with a bank does mean additional expense.

真遗憾，你们坚持用信用证支付方式。对于你们而言，信用证付款是最保险的办法；而对我们而言，问题在于找银行开信用证就意味着额外的费用。

① adhere to 坚持，信守（后接介词 to）

例句：

We should strictly adhere to the terms in the contract.

我们应该严格遵守合同条款。

We always adhere to the principle of equality, mutual benefit and exchange of needed goods.

我们一贯坚持平等互利、互通有无的原则。

② do在此为强调语气的助动词。

例句：

They did tell him to take care of traps in commercial activities.

他们确实告诉过他要小心商务活动中的陷阱。

6. However, let's make a compromise about the terms of payment.

然而，我们还是应该在付款方式上折中一下。

make a compromise 妥协，让步

例句：

  We managed to make a compromise on a price for the machine.

  我们终于就机器的价格达成妥协。

7. Since we are in urgent need of the goods and have to give our clients a specific delivery date, is it possible to persuade your manufacturer for an earlier delivery, say, at the beginning of May?

因为我方急需这批货，并且要给客户一个明确的交货期，能否说服厂家提前一点交货？比如五月初？

be in urgent need of sth. 急需

类似表达：

be in great need of sth.

need sth. urgently

need sth. badly

8. But our manufacturer has a heavy backlog on hand.

但我们的厂家手头未完成的订单很多。

① backlog *n.* （一般用单数）积压未办之事

a backlog of letters 很多未处理的信

② on hand 手头，现有

例句：

  We had no cash on hand to pay for the house.

  我们手头没有现金付房款。

9. You can rest assured of that.

你尽管放心。

① rest assured of/rest assured that 尽管放心

例句：

  You can rest assured of our sincerity.

  你尽管相信我们的诚意。

  You can rest assured that I will not tell anyone.

  你尽管放心，我不会告诉任何人。

② assure sb. of sth./assure sb. 向某人保证……

例句：

  We assure you of our close cooperation.

  我们保证与你方密切合作。

  We assure you that we will cooperate with you closely.

  我们保证与你方密切合作。

10. To meet you half way, what do you say 50% by D/P and the rest by L/C?

我们就做出让步，50% 用付款交单，余款用信用证支付好吗？

meet sb. half way 与某人妥协，迁就某人

例句：

  To meet you half way, we'll give you a commission of 3%.

我们愿做出让步，就付给你百分之三的佣金。

If you can pay some amount of the bill, I'll meet you half way.

如果你能支付账单的一部分，我也支付另一半。

11. All right, thanks for your accommodation.

好吧，谢谢你方的通融。

accommodate *v.* 容纳，提供，供给住宿，使适应

accommodating *adj.* 乐于助人的，肯通融的，随和的，温顺的

accommodation 的几种用法：

① *n.* 通融，和解

例句：

As a special accommodation, we will accept this mode of payment terms.

作为特殊的通融，我们将接受这种付款方式。

They have come to an accommodation over this issue.

他们已就这个问题达成和解。

②（酒店、火车、轮船等提供的）住宿膳食服务

例句：

The travel agency has arranged our accommodation.

旅行社已为我们安排好食宿。

*12. When the goods are ready for shipment and the freight space is booked, you can inform us and we will remit by telegraphic transfer.

当你方的货物备妥待运且舱位订好后，请通知我方，我们即电汇货款。

① book freight space 预订舱位

类似词组：

book shipping space

reserve shipping space

② remit *v.* 汇（款）

例句：

Please remit payment by check immediately.

请速用支票汇出付款。

③ remittance *n.* 汇款，汇款额

例句：

We have received your remittance.

我们已收到你方的汇款。

Part B Practical Key Sentences

1. introduce the topic on terms of payment

Now, there's one question left to discuss, that is, the terms of payment.

现在只剩下一件事需要讨论，那就是付款方式？

替换表达：

  There's one other thing we need to discuss. That is, payment by D/P.

  Would you like to have a talk with us about terms of payment now?

  Shall we have a talk about terms of payment today?

  What is your regular practice concerning terms of payment?

  Let's come to the terms of payment.

  I'd like to have a discussion with you about the modes of payment.

2. discuss the possibility of other terms of payment

I wonder if you could accept other kinds of payment such as D/A or D/P?

我想你们是否能接受其他付款方式，例如付款交单或承兑交单？

替换表达：

  I wonder if you could be more flexible and accept other kinds of payment such as T/T or D/P?

  Is it possible to find alternative terms of payment for this transaction, say, D/A or D/P?

  Could you make an exception and accept D/A or D/P for this transaction?

  In view of the unusually big size of the order, we hope you will offer us more favorable terms of payment, what about D/P or D/A?

  It would help us greatly if you would accept D/P or D/A.

3. insist on payment by L/C

Our usual practice is to accept payment by L/C only.

我们通常的做法就是只接受信用证的付款方式。

替换表达：

  I'm afraid we've got to insist on payment by L/C, which is our usual practice.

  We insist on payment by L/C, which is quite usual in international trade.

  We regret to say that we must adhere to payment by L/C, which is customary in foreign trade.

4. promise to open the L/C

I'll arrange for the L/C to be opened in your favor as soon as I return.

我一回去就着手办理以你方为受益人的信用证。

替换表达：

  I'll arrange for the L/C to be established in your favor as soon as I return.

  I'll apply to the bank for the establishment of L/C in your favor as soon as I return.

  I'll arrange with the bankers to issue an L/C in your favor as soon as I return.

  I'll see about opening an L/C as soon as I arrive home.

5. make a compromise

To meet you half way, what do you say 50% by D/P and the rest by L/C?

我们各退一步吧，50%用付款交单，余款用信用证支付好吗？

替换表达：

  Let's make a compromise, how about 50% by D/P and the rest by L/C?

  To avoid having our transaction tied up, how about 50% by D/P and the rest by L/C?

In order to close the deal, could you bend the rules a little, that is, 50% by D/P and the rest by L/C?

Part C Integration of Theory and Practice

1. terms of payment 付款方式

【知识点】在出口贸易中，卖方收取货款是交易的最终目的，那么付款方式就是合同中很重要的条款，由支付时间、地点和途径等组成。我国在进出口贸易中常用的付款方式有汇付、信用证和托收。汇付（Remittance）有信汇、电汇、票汇三种主要方式，现行的主要方式是电汇T/T（Telegraphic Transfer），即汇出行应汇款人的申请，用电报通知汇入行，指示汇入行对收款人支付一定金额的一种汇款方式，货运单据由出口方自行寄给进口方。一般来说，采用电汇有一定的风险，适用于交易量和涉及的金额较小的交易，但如果买方在卖方发货前已电汇预付货款，这对卖方则十分有利，出口方可以迅速收到货款。使用汇付时，应明确规定汇付的时间、具体的汇付方式和金额等。

【技能训练句型】

The buyer should pay 100% of the sales proceeds in advance by T/T to reach the sellers not later than April 15th.

买方应不迟于4月15日将100%的货款用电汇预付至卖方。

2. letter of credit（L/C） 信用证

【知识点】信用证是国际贸易中常见的付款方式，是一种银行开立的有条件承诺付款的书面文件，通常能保护出口方的利益。一般指开证银行根据进口方的请求和指示向出口方开立的一定金额的并在一定期限内凭规定的装运单据承诺付款的书面文件。有关信用证的常见词组：

confirmed L/C 保兑的信用证
unconfirmed L/C 未保兑的信用证
revocable L/C 可撤销的信用证
irrevocable L/C 不可撤销的信用证
sight L/C (L/C at sight) 即期信用证
time L/C (L/C after sight) 远期信用证
transferable L/C 可转让的信用证
non-transferable L/C 不可转让的信用证
divisable L/C 可分割的信用证
indivisable L/C 不可分割的信用证
documentary L/C 跟单信用证

【技能训练句型】

（1）出口商要求用信用证付款，通常陈述的理由：

An L/C is quite common in the international trade.
信用证在国际贸易中相当普遍。

An L/C is a reliable and safe method of payment.

信用证是一种可靠而安全的付款方式。

An L/C gives the exporter the additional protection of the banker's guarantee.

信用证给出口商品增加了银行的额外担保。

An L/C can assure that the exporter get the right amount of money.

信用证可以保证出口商拿到该得的钱。

An L/C is fair and beneficial to both the seller and the buyer.

信用证是公平的，对买卖双方都有利。

An L/C protects the seller as well as the buyer.

信用证在保护卖主的同时，也保护了买主。

（2）进口商不愿意用信用证付款，通常陈述的理由：

An L/C would cause us a lot of difficulties.

信用证给我们造成许多困难。

An L/C would involve us some unnecessary inconvenience.

信用证给我们造成一些不必要的不便。

An L/C would cost us extra charges.

信用证需要我们另外多付一些费用。

An L/C would add to the cost of our imports.

信用证增加进口成本。

An L/C would need us to pay a deposit and the bank charges.

信用证让我们付订金和银行的费用。

3. collection   托收

【知识点】托收主要有D/P 和D/A 两种。使用托收方式时，应在买卖合同中明确规定交单条件、买方的付款或承兑责任以及付款期限等。D/P (documents against payment) 是指出口方装运货物出口后，备妥商业单据，委托银行托收时，指示银行等付款人付款后，才交付有关单证的方式。按时间不同又分为即期付款交单和远期付款交单。D/A (documents against acceptance)，承兑后交单，是指出口方在货物付运后，开具以进口方为付款人的远期汇票，连同各种货运单据一并交委托银行寄往进口方代收银行。出口方通过托收银行指示代收银行在进口方对汇票承兑后，才交付有关单证的方式。采用这种方式，进口方可先取单后付款，如果进口方在汇票到期日拒付，出口方有货款两空的风险，所以出口方要选择好的银行，并和对方有良好的贸易基础才敢采用此种方式。

Part D Practice

I. Complete the Following Dialogues

(1)

A: What do you think of ___1___ of payment?

B: I wonder if you can make payment ___2___ D/A or D/P?

A: No, I'm afraid not. It's very difficult for us to accept your ___3___.
B: Then what is your regular ___4___ considering the terms of payment?
A: We usually ___5___ payment by irrevocable L/C payable ___6___ shipping documents.
B: But an L/C will need us to pay a ___7___ and the bank charges.
A: Let's ___8___ a compromise, how about 50% by D/P and the ___9___ by L/C?
B: Thank you for your ___10___.

(2)

A: I find everything quite ___1___ except for the terms of payment.
B: Payment by L/C is quite ___2___ in international trade.
A: But to ___3___ an L/C will ___4___ to the cost of our ___5___.
B: I know. However, an irrevocable L/C can give the ___6___ the protection of a banker's ___7___?
A: Sorry you insist ___8___ payment by L/C. However, I'd very much ___9___ it if you could take our suggestion into further ___10___.

II. Interaction Activities

Task 1

Students work in pairs and make a dialogue based on the following situation:

Mr. John, a businessman from America, has ordered a total of USD 25000 worth of sweaters. Mr. Lin is a salesman from China National Textiles Imp. & Exp. Corp., Fujian Branch. Now they have settled everything except the terms of payment. Mr. John suggests D/A or D/P terms. Mr. Lin tries to talk him into accepting payment by L/C, while Mr. John states his difficulties if demanded payment by L/C.

Task 2

Short conversation.
(1) Suppose you urge your client opening the L/C.
(2) State your reasons.

III. Actual Practice

Work in pairs.

Talk about the amendment to the L/C in details. The following information can be used for reference:
(1) The letter of credit is at sight instead of after sight.
(2) The amount of money should be USD 200000 instead of USD 20000.
(3) The expiry date should be the 5th of September rather than the 15th of September.

IV. Creative Discussion

The teacher divides the class into groups and for discussion. Each group chooses a representative after discussion. The student who expresses well will be the winner.

Topic:

What are the main methods of payment? Say something about them.

Explain the payment terms of D/A and D/P.

Explain the payment terms of L/C.

Why is the exporter reluctant to accept D/A or D/P?

What benefit can the exporter receive by L/C?

Chapter 13
Business Negotiation

Learning Objectives
Upon completion of this chapter, you will be able to

- acquire knowledge of insurance and GSP Form A.
- get to know exclusive agency and other business issues.
- learn the ways to reach agreements with your clients through business negotiations.
- improve your skills of communication on business negotiation.
- make yourself closer to be a successful businessman.
- understand promoting unimpeded trade.[1]

---

1 理解加强贸易畅通。

Part A Situational Dialogue

Communicative Scene 1

Insurance and GSP Form A

(Mrs. Brown is talking insurance and Form A issues over with her supplier, Mr. Wang.)

Brown: Mr. Wang, since our price is based on CIF, let's classify what types of insurance clauses should be covered for our shipment.[1]

Wang: According to general practice, the insurance we cover for CIF price is All Risks for 110% of the invoice value.

Brown: Our requirements include not only All Risks, but also the insurance against Strikes Risk and War Risk.

Wang: I don't think we can provide the extensive coverage you mentioned, because there is only 0.3% room left for Insurance in our contract.[2]

Brown: The present world is not peaceful everywhere. Our vessel has to go through the sensitive areas and strikes are very common in our country. We have to make the insurance to avoid losses, just in case.

Wang: We understand your situation. As you know, it's the international trade practice that sellers insure the goods against the usual risks. If you insist on Special Additional Risks, the extra premium is borne by the buyer.

Brown: It makes sense but I'm wondering ...

Wang: Frankly speaking, our price is the most favorable you can get at present. We don't want to lose business, though the insurance only takes up a small percentage in the overall value.

Brown: What should we do then?

Wang: To make things easier, we suggest you cover Special Additional Risks yourself or accept CFR price.

Brown: Then I prefer a CFR basis.

Wang: Of course, we will deduct the cost for insurance from the original price and you can take care of the insurance yourself.

Brown: What is the difference?

Wang: It is different in some ways. First, we don't have to argue about what types of insurance should be covered. Second, if you make the insurance in your local insurance company, you can easily claim compensation in case something happens. Third, the L/C clauses will be simpler for both of us.

Brown: We can do it in this way.

Wang: The renewed contract with CFR price will be made immediately. We promise that we'll inform you immediately after the shipment so that you'll have enough time to carry out your insurance.

Brown: We wish to draw your attention to the GSP Form A. It should be issued as one of the documents for the L/C negotiation. <u>It is of vital importance for us, because it will exempt us from higher tariffs.</u>[3]

Wang: We have noticed that in our contract, to apply for Form A, we need to know some information, such as place of origin, consignee, notify party, port of destination, shipping mark, the country of consumption, and so on.

Brown: Our company will be the consignee and we will let you know the notify party and other information after we make the arrangement with our forwarder.

Wang: You bet.

Communicative Scene 2

Exclusive Agency

(Mr. Baker pays a visit to Ms. Liu's company. <u>He is in negotiations with Ms. Liu over exclusive agency.</u>[4])

Liu: Hello, Mr. Baker. It's a pleasure to see you in our company. You have been one of our best clients since our first meeting in Poland two years ago.

Baker: How time flies! I clearly remember that we started our business from women's garments. Under your encouragement, we have opened up a new market in this line. I appreciate it very much.

Liu: Thank you for saying so. From your email message, we learned that the main purpose of your visit this time is to discuss exclusive agency. Is that right?

Baker: Correct. To secure our ready set-up market, our company hopes to obtain exclusive agency for women's garments.

Liu: That is a very practical and an important matter.

Baker: As you may be aware, we have well-established wide business connections and reputation in the line of clothes in Europe. <u>We know the European markets like the palm of our hand.</u>[5]

Liu: Well-done.

Baker: Our company is the right one to act as your sole agent. If you do so, it will be beneficial for your trade by reducing rivals.

Liu: I appreciate your efforts in pushing sales of our new products. Do you mean your company is requesting exclusive rights of sales in your country?

Baker: Not exactly. As you know, our country is a small European country. The market is quite limited because the population of our country is only above 15 million, even less than that in your province.

Liu: Um. I see.

Baker: Nowadays inside the European Union, all the individual European countries are considered as a whole, especially from the view of economy and business. <u>There is no border line at all between countries for commodity flow. For this reason, exclusive sales in a single European country by no means should be required.</u>[6]

Liu: Well, in this case, what is the "Border Line" you'd like to have?

Baker: We prefer the whole of Europe.

Liu: I'm afraid that is impossible, much as we'd like to. We are selling our products in some of the East European countries already, such as Russia, Ukraine, etc. <u>It is unfair to delete these countries from our customer list. What we can do is that we give you exclusive rights inside the European Union.</u>[7]

Baker: Sounds reasonable. <u>We agree to define our "Border Line" inside European Union.</u>[8] Here is a draft agreement on the exclusive agency. Please take a look and we'll discuss it this afternoon.

Liu: OK.

The Volume of Sales and Penalty

(A further discussion about sales volume and penalty is going on in the afternoon.)

Liu: Mr. Baker, we have had a careful look at your proposal. Besides the territory we discussed this morning, we basically agree on the starting time, product range of exclusive agency and other issues.

Baker: Fine.

Liu: Here we'd like to discuss some more about the volume of sales and penalty. Compared with other tool kits we sold, the annual value for women's garment is still much smaller though the business between us is growing fast. We really want the market to be much, much bigger than the present one.

Baker: This is why we are asking for the exclusive right. We have the same goal to make the business big enough so that we can both make more money.

Liu: Well, Mr. Baker, we'd like to talk about the annual quantity you will propose to sell.

Baker: <u>We don't think it practical to make the volume of sales too high in the initial stage. We may encounter strong resistance.</u>[9]

Liu: To solve this problem and reach our common goal, why don't we set a progressive limit for the volume of sales?

Baker: That's marvelous! Half a million sets per year for the first two years and a quarter million sets increase each year in every following two years. We expect to get 6% commission on the net value for sales.

Liu: Sounds good. The next point is the article of penalty, which seems unfair for our side.

Baker: Why do you say so?

Liu: <u>The article specifies that we will be punished if we sell our products to other companies in the European Community.</u>[10] We did not see any corresponding article of punishment if you buy the same or similar products from other companies or manufacturers. We'd like to have this portion added to the Agreement.

Baker: OK. I know <u>"No victory comes out without price."</u>[11]

Liu: In the interests of both companies, we agree to appoint you as our exclusive agency for a period of 4 years.

Baker: I am very pleased to get everything settled so quickly. I'm very grateful for your kindness and efficient work. I believe our cooperation in the future will be more fruitful and successful.

Liu: I'm very delighted to see the business between our two companies growing so smoothly and healthily.

Words and Expressions

1. GSP Form A (Generalized System of Preferences Certificate of Origin)		普惠制原产地证
2. All Risks		综合险
3. Strikes Risk		罢工险
4. sensitive	adj.	敏感的；灵敏的
5. Special Additional Risks		特别附加险
6. premium	n.	保险费
7. overall value		总值
8. renew	vt.	使更新；修补；重做
9. classify	vt.	分类；归纳
10. exempt	vt.	免除，豁免
	adj.	被免除的，被豁免的
11. tariff	n.	关税
12. consignee	n.	收货人；受托人
13. notify party		通知方
14. shipping mark		唛头
15. forwarder	n.	运输人，运输商
16. exclusive agency (sole agency)		独家代理
17. encouragement	n.	鼓励；赞助
18. territory	n.	地域；领土

19. Border Line		边界
20. Ukraine	n.	乌克兰
21. define	vt.	定义；详细说明
22. consumption	n.	消费，消耗
23. the volume of sales		销售量
24. encounter	v.	遇到；遭受
25. specify	vt.	规定；指定
26. progressive	adj.	累进的；逐渐的；进步的
27. marvelous	adj.	妙极的；了不起的
28. corresponding	adj.	相应的，对应的；符合的

Notes

1. Since our price is based on CIF, let's classify what types of insurance clauses should be covered for our shipment.

    既然我们的价格条款是成本加保险费、运费价，那么来确定一下我们的货物该上什么保险。

    ① classify v. 分类，归纳

    例句：

    The insurance is classified as 3 basic types of coverage, General Additional Risk and Special Additional Risk.

    保险分为三种，基本险、一般附加险和特殊附加险。

    ② cover v. 给（货物等）保险，包含

    例句：

    All the expenses, including room and board, round-way tickets, will be covered by ourselves.

    所有费用，包括食宿和往返机票，均由我方自己承担。

    We will have to cover the porcelain against Risk of Breakage to avoid losses in transit.

    我们将只好对陶瓷投保破碎险以避免运输中的损失。

2. There is only 0.3% room left for Insurance in our contract.

    我们合同中的"保险"仅有0.3%的余地。

    ① room n. 空间，余地（常指抽象事物）

    例句：

    We could not load all the goods into the container. The room was fully occupied.

    我们无法把全部货物装进集装箱。空间被占满了。

    There is no room for improvement due to our limited working conditions.

    由于我们工作条件的限制，无法再改进了。

3. It is of vital importance for us, because it will exempt us from higher tariffs.

    它对我们很重要，可使我们免交高额关税。

    ① exempt from 免除，豁免（常与from连用）

例句：
> The new law exempts low-income families from taxation.
> 新法律使低收入的家庭免除税收。

4. be in negotiations with sb. over sth.

与某人洽谈某事

例句：
> The exporter is in negotiations with the representative of Technical Import & Export Corporation over compensation trade.
> 出口方与技术进出口公司的代表在洽谈补偿贸易。

5. We know the European markets like the palm of our hand.

我们对欧洲市场的情况了如指掌。

know sth. like the palm of one's hand 对……了如指掌

例句：
> Our exclusive agent knows the local custom of the buying country like the palm of his hand.
> 我们的独家代理对购买地国家的风俗习惯了如指掌。

6. There is no border line at all between countries for commodity flow. For this reason, exclusive sales in a single European country by no means should be required.

商品流通根本没有什么国界。因此要求一个欧洲国家的独家经营权毫无意义。

by no means 决不

例句：
> The special compromise we made by no means should be taken as usual practice.
> 决不能把我们这次所做的退让视为惯例。

7. It is unfair to delete these countries from our customer list. What we can do is that we give you exclusive rights inside the European Union.

我们不宜把他们从客户名单上划掉，我们只能给您欧盟内的独家经营权。

① It is unfair to ... 不公平的，不合适的

例句：
> It is unfair to insist on the shipment on time because of your delay opening L/C.
> 由于你方延误开立信用证，坚持要求我方准时发货是不合适的。

② What we can do is that ... 我们所能做的是……

例句：
> What we can do is that you take measures to avoid such inferior goods reoccurring.
> 我们所能做的是要求你方采取措施避免再出现劣质产品。

8. We agree to define our "Border Line" inside European Union.

我们同意将"边界"限定在欧盟内。

define vt. 下定义，阐释，详细说明

例句：
> I wonder if you can define "With Particular Average" more clearly? (I wonder if you can give a more clear definition of "With Particular Average"?)

你能就水渍险给出更清晰的定义吗？

9. We don't think it practical to make the volume of sales too high in the initial stage. We may encounter strong resistance.

我们认为在初期把销售额定得太高是不现实的，我们可能面临强大的阻力。

We don't think it practical to ... 我们认为……是不可行的

例句：

    We don't think it practical to submit the disputes for arbitration before friendly negotiation.

    我们认为在友好协商之前就把争端提交仲裁是不可取的。

10. The article specifies that we will be punished if we sell our products to other companies in the European Community.

条款规定如果我们的产品销往欧盟的其他公司，将受到处罚。

specify vt. 规定，确定，具体说明

例句：

    Please specify the name of commodity, specification and quantity you require.

    请具体说明所需的商品名称、规格和数量。

11. No victory comes out without price.

没人能随随便便成功。

*12. make sense 有道理，（讲话等）有意义

例句：

    His definition of Exclusive Agency doesn't make sense.

    他对独家代理的定义没有解释清楚。

make sense of 了解……的意义，明白

例句：

    Through trade training, they make sense of *INCOTERMS* 2000.

    通过贸易培训，他们了解了《国际贸易术语解释通则2000》的含义。

Part B Practical Key Sentences

1. insurance

    insurance on 表示所投保货物

    insurance against 表示保险种类

    insurance with ... 表示向……保险公司投保

    insurance for 表示保额

We effect insurance on the 1200 cartons of sea food for 110% of invoice value against All Risks.

我们按发票金额的110%对1200箱海产品投保了一切险。

Insurance is to be covered by the seller on behalf of the buyer for 110% of invoice value against Overland Transportation with the People's Insurance Company of China.

卖方代买方按发票金额的110%向中国人民保险公司投保陆上运输险。

替换表达：

I wonder what exactly insurance takes out according to your usual CIF terms.

Free from Particular Average is too narrow for the shipment of this goods, please extend the coverage to include All Risks.

2. premium

The insurance rate for such kind of risk will vary in accordance with the nature of the cargo.
这类险别的保险费率将取决于货物的种类。
As our general practice, insurance effects basic risks only, the extra premium involved would be for the buyer's account.
按照我们的惯例，只保基本险，而额外的保险费则由买方负担。

替换表达：

The buyer requires the insurance against Special Additional Risks and agrees to pay the additional premium.

We have found out this risk is coverable at the premium rate of 0.3%.

3. the trade practice

We can't break international practice to allow Extraneous Risks by the seller.
我方不能违背国际惯例，让卖方投保附加险。
According to the regular trade practice, the L/C should be opened by the buyer 30 days before the date of shipment.
根据贸易惯例，信用证应在装船前30天由买方开出。

替换表达：

It's the international trade practice that the agent is given the authority to represent the principle in dealing with buyers.

As for terms of payment , our company mainly adopted some usual international practices.

4. we wish to draw your attention

本句型适用于提醒谈判对手可能忽视的重要事情。
We wish to draw your attention that the seller should send shipping advise to buyer before shipment on CFR basis.
我想提醒你注意，在CFR价格条件下，装运前卖方必须向买方发出装船通知。

替换表达：

We'd like to remind you that you must take delivery date into consideration because we need the goods urgently.

May I invite your attention to the fact that the GSP Form A should be issued as one of the documents for the L/C negotiation?

5. it is impossible, much as we'd like to

I'm afraid that it is impossible, much as we'd like to give you further discount.
尽管我们很想给你更低的折扣，但恐怕不行。

替换表达：

I'm afraid that it won't be possible, much as we want to.

I don't think it is workable, much as we'd like to.

I really don't like to say no, but I have to.

6. as you may be aware

As you may be aware, we are interested in setting up a joint venture company with you in Canada.

正如你所知，我们有兴趣与贵公司在加拿大建立合资企业。

替换表达：

As we may be aware that the purpose of my visiting is seeking for a possibility of general agency.

As you know, we have extensive business connections and reputation in the field of aquatic products.

7. in the interests of

In the interests of our long-term cooperation, we are glad to sign an agency agreement with you.

为了双方长期合作的利益，我们很高兴与贵公司签署代理协议。

替换表达：

For the sake of the development of business, a 10% commission will be granted for you to push the sales.

To the advantage of our trade, we are ready to give you a 10% discount.

Part C Integration of Theory and Practice

1. cover insurance on the goods　货物投保

【知识点】按CIF和CIP条件成交的出口商品，卖方在确定装运期和运输工具后，按约定的保险金额和险别，向保险公司办理投保。

其他交易条件的投保，卖方务必及时发出装船通知，以便买方决定是否投保。延误发出装船通知，若造成损失由卖方承担。

【技能训练句型】

We promise that we will inform you immediately after the shipment so that you will have enough time to carry out your insurance.

我们保证在货物装运后会立即通知贵方，以便贵方有足够的时间投保。

三种基本险别：

（1）平安险 Free from Particular Average，简称FPA

平安险的保障范围一般只赔全部损失。

（2）水渍险 With Particular Average，简称WPA

水渍险的责任范围除包括"平安险"的各项责任外，还负责被保险货物由于恶劣气候、自然灾害所造成的部分损失。

（3）综合险（一切险）All Risks

综合险的责任范围除包括"平安险"和"水渍险"的责任外，还包括保险货物在运输过程中，因各种外因造成不论全部或部分的损失。一般附加险别包括其中。

只能在投保三种基本险中的某一种后，才能投保附加险。特别附加险，例如战争险（War Risk）和罢工险（Strikes Risk）等，不属于综合险的范围之内，按国际惯例应由买方投保。

Chapter 13 Business Negotiation

【技能训练句型】

As you know, it's the international trade practice that sellers insure the goods against the usual risks. If you insist on Special Additional Risks, the extra premium is borne by the buyer.

但你知道，按国际惯例，卖方对货物只投保惯常险别。如贵方坚持保特殊险，则额外的保险费由贵方承担。

2. GSP Form A　普惠制原产地证

【知识点1】普惠制是发达国家给予发展中国家出口产品普遍的、非歧视的、非互惠的一种关税优惠制度，是一项有利于发展中国家和地区扩大出口的关税优惠制度。普惠制原产地证（Generalized System of Preferences Certificate of Origin，简称Form A）是依据给惠国要求而出具的能证明出口货物原产自受惠国的证明文件，并能使货物在给惠国享受普遍优惠关税待遇。国家出入境检验检疫局是中国签发普惠制原产地证的官方机构。

如需办理普惠制原产地证，买方会在合同和信用证中作出规定。

【技能训练句型】

We have noticed that the GSP Form A is written down in our contract. To apply for the Form A, we need to know some information, such as place of origin, consignee, notify party, port of destination, shipping mark, the country of consumption, and so on.

我们注意到此事已写在合同中。为了申请普惠制原产地证，我们还需要一些信息，比如原产地、收货人、通知方、目的港、唛头和消费国等。

【知识点2】正确运用该优惠政策，有助于企业在欧盟等进口国享受到大幅关税减免，扩大外贸出口。普惠制原产地证由受惠国出品商填制申报，受惠国签证机构审核、证明及签发。

3. certificate of origin　原产地证

【知识点】原产地证（Certificate of Origin）简称C/O，证明货物原产自某一特定国家或地区，是享受进口国正常关税（最惠国）待遇的证明文件。中国原产地证是证明我国出口货物生产和制造于中国的证明文件，是出口产品进入国际市场的护照。

Form A不同于一般原产地证C/O，一般原产地证是享受最惠国待遇的有效证件，普惠制原产地证则是享受普惠制减免税待遇的有效证件。

4. exclusive agency　独家代理

【知识点】独家代理是外贸的一种重要形式。出口方与代理商达成协议，利用代理商熟悉销售地市场和广泛的销售渠道的优势，代表出口方推销商品、签订合同，开拓出口市场。代理商在委托人授权的范围内经营，不承担销售风险和费用，通常按达成交易的金额提取约定比例的佣金。

谈判独家代理时应注意：

（1）了解代理商是否确实具有优势，选择好代理商，充分借助代理公司的销售渠道优势和良好信誉去开拓市场。

（2）独家代理通常要承诺最低成交数量或销售金额。若未能达标，委托人有权中止协议或按协议规定调整佣金。

（3）独家代理必须明确代理业务的地理范围，并约定代理协议有效期。

（4）确定代理商品的种类，规定委托人和代理商的职责和义务。

（5）规定佣金率、支付佣金的时间和方法。独家代理具有专营权，若委托人与其他买主直接发生交易，仍应按交易金额向独家代理支付佣金。这是独家代理与一般代理的主要区别。

5. win-win negotiation 双赢的谈判

【知识点】成功的商务谈判要争取达成双赢的效果。谈判结果应使双方都得到商务发展的机会，让双方共赢。

在当今的外贸谈判中如坚持传统的谈判方式，斤斤计较，寸土必争，捞尽所有好处是不明智的。这样必然使谈判各方不欢而散，生意不成，自己也无胜利可言，甚至还破坏了今后双方进一步合作的机会。

争取双赢的技巧：

（1）做好谈判前的准备，制订详细的谈判计划。

（2）在谈判中寻找双方的共同点，互作让步。不光考虑自己，还要替对方着想，留点好处给对方，让对方有谈判赢了的感觉。

（3）具有灵活的谈判策略，高效的谈判方式。

（4）相互信任，相互协调，相互合作。所提的方案，应让对方觉得有道理。

（5）达成明智的双赢协议，使双方在贸易中都有利可图。

【技能训练句型】

A: We prefer to get the exclusive rights in the whole Europe.
我想要整个欧洲的独家经营权。

B: I'm afraid that it's impossible, much as we'd like to. It is unfair to delete our existing Eastern European countries from our customer list. What we can do is to give you exclusive rights inside the European Union.
我们很想满足您的要求，但恐怕不行。我们不宜把已有的东欧国家的客户从我们的客户名单上划掉，我们只能给您欧盟内的独家经营权。

A: Sounds reasonable. You win.
很合理。你赢了。

I am very pleased to get everything settled so quickly. I'm very grateful for your kindness and efficient work. I believe our cooperation in the future will be more fruitful and successful.
非常高兴所有问题这么快就解决了。非常感谢您的友好态度和高效工作。我相信我们之间将来的合作会更有成效。

Part D Practice

I. Complete the Following Dialogues

Fill in the blanks with the proper words.

(1)

A: Peter, I quote the price on CIF basis. If you prefer to effect ___1___ at your end, please don't hesitate to tell us.

B: Well, we'd like to ___2___ what types of insurance we should take ___3___ according to your usual CIF terms.

A: Insurance to be covered ___4___ the 3000 pieces of sculptures for 110% of invoice value ___5___ All Risks.

B: I'd like to draw your ___6___ to the fact that the sculptures are valuable. We have to request for 130% of the invoice ___7___.

A: As the regular trade ___8___, we regret to tell you that you have to bear the cost of the additional part since the amounts of value exceed the stipulated limit.

B: I guest there must be some ___9___ for discussion.

A: I don't think it ___10___, much as we'd like to.

(2)

A: Our business is concluded ___1___ a CFR basis. May I draw your attention to ___2___ insurance as soon as we send you the ___3___ advice?

B: Sure. Thank you for reminding me. To be ___4___, I'd like you to cover the insurance for us. The premium will be for our ___5___.

A: No problem. We'll arrange for the goods ___6___ All Risks for 110% of the invoice value ___7___ the People's Insurance Company of China.

B: Good. We wish to draw your attention to the GSP Form A. It should be issued as one of the documents for the L/C ___8___. It is important for us because it will ___9___ us from higher tariff.

A: OK. We'll make it according to the contract. I need more ___10___ to complete the GSP Form A. Could you send it to me soon?

B: All right. I'll check it and send it to you at once.

II. Interaction Activities

Task 1

A foreign importer asks the seller to insure the domestic glassware against Risk of Breakage, War Risk and WPA. Suppose you are the seller. You agree to accept the request on the condition that the extra premium should be borne by the buyer.

The teacher divides students into pairs. Students make short dialogues and role-play them. The following expressions should be included in the dialogue:

(1) invite your attention to
(2) what types of insurance are covered
(3) be too narrow for
(4) extend the coverage to
(5) as you may be aware
(6) the trade practice
(7) the extra premium is borne
(8) I'm afraid that it is impossible

(9) can't break practice to

(10) it makes sense

(11) have to pay Extraneous Risks

Task 2

The representative of Machinery and Equipment Corporation is in negotiations with the exporter over the commission rate for sole agency. Compose a conversation with your partner. Your conversation should cover the expressions below:

(1) as you may be aware

(2) well-established marketing channels

(3) talk over the possibility

(4) be experienced in

(5) appreciate the efforts

(6) invite your attention to commission

(7) as our general practice

(8) don't think it practical to

(9) push sales

(10) I'm afraid that

(11) In the interests of both sides

(12) be ready to

(13) appoint you as

III. Actual Practice

Mr. Victor is having a negotiation with Mr. Hong on sole agency. He praises that the silk products of Mr. Hong's company are popular in Indian market. He states the advantages of his company to deal with silk products and expresses his intention to be a sole agency.

Mr. Hong points out the trade turnover of Mr. Victor's company is still too low to be a sole agent. In view of low volume of sales, Mr. Hong suggests that Mr. Victor try to sell more of silk products at an initial stage. When time is ripe, they will discuss sole agency again.

Students work in pairs and role-play the conversation.

IV. Creative Discussion

From Communicative Scenes 2 and 3, you learn Mr. Backer is in negotiations with Ms. Liu over exclusive agency.

The teacher divides the class into groups and asks students to discuss the topics with their partners and then share their opinions with other groups.

Topics:

1. Why does Mr. Baker request sole agency not just in a single European country?

2. Why doesn't Ms. Liu agree to give Ms. Baker exclusive rights in the whole Europe? Does it do something good if Ms. Liu approves Mr. Baker's requests for exclusive right in the whole Europe?

3. What consideration do we need when appointing an agent?

4. How should we improve trade by means of sole agency?

Chapter 14

Sign a Contract

Learning Objectives
Upon completion of this chapter, you will be able to

- get familiar with the process of negotiating the terms of contract.
- check the contract carefully.
- know how to sign a contract.
- conduct the activities related to signing a contract.
- understand the meaning of sustainable development.[1]

1　理解可持续发展的含义。

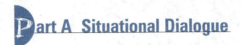

Going over a Draft Contract

(Mr. Smith, a businessman from Britain, is talking about a draft contract with Miss Chen working at Fujian Wonderful Import & Export Corporation.)

Smith: Miss Chen. I read very carefully the draft contract last night. <u>It seems to me we've come quite a long way. However, there are still some points which I'd like to bring up.</u>[1]

Chen: Please go ahead. I also think it is necessary for us to clarify some important terms before they are finally included in the formal contract.

Smith: First, about the packing. <u>I'm afraid the cardboard boxes are not strong enough for transport by sea.</u>[2] Would you please use wooden cases instead?

Chen: I'm sorry. <u>It's stipulated in the contract that the products are packed in cardboard boxes.</u>[3] And, what's more, they are easier to handle and cheaper in cost.

Smith: Well, carton is all right. But the packing must be strong enough to withstand rough handling. <u>So could you please take some measures to reinforce them?</u>[4]

Chen: OK. We can strengthen the cartons with double straps.

Smith: Thank you. Second, about the terms of payment. I wonder whether the payment is to be made by D/A or D/P?

Chen: I'm afraid not. As we all know, that might cause great trouble to the sellers. We want payment to be made by confirmed, irrevocable letter of credit, payable against shipping documents. That's our usual practice.

Smith: I see, but opening an L/C with a bank means additional expense.

Chen: I'm sorry, that can't be helped.

Smith: Then payment by L/C. But I must stress again that shipment should be effected and completed by the end of July. We can't accept any delay.

Chen: Of course not, as long as you open the covering L/C in due time.

Smith: I'll arrange for the establishment of the relative letter of credit with Bank of China, London as soon as I return, and let you know by fax at the moment it is opened.

Chen: Fine. Is there anything else?

Smith: What about the quality standard?

Chen: It is clearly stipulated in the contract that <u>"quality as per sample 23 and technical feature indicated in the illustrations submitted by seller"</u>[5] Have you any questions about this stipulation?

Smith: No, it's all right. Next, I'd like to talk about arbitration. It is stipulated that arbitration shall take place in China. Is it possible to have it carried out in a third country?

Chen: No problem, since arbitration is very rarely resorted to. I hope all disputes can be settled through friendly consultations.⁶

Smith: Certainly. Well, it seems we have talked about the disputes in the draft contract. However, would you please check all the terms listed in the contract and see if there is anything not in conformity with the terms we agree on?⁷

Chen: Fine. I'll get it ready and send it to your hotel tomorrow morning. Is that alright?

Smith: That's fine. Thank you.

Communicative Scene 2

Checking the Contract One More Time

(Miss Chen is checking the draft contract with Mr. Smith one more time to make sure that everything is all right.)

Chen: Now, Mr. Smith, the contract is ready. Shall we check the contract one more time to make sure we have reached an agreement on all the terms?

Smith: OK. I think that's a good idea and will help avoid disputes and claims in the future. ⁸(*After checking*) Well, everything seems all right except some minor points. First of all, don't you think we should add this sentence here? "If one side fails to carry out the contract, the other side is entitled to cancel the contract."⁹

Chen: Yes, I'll add it to the contract.

Smith: Second, what insurance will you take out for the goods, if we conclude the business on CIF basis?

Chen: We'll only insure WPA.

Smith: Could you cover the Risk of Breakage?

Chen: Your request is acceptable on condition that the additional charge is for your account. But I should remind you that claims are payable only for that part of the loss, that is, over 5%. So I don't think it necessary.

Smith: What you said is reasonable. WPA is enough.

Chen: Now that the insurance is decided on, shall we go on to other terms and conditions?

Smith: Go ahead.

Chen: Have you any further questions concerning the packing and shipping marks?

Smith: I agree to the terms. Then do you have any problems that need to be worked out?

Chen: Oh, I think the "force majeure" clause is missing. We often have typhoons and floods during the summer, production might be affected and the execution of the contract would be delayed. <u>I hope that you won't object to adding such a clause in the contract.</u>[10]

Smith: All right. If it's nothing we can do to protest the nature, we'll add it to the contract. In case of "force majeure", you should notify us as soon as possible.

Chen: I will. Thank you for your friendly cooperation. I hope everything will go smoothly and no disaster will happen.

Smith: Now, I think it is essential to include in this clause, that is, "Any modification or alteration to the contract shall only be made with the consent of both parties."

Chen: No problem, I'll do it. Then I think we have reached an agreement on all the terms and the contract contains basically all we have agreed upon during our negotiation. However, if there are any problems, you can contact me at any time before we sign the formal contract.

Smith: Great. When can the contract be ready for signature?

Chen: I hope it can be signed next Monday, will that work?

Smith: Yes. I'll see you then.

Chen: See you.

Communicative Scene 3

Signing a Formal Contract

(Mr. Smith and Miss Chen check the items in the contract one by one and sign a formal contract.)

Chen: Well, I think there will be no misunderstandings between us. Here is our contract. Would you please read it carefully again?

Smith: Fine, let's check the items in the contract one by one, the name of the commodity, specifications, unit, quantity, unit price and the total amount ... (*After checking all the items*) I'm glad that we've finally come to an agreement after repeated negotiation. Things that should be there are there. Do you have an English copy of the contract?

Chen: Yes, here it is. Please have a look.

Smith: (*After reading the contract*) No problem.

Chen: Now since everything is settled, shall we sign the contract now?

Smith: OK.

Chen: Please sign here. (*After all signatures*) Each has two formal copies of the contract. These two copies are for you. One is in English and the other is in Chinese. They are all in agreement with each other.

Smith: Thank you. <u>Let's congratulate ourselves that this transaction has been brought to a successful conclusion.</u>[11] The next step is to carry out this contract well. As we all know, once a contract is signed, it has legal effect.

Chen: I am sure both of our parties will value our commercial reputation highly and the contract will be executed smoothly. This deal will promote further expansion of the trade between us.

Words and Expressions

1. draft contract		合同草案，草约
2. bring up		提出
3. clarify	v.	澄清，阐明
4. reinforce	v.	加固；加强
5. as per		根据，按照
6. indicate	v.	表示，标示
7. submit	v.	提交，呈递
8. arbitration	n.	仲裁
9. resort to		诉诸
10. consultation	n.	协商
11. conformity	n.	一致
12. be entitled to		给予（某人获得某物或做某事的）权利
13. force majeure		不可抗力
14. typhoon	n.	台风
15. execution	n.	执行
16. object to		反对
17. modification	n.	修改
18. alteration	n.	变化
19. consent	n.	同意
20. withstand	v.	经受住，抵挡
21. misunderstanding	n.	误解
22. original	n.	原件
23. legal effect		法律效力

Notes

1. It seems to me we've come quite a long way. However, there are still some points which I'd like to bring up.
我认为我们已有很大进展，但仍有一些问题需要磋商。
① come a long way 有很大进展
例句：
  They have come a long way in the research.
  他们的研究取得很大进展。
② bring up
▶ 提出（供讨论）
例句：

He brought up the subject of money at the meeting.

他在会上提出钱的问题。

▶ 养育（孩子）

例句：

She brought up three children alone.

她独自养育三个孩子。

2. I'm afraid the cardboard boxes are not strong enough for transport by sea.

这种纸箱用于远洋运输，恐怕不够结实。

enough 用作后置定语，在形容词或副词之后，而不是之前，后面可接to do sth.或for sth.

例句：

The quality of the product is good enough for me to make a decision.

产品的质量让我有足够的信心做出决定。

3. It's stipulated in the contract that the products are packed in cardboard boxes.

合同规定产品用纸箱包装。

① stipulate *v.* 规定

例句：

The contract stipulates that you should pay in advance.

合同规定你方应预付款。

② stipulation *n.* 规定，规定（约定）的条件

例句：

She agreed to the clauses, but with the stipulation that she would take 2% commission.

她同意了这些条款，条件是她要得到2%的佣金。

4. So could you please take some measures to reinforce them?

那么，你们可以采取一些加固措施吗？

take measures 采取措施

例句：

The government has taken stronger measures to combat smuggling.

政府已采取更强有力的措施与走私作斗争。

5. ..."quality as per sample 23 and technical feature indicated in the illustrations submitted by seller"

"品质以卖方提供的第23号样品和说明书的技术标准为准"

① as per 根据，按照

例句：

We carried out the market research as per your instructions.

我们根据你的指示开展市场调研工作。

② submitted by seller 修饰sample 23 和technical feature。indicated in the illustrations 修饰technical feature。

③ submit to

▶ 提交，呈递

例句：

　　He submitted the application to the committee for approval.

　　他向委员会递交申请以求批准。

▶ 同意服从 (正式用语)

例句：

　　We are willing to submit to arbitration.

　　我们愿意接受仲裁。

6. No problem, since arbitration is very rarely resorted to. I hope all disputes will be settled through friendly consultations.

没问题，因为很少进行仲裁。我希望所有的争议均通过友好协商解决。

resort to （不得已时）诉诸（坏的或极端的办法）（正式用语）

例句：

　　If other means fail, it is necessary for us to resort to force.

　　如果其他手段失败，我们有必要诉诸武力。

7. However, would you please check all the terms listed in the contract and see if there is anything not in conformity with the terms we agree on?

然而，您是否能逐项检查一下合同的所有条款，看看还有什么意见不一致的地方？

① listed in the contract 修饰 all the terms

② in conformity with 与（规定、习俗等）一致，符合（正式用语）

例句：

　　We must act in conformity with the commercial law.

　　我们必须遵守商法。

8. I think that's a good idea and will help avoid disputes and claims in the future.

我想这是个好主意，这样能避免今后的纠纷和索赔。

claim 既可以当名词也可以当动词，在国际贸易中表示"索赔"时，注意以下词组：

lodge a claim 提出索赔

claim for 因……提出索赔

claim on / against sb. 向……提出索赔

accept a claim 接受索赔

dismiss a claim 驳回索赔

reject a claim 拒绝索赔

withdraw a claim 撤回索赔

claim a compensation of the shipment from sb. for sth. 因为……向某人要求赔偿

asking for amends for the losses by replacing the inferior goods 要求更换劣质产品

9. If one side fails to carry out the contract, the other side is entitled to cancel the contract.

如果一方未按本合同条款执行，另一方有权中止本合同。

① fail to do sth. 未做应做的事

例句：

　　He failed to keep his promises.

他没有履行诺言。

② be entitled to do sth. 给予（某人获得某物或做某事）的权力

例句：

We are entitled to ask for compensation according to the contract.

根据合同，我们有权要求赔偿。

10. I hope that you won't object to adding such a clause in the contract.

我希望你方不会反对在合同中加入这一条款。

object to 反对（to是介词，后面跟动词时要加 ing）

例句：

He strongly objects to accepting the clause.

他强烈反对接受此条款。

11. Let's congratulate ourselves that this transaction has been brought to a successful conclusion.

祝贺我们圆满达成交易。

bring to a successful conclusion 达成交易

相似表达法：

come to terms

come to a transaction

conclude a transaction

close a deal

put through the deal

Part B Practical Key Sentences

1. discuss changing some points

    There are still some points which I'd like to bring up.

    我想仍有一些问题需要磋商。

    替换表达：

    Don't you think we should add this sentence here?

    I want to point out that...

    I wonder if we can add this sentence here?

2. confirm the terms in the contract

    Would you please check all the terms listed in the contract and see if there is anything not in conformity with the terms we agree on?

    您是否能逐项检查一下合同的所有条款，看看还有什么意见不一致的地方？

    替换表达：

    Shall we check the contract one more time to make sure we have reached an agreement on all the terms?

    Would you please go through it to see if everything is all right?

Would you please go over it and see whether there is anything wrong with it?

Would you check all the details and make sure that everything conforms with what we have agreed on?

3. confirm the time for signature

I hope to be able to sign the contract next Monday, is that alright?

我希望在下星期一签字，可以吗？

替换表达：

The contract will be ready next Monday. Will you come to sign it?

I'll send the contract to you for your signature next Monday. Will that work?

Now everything is settled and I expect to have the contract ready for signature next Monday.

4. reach an agreement

I'm glad that we've finally come to an agreement after repeated negotiation.

我很高兴我们在反复协商之后最终达成协议。

替换表达：

I'm glad we have reached an agreement on all the terms.

I'm very glad we have no questions about all the terms.

I'm glad the contract contains all we have agreed upon during our negotiation.

I'm glad our discussion has come to a successful conclusion.

I'm glad our discussion has successfully concluded.

I'm glad our negotiation has reached a successful result.

Part C Integration of Theory and Practice

【知识点】在商务活动中，交易双方通常对合同草案的条款进行逐一确认，然后由一方制定书面合同，经双方核对无误后签字。双方各持正本一份（国际贸易中含中英文文本），据此履行合同条款。合同的形式一般包括三个部分。

1. the first part of the contract 合同的第一部分

第一部分包括合同的标题及编号、签约的日期和地点、签约双方的名称和地址等。标题在合同第一页顶端的正中位置，如由卖方草拟并提出的合同称"销货合同"（Sales Contract），由买方草拟并提出的合同称"购货合同"（Purchase Contract）。签约的日期，也就是说合同从这一天开始生效，通常的格式是"date-month-year"或"effective date-month-year"。

合同的第一句话通常是"根据合同的规定条款，卖方同意出售，买方同意购买下述商品"。（"Seller agrees to sell and buyer agrees to buy the under-mentioned goods subject to the terms and conditions."）

2. the second part of the contract 合同的第二部分

【知识点】第二部分是合同的主体，主要是具体的交易条款。合同的内容应尽可能全面，不仅要包括商品的名称（name of commodity）、规格（specifications）、单价（unit price）、装运港和目的港（port of shipment and port of destination），还要包括商品的品质

（quality）、包装（packing）、运输标志（shipping mark）、交货期（delivery day）、付款方式（terms of payment）、保险（insurance）、商品检验（inspection）以及索赔（claims）、仲裁（arbitration）、不可抗力（force majeure）等条件。以下是签订合同时需要特别注意的事项。

（1）包装条款（Packing terms）：进出口双方应在合同中明确所要求的包装，因为不符合规定的包装会影响货物安全到达目的地或引起当地海关拒绝货物入境。

【技能训练句型】

在签订正式合同前，常用以下这些谈判用语：

We hope that you can make some improvements in the packing.

我方希望你方在包装上能稍作改进。

I'm afraid the cardboard boxes are not strong enough for transport by sea.

这种纸箱用于远洋运输，恐怕不够结实。

Could you please take some measures to reinforce them?

你们能采取一些加固措施吗？

When you pack, please put 3 different colors in each box.

装箱时，请每箱装三种颜色。

（2）【知识点】费用（Expenses）：包括价格、使用何种货币、利息、价格的递增和付款方式等，要注意价格可能不仅仅是货物的基本费用，还可能包含佣金和各种折扣的比率等。出口方应谨慎选择使用何种货币，不致因汇率变动而受损失，在我国，一般使用硬通货。利息条款应规定在何时、何地由买方支付，可以这样制定："在合同规定的信贷期内，利息按年率百分比收取。"（"Interest will be charged at the rate of ...% per annum on the credit period agreed in the contract."）如果签约日期与最后发货期间隔时间较长，出口方就需要在签订合同时，采取措施来防止一些变动可能带来的损失，例如确认合同价时就把可能上涨的幅度充分体现出来，在签订合同时说明在一些情况下允许提高费用。采用何种付款方式，不仅取决于国际上行业的惯例，还取决于交易双方的关系及讨价还价的能力。

【技能训练句型】

在签订正式合同前，常用以下这些谈判用语：

I'd like to discuss the matter of discount with you.

我想跟你们谈谈折扣问题。

We have to adjust our price because the price of raw materials is constantly going up.

因为原材料不断涨价，所以价格也不得不调整。

We hope you can open a letter of credit in our favor as soon as possible, to be settled in US dollars.

我方希望你方能尽快开立以我方为受益人的信用证，以美元结算。

Could you make an exception this time and accept D/A or D/P?

你方这次能否破例一下，接受承兑交单或付款交单？

（3）【知识点】单证（Documents）：在合同中要明确说明所需的单据种类及份数，因为如果没有这些单据，出口方就不能从银行得到货款，进口方就提不到货。

【技能训练句型】

A: Could you tell me what documents you'll provide?

请问你们将提供哪些单据？

B: Besides the draft, we'll send you a full set of bills of lading, an invoice, an insurance policy, a certificate of origin and a certificate of inspection.

除了汇票外，我们还将给你们一整套提单、发票、保险单、产地证书和检验证书。

（4）【知识点】装运条件（Shipping terms）：合同应明确规定交货日期及由谁来支付费用等，尽量避免"尽快装运"等含糊性词语。

【技能训练句型】

I must stress again that shipment should be effected and completed by the end of July. We can't accept any delay.

我必须再次强调你方要在七月底前完成装运，不得延误。

You should bear all the costs of transportation of the goods.

你方应该承担货物的一切运输费用。

（5）【知识点】仲裁条款（Arbitration clauses）：当国际贸易发生纠纷，交易双方无法以友好方式解决问题时，通常选择事先约定的仲裁机构来对当事人之间的纠纷予以公正合理地裁决。仲裁条款通常包含仲裁地点、机构、程序和仲裁的裁决力。仲裁地点通常由双方当事人协商决定。采用国际商会仲裁，合同可以包括类似的条款："与该合同有关的一切争议，将按国际仲裁调解规则，由一个或多个根据规定指定的仲裁员做出最终裁决。"（"All disputes arising in connection with the present contract shall be finally settled under the Rules of Conciliation and Arbitration of the International chamber of Commerce by one or more Arbitrators appointed in accordance with the rules."）

3. the last part of the contract　合同的第三部分

【知识点】第三部分包括合同的份数及双方的签字等。交易双方各保留一份经过会签的合同。合同在商务活动中起着重要的作用。它划分双方的责任和义务，约束双方的行为。在出现争议时，它也能保护双方的利益。只有正式的书面合同才具有法律效力。因此，在正式签字前，至少要做到以下三点：第一，与交易有关的任何条款都尽可能地商讨，特别注意容易被忽视的细节问题。第二，所有的条款都必须清楚明白，以避免产生歧义，损害双方的利益。第三，合同的格式要规范，必须由合适的人签字。

Part D Practice

I. Complete the Following Dialogues

(1)

Fill in the blanks with the proper words.

A: Here's the ___1___ contract. Please ___2___ and see if there is anything else that should be ___3___.

B: (*After checking the contract*) Well, everything seems all right ___4___ for a minor point. This question is related ___5___ the packing. Would you please use wooden cases ___6___ of cartons? I'm afraid the cartons are not strong enough for transport by sea.

A: I'm sorry. It's ___7___ in the contract that the products are ___8___ in cartons.

B: Is it possible to be a little more ___9___? If not, could you please take some measures to ___10___ them?

(2)

Fill in the blanks with the proper words.

A: When can the contract be ready for ___1___?

B: If you have nothing else to bring ___2___, let us sign the ___3___ now. Well, would you please ___4___ your name here?

A: With ___5___. (*After signing his name*) Here you are.

B: Thanks.

A: Let's ___6___ ourselves that this ___7___ has been brought to a successful ___8___.

(3)

Fill in the blanks with the following expressions, and change the form if necessary.

be entitled to	come to a successful conclusion	to be signed
take some measures	in conformity with	be responsible for
on condition that	with the consent of	as per
resort to		

1. Will you _____ to reinforce the cardboard boxes?
2. Your request is acceptable _____ you pay for the extra charges.
3. Let's congratulate ourselves that this transaction _____.
4. You will _____ any delay in the shipment.
5. Any modification or alteration to the contract shall only be made _____ both parties.
6. If one side fails to honor the contract, the other side _____ cancel it.
7. If other means fail, it is necessary for us to _____ force.
8. Please check the contract carefully and see if there is anything not _____ the terms we agreed on.
9. The contract is ready _____, please check if there is anything wrong.
10. We carried out the research _____ your instructions.

II. Interaction Activities

The teacher divides students into pairs. Students make short dialogues and role-play them.

Task 1

Students work in pairs and make a dialogue based on the following situation:

Mr. Johnson, is going to import 1000 Olive Brand Sewing Machines. He negotiates with Mr. Chen, the Sales Manager of Oriental Machinery Imp. & Exp. Corp., about the terms of the draft contract. After they go over the packing, terms of payment, delivery and other general terms, the business is concluded. The following expressions might give you a hand:

(1) make a close study of, go over; check

(2) first, second, as for

(3) It's stipulated in the contract that ...

(4) any other questions?

(5) Let's congratulate ourselves that ...

Task 2

(1) Suppose you negotiate with your client about some minor points of the draft contract.

(2) Ask your client to check the draft contract again and discuss next time.

III. Actual Practice

Students work in pairs and role-play the conversation.

Talking about signing a formal contract. The following information can be used for reference:

(1) Take one more look before you sign.

(2) Things that should be there are there.

(3) Each has two formal copies of the contract: one in Chinese and one in English.

(4) Congratulation

IV. Creative Discussion

The teacher divides the class into groups for discussion. Each group chooses a representative after discussion. The student who expresses well will be the winner.

Topics:

What should be negotiated before we sign a formal contract?

What skills can be adopted during the negotiation of the terms of the draft contract?

Chapter 15
Cargo Delivery

Learning Objectives
Upon completion of this chapter, you will be able to

- get familiar with the most important features of cargo delivery.
- resolve a variety of problems connected with cargo shipping.
- acquire the skills of communication.
- understand the significance of international multimodal transport.
- understand deepening reform and opening up.[1]

1　理解深化改革开放。

Part A Situational Dialogue

Communicative Scene 1

Interview: A Cargo Delivery Service

(Li Hua is the Delivery Service Director of Fast Delivery Company. Mr. Wang, an interviewer from the local television station, interviews her about the typical features for the cargo delivery service in her company.)

Wang: *(To audience)* Li Hua is the Delivery Service Director of Fast Delivery Company. Li Hua, could you tell us some typical features for the cargo delivery service in your company?

Li: Yes, you know, delivery affects all the results of the trade and the reliability of the company.[1] We have a good reputation in this area. We offer quality, reliability and scheduled delivery for all the cargos.

Wang: What kinds of cargo delivery services does your company offer?

Li: We have Express Plus service. It is the fastest service for the most urgent cargos.[2] It guarantees delivery within 2 days to all the cities in the world. You know, the service also includes telephone confirmation of delivery as soon as the goods are delivered.

Wang: OK. Do you have another service for cargo shipping?

Li: Of course, besides this, we have Express service; it is an ideal choice for most of the less urgent deliveries. For common cargos, we also have Expedited service.

Wang: What about the shipping cost?[3]

Li: There is no need to worry about it. Three models of cargo shipping can meet different requirements of the customers. Our charges are reasonable. The prices of Express service and Expedited service are certainly cheaper than that of Express Plus service.

Wang: Yes, which features do you think are the most important for the cargo delivery service?

Li: Well, I think punctuality and security are of the most important. The quality of service is also important as well as the length of time taken. As long as we can offer high quality service, our business will develop quickly.

Wang: Thank you. It's been nice talking with you.

Chapter 15 Cargo Delivery

Choosing Air Transport

(Bill comes from Bright Company. He talks about shipping to London with Dhana of Dispatch Department. Bill would like to choose air transport.)

Dhana: Dispatch Department. Dhana speaking.
Bill: Dhana, this is Bill from Bright Company.
Dhana: Hello, Bill. What can I do for you?
Bill: Please ship thirty cases of flowers from Hong Kong to London, which is to be delivered within 2 days.
Dhana: It's a long way to reach London, isn't it? Anyway, I think we can meet your requirement. We can assure you that it will be on time.
Bill: You know that it is very urgent, so please consider air transport. I hope you can give our request your special consideration. I would like to know the shipping cost.
Dhana: It depends on the goods. Usually we should calculate charges according to the size, weight or value of the goods and sometimes risks.[4]
Bill: OK. We have 30 cases of flowers. Every case weighs 20 kilograms, and the volume is 0.5 cubic meters.
Dhana: Um, 30 cases, 20 kilograms, 0.5 cubic meters. OK. The weight and size are all available. Please wait a moment. Don't worry. There's enough time. Um, they will arrive in London the day after tomorrow if there is no surprise.
Bill: Thank you.
Dhana: The freight charges are £4.00 for each kilogram, plus £2.00 for Airway bill of loading and £21.00 for customs clearance.[5] Um, I believe that the flowers will reach you in time and in good order. Hope they will give you complete satisfaction.
Bill: Great. Thanks a lot.
Dhana: You're welcome. If you have any problems, you can contact me at any time.
Bill: OK. Bye.
Dhana: Bye.

International Multimodal Transport

(Barry and Eileen are talking about the delivery of the furniture. They would like to choose international multimodal transport.)

Barry: Jupiter Products. Barry speaking.

Eileen: Hello, this is Eileen.

Barry: Hello, Eileen.

Eileen: I'm phoning about the delivery of these 30 sets of furniture from Tianjin to Chicago this month.

Barry: I see. I believe it will be better to transport the furniture by multimodal transport.

Eileen: So do I. <u>Containers are safe, and the goods don't need to be conveyed many times.</u>[6/7]

Barry: Yes, we can unload at the port and then we deliver the furniture to the customers by trucks.

Eileen: Could the expenses be very high?

Barry: International multimodal transport is a very effective way of transportation. The combined transport operator is responsible for the whole process of different ways of transportation. It's a safe and competitive way of transportation. It saves the transportation cost and time so the freight is reasonable.

Eileen: That's good. <u>What about the Bill of Lading?</u>[8]

Barry: <u>We supply Combined Transport Bill of Lading.</u>[9]

Eileen: <u>So we should advise our bank to accept it during establishment of L/C instead of the usual B/L.</u>[10]

Barry: OK. When do you want the delivery made?

Eileen: We are going to book shipping space before this weekend.

Barry: No problem. Is your furniture ready?

Eileen: Yes. Could the container reach our warehouse?

Barry: It will be to your warehouse this Thursday.

Eileen: Great!

Words and Expressions

1.	Delivery Service Director		递送服务部主管
2.	cargo delivery service		货物递送服务
3.	reliability	*n.*	信度
4.	Express Plus service		加急快递服务
5.	Express service		特快服务
6.	Expedited service		快件服务
7.	scheduled	*adj.*	预定的，预先安排的
8.	punctuality	*n.*	准时，守时
9.	security	*n.*	安全；抵押品
10.	dispatch department		配送部
11.	air transport		空运
12.	shipping cost		运费
13.	delivery charge		送货费用（指将货物运送到指定地点交给指定人过程中所产生的费用，如运费、装卸费等）

Chapter 15 Cargo Delivery

14. cubic meter　　　　　　　　　　　立方米
15. freight charges　　　　　　　　　 运费
16. Airway bill of loading　　　　　　空运单
17. customs clearance　　　　　　　 结关；海关出口放行；海关出口许可证
18. container　　　　　　　　　 n.　 集装箱
19. International multimodal transport　国际多式联运
20. Combined Transport Bill of Lading　联运提货单

Notes

1. Delivery affects all the results of the trade and the reliability of the company.
   配送服务影响着公司贸易的最终结果，并关系着公司的信誉。
   ① delivery *n.* 交货
   交货指卖方将货物转交给买方。交货的概念主要包括三个方面，即交货地点、交货方式和交货时间。国际贸易中有实际交货和象征交货两种。在实际操作中，多用象征交货，即卖方将货物交付给运送人之后，取得足以证明交运货物所有权的文件，把文件提供给买方或银行，即已履行交货义务。
   ② reliability *n.* 信度
   例句：
   　　Letter of credit is characterized by its reliability.
   　　信用证以可靠性著称。
   ③ reliable *adj.* 可靠的
   例句：
   　　We can give you a loan if you can provide us with reliable guarantee.
   　　如果贵方能够提供可靠的担保，我方可以向你方提供贷款。

2. It is the fastest service for the most urgent cargos.
   （加急快递服务）适合于紧急货物的最快速的递送。
   ① express *v.* 快递，快运
   ② express consignment　快件，快达货物
   ③ express fee　快递费
   ④ express goods　快运货物
   ⑤ express mail　快信（邮）

3. What about the shipping cost?
   装运费是怎么样的？
   ① shipping cost 相当于 shipping charges，shipping expenses
   ② shipping container　海运集装箱
   ③ shipping invoice　装运发票
   ④ shipping list　发货清单
   ⑤ shipping permit　装运许可证

4. Usually we should calculate charges according to the size, weight or value of the goods and sometimes risks.

我们通常按货物的规格、重量、价值来计算运费，有时还要考虑风险。

① calculate *v.* 计算，考虑，计划

calculate the output 计算产量

② calculated *adj.* 计算出的

calculated risk 计划风险，预期风险

③ calculation *n.* 计算，考虑

calculation center 计算中心

5. The freight charges are £4.00 for each kilogram, plus £2.00 for Airway bill of loading and £21.00 for customs clearance.

运费是每千克4.00英镑，外加2.00英镑空运单和21.00英镑结关。

clearance (cl.) 结关，通关

相关词汇：

clearance fee 结关手续费

clearance papers 报关许可证

6. Containers are safe.

集装箱运输安全可靠。

相关词汇：

① container vessels 集装箱船

② container rate 集装箱运价

③ container terminal 集装箱码头，集装箱装卸区

④ Container Transport International 国际集装箱运输公司

7. The goods don't need to be conveyed many times.

货物不必转运好几次。

① convey *v.* 运输，运送

例句：

This train conveys both passengers and goods from Beijing to Russia.

这趟火车装载乘客和货物从北京到俄罗斯。

② conveyance *n.* 运输，运输工具

8. What about the Bill of Lading?

提货单的情况怎么样？

Bill of Lading 提货单，有三种功能：（1）承运货物的收据；（2）承运人和托运人之间运输合同的证明；（3）货物所有权的凭证。

9. We supply Combined Transport Bill of Lading.

我们这一次用的是联运提货单。

① combined transport 联运，联合运输（指用水路、铁路、公路、航空中至少两种方式的运输）

② Combined Transport Bill of Lading (CTB / L) 联运提单

③ Combined Transport Document (CTD) 联运单据，由联运货人签发的运货凭证

④ Combined Transport Operator (CTO)　联运经营者，联运承运人

10. So we should advise our bank to accept it during establishment of L/C instead of the usual B/L.

那我们开立信用证时会建议银行接受联运提单而不是通常所用的普通提单。

① advise *v.* 通知，建议

advise sb. of sth. 通知某人某事

② advice *n.* 通知，通知单，通知书

Shipping Advice　装船通知书

Part B Practical Key Sentences

1. time of delivery

（1）根据实际情况询问发货时间时，买方可以说：

When at the earliest can we expect the shipment?

最早能在什么时候发货？

替换表达：

　　When time is the earliest you can make delivery?

　　What is the earliest time you can make delivery?

　　When will you deliver the goods to us?

　　When will the products reach our port?

还可以说：

How long does it take you to make delivery?

多长时间可以交货呢？

When do you want the delivery made?

你想何时发货？

替换表达：

　　When will the goods be delivered?

　　How long does it probably take for delivery?

　　When is the delivery time?

（2）卖方对于发货时间询问的回答，可以说：

I think we can meet your requirement.

我想，我们可以满足您的要求。

替换表达：

　　I'm sure the shipment will be made on time.

　　We will get the goods dispatched within two weeks.

2. an early shipment

（1）买方要求提前装运时，可以开门见山地问：

Is it possible to make an early shipment?

有可能提前装运吗？

替换表达：

You may know that time of delivery is a matter of great importantce. Is it possible to deliver the goods two weeks ahead of time?

Could we expect an earlier shipment within three weeks?

Will it be possible for you to ship the goods before early May?

Is there any way to make an early shipment?

Could you make shipment 7 days earlier?

Can't it be delivered in early April?

We hope the delivery can be pushed to mid-May.

（2）卖方可以这样回答：

The earliest time we can make is mid-May.

我们最快只能在五月中旬发货。

Sorry, we cannot advance the time of delivery.

对不起，我们不能提前发货。

替换表达：

I'm afraid it won't be ready until mid-May.

Early May is unlikely. The earliest would be mid-May.

Sorry, we cannot advance the time of delivery.

We cannot make the delivery earlier.

Part C Integration of Theory and Practice

1. background information 背景知识

【知识点】随着时代的发展，传统的运输方式已远远不能满足企业的需要。货物运输主要分为航空货物运输、铁路运输、公路运输、海上运输、集装箱运输及国际多式联运等。运输公司同样也有包裹递送服务的各项业务，主要包括加急快递服务、特快专递服务和递送服务。

航空货运速度快，安全性高，但运量小，运价高。铁路运输受天气等不可抗力因素的影响较小，准确性较高，运输安全，且速度快、运量大，成本也较航空货运低。海上运输是指船舶在不同地区和港口运送货物，具有运量大、运费低、速度慢的特点。据统计，我国进出口货运90%都是由海上运输承担的。

集装箱运输能很好地保护货物的安全，货物的交接地点可以在目的港，也可以通过其他运输方式有机结合的多式联合运输延伸到内陆地区，最终完成货物运输。

2. transportation terms and frequently-used sentences 运输专有词汇及常用句式

【知识点】在国际商务口语的学习中，光有国际商务理论知识是远远不够的，学习者必须努力拓宽国际商务专业词汇范围，举一反三，做到多听、多说、多记，尽量缩小母语与外语的差别。例如：

Bill of Lading（B/L）提货单（指承运人在收到货物时签发给托运人的货物收据，也是持

有者在目的地的提货凭证）

　　Delivery Advice 交货单，交货通知（指出口国指定地点交货成交条件下，卖方将货物运送到指定地点或装上指定运输工具时向买方发出的已交货通知书）

　　immediate shipment / prompt shipment 立即装运
　　initial shipment 第一批船货
　　monthly shipment 每月装运量
　　partial shipment 分批装运
　　port of shipment 装运港
　　total shipment 总发货量，总装运量

　　除词汇、短语外，国际商务交流中句子的表达也要力求地道，言简意赅，准确达意，要尽力避免用语失误造成的损失。

　　（1）要求采取某种运输方式时，常用的表达方式有：

【技能训练句型】

Please use direct shipping instead of installment.
请用直运而不是分批装运。
Is it possible to use container for shipping?
可以用集装箱进行货运吗？
We deliver our goods by lorries.
我们用卡车运送货物。
We advise the cargos to be sent by express trains.
我们建议用特快火车发货。
I propose multimodal combined transport by air and sea.
我提议用海空联运。
We'd like to ship them by air.
我们决定空运这批货物。
It is very urgent, so please consider air transport.
这批货急用，能否考虑空运？
It is better to use container for freight.
最好用集装箱来运输。
We will be more careful with shipping.
我们在装运时会更加小心。

　　（2）【知识点】当无法确认是否能满足对方的运输要求时，稳住客户尤为重要，我们应该有礼有节，提出尽力提前发货的措施。

【技能训练句型】

We will speed up the production in order to ship your order in time.
我们一定加速生产以确保准时发货。
相关表达：
If you desire earlier delivery, we can only make a partial shipment.
如果你方要想提前发货，我们只能分批装运。

The earliest delivery we can make is in May, but I can assure you that we'll do our best to advance the shipment.

我方最快在五月发货,我保证我方会尽力将发货时间提前。

Thank you very much for your cooperation. I'll find out with our home office. We'll do our best to advance the time of delivery.

非常感谢您的合作。我必须和总部联系。我们将会尽力将发货时间提前。

I believe that the products will reach you in time and in good order and hope they will give you complete satisfaction.

我相信货物会准时完好地到达贵方。希望您能满意。

3. freight calculation　运费的计算

【知识点】运费的计算要考虑到双方的协议,根据货物的重量、体积、商品的价值等进行合理支付。航空公司规定,当货物体积小、重量大时,按实际重量计算;当货物体积大、重量小时,按体积计算。在集中托运时,一批货物由几件不同的货物组成,有轻货也有重货。其计费重量则采用整批货物的毛重或总的体积重量,按两者之中较高的一个计算。

总之,相关工作人员对货物运输的策划、海关申报、运费、风险规避到货物抵达装卸等每一个环节都要十分熟悉,包括其流程及规章制度,并在此基础上有效地运用国际商务英语进行交际,力求做到清晰达意,不失礼节。

4. international multimodal transport　国际多式联运

【知识点】国际多式联运是一种以方便托运人和货主为目的的先进的货物运输组织形式。它是一种重要的国际集装箱运输方式,也是现在国际运输发展的主要趋势。

国际多式联运是指按照多式联运合同,以至少两种不同的运输方式,由多式联运经营人将货物从一个国家的国境内接管货物的地点运至另一个国家的国境内指定地点交付的货物运输。

国际多式联运是一种利用集装箱进行联运的新的运输组织方式。它通过采用海、陆、空等两种以上的运输手段,完成国际间的连贯货物运输,从而打破了过去海运、铁路、公路、空运等单一运输方式互不连贯的传统做法。提供优质的国际多式联运服务已成为当今集装箱运输公司提高竞争力的强有力方式。

国际多式联运是一种以实现货物整体运输的最优化效益为目标的联运组织形式。其主要特点是,由多式联运经营人对托运人签订一个运输合同统一组织全程运输,实行运输全程一次托运、一单到底、一次收费、统一理赔和全程负责。

【技能训练句型】

International multimodal transport is a very effective way of transportation. The combined transport operator is responsible for the whole process of different ways of transportation. It's a safe and competitive way of transportation. It saves the transportation cost and time so the freight is reasonable.

国际多式联运是一种货物整体运输最有效的运输方式。多式联运经营人负责不同方式的运输全程。它是一种安全和富有竞争性的运输方式。能节省运输费用和时间。因此,运费十分合理。

Chapter 15 Cargo Delivery

Part D Practice

I. Complete the Following Dialogues

(1)

Li: Dispatch Department. Li Ming speaking.
Bill: Hello, Li Ming. This is Bill from LTT Company.
Li: Hello, Bill. What can I do for you?
Bill: When will you ___1___ the products to us?
Li: The earliest delivery we can ___2___ is at the end of October.
Bill: Will it be ___3___ for you to ship the goods before early September?
Li: I'm sorry. We can't ___4___ the time of delivery.
Bill: You know that ___5___ of delivery is very important to us. I sincerely hope you can give our ___6___ your special consideration.
Li: We'll try our best to speed up the production in order to ___7___ your requirement.
Bill: Thank you very much.

(2)

A: Excuse me. What's the ___1___ on this parcel to Australia, please?
B: That's USD 72 cents per ounce for overseas mail. Please wait a moment. I have to weigh it first. Um, it's a little overweight. You have to pay 23 cents ___2___.
A: OK. Anything else?
B: The insurance is ten cents.
A: When will the post be ___3___?
B: The first ___4___ is at 8 a.m.
A: Thank you. Please ___5___ this parcel off by special delivery.
B: Be sure to put down the address of the ___6___ clearly.
A: Thank you.

II. Interaction Activities

Task 1

The teacher divides students into several groups to make discussions. Each group is suggested to be 5 students.

Topics:

Which features do you think are the most important for dispatch department?

There are some useful expressions for you to complete this task.

(1) I believe that ... is of the most importance for dispatch department.

(2) high quality of service

(3) shipping charges

209

(4) lower cost

(5) reputation and reliability

(6) security

Task 2

Students work in pairs.

One of your customers has sent you an e-mail and wants to know why 30 high definition televisions he ordered have been delayed.

There are some useful expressions for you to complete this task.

(1) I'll check it out immediately.

(2) What's the number of your bill of lading?

(3) I would like to know why the ship has been delayed.

(4) The ship was delayed by ...

(5) We apologize for the delay.

(6) contact sb. at any time

III. Actual Practice

Task 1

Students work in pairs.

Suppose you work in ABC Company. Last month you placed an order with Bright Future Inc. for 1,000 pairs of shoes. The goods were delivered on Monday. But you found out that 50 pairs of shoes didn't meet your requirement. Decide what you are going to do.

There are some useful expressions for you to complete this task.

(1) I'm sorry to let you know that ...

(2) I'm sorry to have to say this but ...

(3) I bought ... and I've got a bit of problem here, you see ...

(4) There seems to be a mistake.

(5) We ordered ... but we received ... instead.

(6) There has been a slip-up in our... department.

(7) We are very sorry about the mistakes ...

(8) I'm extremely sorry to hear about your complaints. I can assure you that ...

(9) It's perfectly all right.

Task 2

Students work in pairs.

Suppose you work in dispatch department of ABC Company. Your partner calls for the early delivery of 1,000 packages of the LTT fans his company has ordered. Try to give his request your special consideration.

There are some useful expressions for you to complete this task.

(1) What is the earliest time when you can make delivery?

(2) We can assure you that the shipment will be made not later than ...

(3) I hope you can give our request your special consideration.

(4) We'll do our best to advance the time of delivery.

(5) Please let me know whether it is available or not.

(6) I believe that the products will reach you in time and in good order and hope they will give you complete satisfaction.

IV. Creative Discussion

The teacher divides the class into groups, and the students make a discussion with their partners and share their opinions with other groups.

Topic:

Suppose you work in a dispatch department. One of your customers would like to know how to decide the best way to send the goods to its destination.

There are many ways of delivery. Discuss which one you prefer and show the reasons. If possible, discuss the advantages and disadvantages of each way.

There are some useful expressions for you to complete this task.

(1) It just depends on ...

(2) We need to consider that ...

(3) We choose different delivery methods according to ...

(4) It's suitable for / ideal for ...

(5) There are some advantages of ...

Chapter 16
Business Conference

Learning Objectives
Upon completion of this chapter, you will be able to

- get familiar with the process of business conference.
- make good preparation for business conference.
- learn how to express one's opinions and ask for others' opinions.
- take an active participation in business conference.
- understand intensifying our international right to a voice.[1]

1　理解提高国际话语权。

Part A Situational Dialogue

Conference Arrangement

(Mr. Brown is discussing about the arrangement of the sales conference with Miss Li, the secretary.)

Brown: Miss Li, could we have a quick discussion about the sales conference?
Li: Yes, I'm glad to go through it now.[1]
Brown: You know, the meeting is scheduled at 2:00 p.m. this Friday afternoon, which will last for 3 hours. And there will be 150 top managers from 10 countries to participate in this conference.[2] Will you please arrange it for me?
Li: Of course, Mr. Brown, but could I have your plan?
Brown: Please send formal invitations first. Oh, all things to be done are written here.
Li: May I keep it? I need it when I draw up the notice of the meeting and the agenda.[3]
Brown: Go ahead, it's for your reference. By the way, please make a special agenda for me.
Li: You mean you need a more detailed agenda for yourself?
Brown: That's right. I'm going to chair the meeting.
Li: OK, I see. I will prepare it carefully and distribute all the agendas in advance so that the participants will have time to think about all the agenda items before the meeting.[4]
Brown: Good. And I wonder if you have any good place for the meeting in your mind.
Li: Yes, it can be in West Lake Hotel. The conference room there is of adequate size. In addition to size, the facilities offered there are sufficient and the cost of hiring is reasonable.
Brown: Could you tell me what the budget is?
Li: 20,000 yuan maximum.
Brown: That'll be fine. But you'd better check if the lighting, air-conditioning and the video projector are OK, and if water, glasses, ashtrays, pens and papers are available before the conference.[5]
Li: You're right.
Brown: By the way, we'll have several foreign guests attend the meeting. What have you got then?
Li: I'll arrange for an interpreter to be present.
Brown: There are simultaneous translation facilities in the auditorium, aren't there?
Li: Yes. The participants can also count on them.[6]
Brown: That's OK. Another thing, how would you seat our guests?
Li: I'm not familiar with every participant.[6]

Brown: Oh, that's easy. I'll write you a list of the names.

Li: Very good. So I can make a seating plan with the names and I'll prepare name cards to be put on the conference table for guests to sit by. Well, what time would you like the refreshments served?

Brown: After Mr. White's report there'll be an interval for rest and refreshments.

Li: And then what are we doing for refreshments?

Brown: Why not have a buffet?

Li: OK, I'll arrange it. <u>If you don't mind, I'll withdraw and get down to it.</u>[7]

Communicative Scene 2

At the Conference

(Mr. Brown, Mr. Heine, Mr. Glover, Mr. Jobe, Mr. Boiler and Mr. Graber are at the conference. They are discussing about whether to carry out a new plan.)

Brown: Ladies and gentlemen, may I have your attention? Please take a seat. We are about to start our meeting.

Heine: Where's Mr. Glover? <u>He's supposed to join us.</u>[8]

Brown: Oh, here he comes. <u>Speak of the devil ...</u>[9]

Glover: I'm sorry to keep you waiting.

Brown: OK, everyone's here. Let's begin. We all know what we're here for. <u>The client's meeting is tomorrow and between now and then we've got to come up with some original ideas.</u>[10] So everyone just speak your minds, because there's no such thing as stupid idea in the brain-storming session. Now we'd like to hear your ideas about the whole issue, Mr. Glover?

Glover: Well, I must admit I still somehow doubt this business. Here is the chart showing our company's latest financial status. From the chart, we can see clearly that our profits have dropped recently because of the high rate of inflation. The Purchasing Department is now having to pay double for supplies of raw materials.

Brown: <u>What have you got to say about this matter, Mr. Jobe?</u>[11]

Jobe: I have no strong feelings about the ideas. I am just wondering if Mr. Heine has got any ideas for us.

Brown: Mr. Heine?

Heine: Can we cut down any of our costs?

Jobe: Transport costs seem very high, too.

Boiler: This is due to the increasing charges for air-freighting goods.

Jobe: Why don't we ship our goods down the Yellow River from Hankou? That would reduce costs considerably.

Graber: I'm afraid I have different views on this.

Brown: Could you be more specific on this point?

Graber: If we do that, we'll have to revise all our schedules to allow for the longer time it would take.[12]

Boiler: Yes, we would have to dispatch goods well in advance to make sure the customers got them on time.

Heine: Isn't there a risk of delays? The volume of traffic on the Yellow River is very heavy.

Jobe: Delays certainly would be very bad for public relations. We can't afford to lose customers through delayed deliveries.

Glover: It seems to me that our first job is to find out what it's likely to cost us to get started, and what kind of return we can expect over the next two or three years.

Heine: You see, costs are not our only concern. We've been waiting for an opportunity like this for years. I suggest we carry out this plan right now.[13] It's a chance of a lifetime.

Glover: I'm not saying that I'm against this plan, but we'll need some verification before we can rush into any decision.

Jobe: You said it. We need to be more cautious regarding the present market situation.

Brown: Well, we seem to agree with the project, but let me just clarify one thing before we go. If this plan is to be carried out successfully, it needs everyone to work together. The financial support is going to be available if we can convince our sponsor that the plan will finally benefit all investors.[14] So, to sum up, it's vitally important that all departments cooperate with each other and make sure it goes smoothly. OK, let's call it a day.[15]

Communicative Scene 3

Taking Notes in Meetings

(The new secretary, Miss Fang, is asking Miss Li, an experienced secretary, some questions about how to take minutes at the meeting.)

Fang: Miss Li, shall I take minutes in the conference?

Li: Yes, of course. The minutes should be taken carefully.

Fang: So could you explain how to do it?

Li: OK. Oh, I have my notebook here ready for the meeting. You can read it.

Fang: Thank you. Err... what's this?

Li: This is the heading... the Star Machinery Import & Export Corporation. Then underneath that... Minutes of Meeting of Branch Managers at 2:00 p.m. on Thursday, 8th, March, 2006, then underneath that... Present: Mr. Brown, CEO, in the chair.

Fang: And you've left a space underneath to fill in the name of the managers, haven't you?

Li: Yes, that's right. Then the first item is always ... apologies for absence.

Fang: What comes next?

Li: The next item is always ... Minutes of Last Meeting. As soon as the minutes of the last meeting have been read, you can write "The minutes of the last meeting were read, confirmed and signed."

Fang: Signed?

Li: Yes, when the minutes have been confirmed, the chairman will sign them.

Fang: Do I have to write down every word that everyone says?

Li: Oh, no. It's very difficult and hardly necessary. You just need to make a note of the topics that are discussed and the result of the discussion.

Fang: The result of the discussion?

Li: When a topic has been discussed for some time, someone usually proposes that some action should be taken.

Fang: Then what happens?

Li: Then the chairman asks whether the members agree to the proposal. And if they do agree, you can write down "It was agreed that ..." or "It was resolved that ...".

Fang: Is there a difference?

Li: Not really. "Resolved" is a special committee word. When a proposal has been agreed by the committee, it is called a "resolution". Look, here is a copy of the minutes of the last meeting and here are my notes.

Fang: Oh, that's wonderful. I'm interested in what you wrote in your notes: It was resolved that the office would be closed on 15 March.

Words and Expressions

1. chair	n.	（主持会议的）主席的职位
	v.	主持（会议）
2. distribute	v.	分配，分送
3. facilities	n.	设备
4. sufficient	adj.	足够的
5. budget	n.	预算
6. projector	n.	投影仪
7. interpreter	n.	口译员
8. simultaneous	adj.	同时的
9. auditorium	n.	会堂；礼堂
10. interval	n.	（戏剧、音乐会各段落间的）间隔时间
11. refreshments	n.	点心
12. buffet	n.	自助餐
13. the brain-storming session		头脑风暴环节
14. inflation	n.	通货膨胀
15. air-freighting		空中货运的

16. verification	n.	鉴定，证实
17. resolve	v.	投票表决，决议
18. resolution	n.	决议
*19. definitely	adv.	明确地
*20. take minutes		会议记录
the minute book		会议记录本

Notes

1. I'm glad to go through it now.
   我很高兴现在谈论这个问题。
   go through
   ① 详细讨论
   例句：
   > Let's go through the data again.
   > 让我们将这些数据再详细讨论一遍。

   ② 履行，参加
   例句：
   > She made him go through a religious wedding.
   > 她让他举行了宗教仪式的婚礼。
   > He went through the degree ceremony without getting too nervous.
   > 他自如地参加了学位授予仪式。

2. And there will be 150 top managers from 10 countries to participate in this conference.
   而且将会有来自10个国家150名高级经理参加这次会议。
   ① participate in 分享，参与
   例句：
   > In a modern democracy, people want to participate more fully.
   > 在现代民主政体中，人们要求更多地参与。

   ② participate with sb. in one's sufferings 与某人共患难
   ③ participant n. 分享者，参与者

3. I need it when I draw up the notice of the meeting and the agenda.
   我草拟会议通知和会议日程时需要它。
   draw up
   ① 草拟
   draw up a memorandum 起草一份备忘录
   ② 使停住
   例句：
   > A freight car drew up outside their house.
   > 一辆运货车在他们房子外面停下。

4. I will prepare it carefully and distribute all the agendas in advance so that the participants will have time to think about all the agenda items before the meeting.

我会认真准备并且在会议开始前送出日程表，以便与会者有时间在会议开始前考虑日程表上的议程。

① in advance 事前，预先，该词组常与介词 of 搭配

例句：

It's unwise to spend your income in advance.

把你的收入预先花掉是不明智的。

② in advance of 超过

例句：

Galileo's ideas were in advance of the age in which he lived.

伽利略的思想超越了他生活的时代。

5. But you'd better check if the lighting, air-conditioning and the video projector are OK, and if water, glasses, ashtrays, pens and papers are available.

不过你最好检查一下灯、空调和投影仪是否都正常，还有水、玻璃杯、烟灰缸、钢笔和纸是否都已备好。

6. The participants can also count on them.

与会者也可以依靠同声传译设备。

count on 指望，依赖

例句：

You had better not count on an increase in your salary this year.

你今年最好不要指望加薪。

7. If you don't mind, I'll withdraw and get down to it.

如果你不介意，我就着手办了。

get down to 开始认真对待（工作等）；开始认真注意（细节等）

例句：

The company really gets down to improving working conditions.

公司确实开始改善工作条件。

I get down to discussing my workload.

我开始讨论我的工作量。

8. He's supposed to join us.

他是要出席会议的。

be supposed to do sth. 认为必须，认为应该

例句：

When is the cargo ship supposed to leave?

货船应该在什么时候开？

We are supposed to be there at six.

我们得在6点钟到达那里。

9. speak of the devil ...

  这句话完整的表达是： Speak of the devil and he will appear.

  说曹操，曹操到。

10. The client's meeting is tomorrow and between now and then we've got to come up with some original ideas.

  明天就要见客户了，从今天到明天的这段时间里，我们一定要想出些有创意的点子。

  come up with（针对问题、挑战等）提出，想出

  例句：

    He could always come up with a reason for them to linger another month.

    他总能想出个理由来让他们再延迟一个月。

11. What have you got to say about this matter, Mr. Jobe?

  那你是怎么看的呢，朱比先生？

12. If we do that, we'll have to revise all our schedules to allow for the longer time it would take.

  如果那样的话会花更长的时间，我们将不得不修改所有的日程安排。

  allow for 考虑到，顾及

  例句：

    Allowing for inflation, the cost of the project is USD 2 million.

    考虑到通货膨胀因素，这个项目的费用为200万美元。

13. I suggest we carry out this plan right now.

  我提议我们马上实施这个计划。

  文中另外两句话：So, to sum up, it's vitally important that all departments cooperate with each other and make sure it goes smoothly.

  总之，至关重要的是，所有的部门能够通力合作，确保计划的顺利进行。

  When a topic has been discussed for some time, someone usually proposes that some action should be taken.

  一个话题经过一段时间讨论后，通常就有人建议实施。

  这三句话中都使用了虚拟语气。一般在动词suggest，propose或it's important等后面的从句谓语动词常使用虚拟语气，结构为should + v.，其中should可以省略。

  例句：

    He proposes that we should talk to each other in teleconference.

    他建议我们通过电话会议交谈。

    It is essential that this mission not fail.

    这项任务不失败至关重要。（至关重要的是这项任务没有失败。）

    He suggested that a contract be signed.

    他建议签订契约。

14. The financial support is going to be available if we can convince our sponsor that the plan will finally benefit all investors.

  如果我们能使赞助商相信这个项目最终可以让所有的投资人受益的话，那么资金就一定会到位。

convince sb. of sth. 使某人确信

例句：

    I am convinced of his honesty.

    我深信他的诚实。

15. OK，let's call it a day.

    好的，今天就到这儿吧。

Part B Practical Key Sentences

1. **asking for somebody's opinion**

   What have you got to say about this matter, Mr. Jobe?

   你对这个问题有什么看法，朱比先生？

   替换表达：

       Do you have any views on this matter, Mr. Jobe?

       How do you feel about this matter, Mr. Jobe?

       What do you think of this matter, Mr. Jobe?

       Do you have any points on this matter, Mr. Jobe?

       What's your opinion of this matter, Mr. Jobe?

       What's your view on this matter, Mr. Jobe?

       What do you reckon to this matter, Mr. Jobe?

       What are your feelings about this matter, Mr. Jobe?

       What do you make of this matter, Mr. Jobe?

2. **expressing your opinion**

   It seems to me that our first job is to find out what it's likely to cost us to get started, and what kind of return we can expect over the next two or three years.

   我觉得我们首先要弄清楚启动这项计划要花费多少，以及在接下来的两三年里我们会有什么样的回报。

   相似表达：

       I think the quality is fine.

       I believe the payment term is rather reasonable.

       As I see it, extending L/C is a common thing.

       As far as I'm concerned, I think the price is rather reasonable.

       In my opinion, the business talk is very successful.

       I reckon that the customer isn't likely to come.

       From my point of view, the shipping date is too late.

3. **stating you have no opinion**

   I've no strong feelings about this ideas.

   我对这个计划没有什么看法。

替换表达：

I have nothing to say about this plan.

I really don't know what to say.

I don't have any ideas yet.

I really don't have any opinion about this plan.

4. stating you have different opinions

I'm afraid I have different views on this.

恐怕在这方面我的意见与你有所不同。

替换表达：

You approach it in a different way than I do.

I'm afraid I can't agree with you there.

5. asking for further explanation

Could you be more specific on this point?

你能把这点说得再具体一些吗？

替换表达：

Can you further explain what you mean by that?

Could you elaborate on it?

Part C Integration of Theory and Practice

meeting   会议

【知识点1】会议是商务活动中常常被采用的一种手段。通过会议人们可以互通信息、讨论问题，各部门对现有问题或下一步计划进行磋商。在会议前，会议组织者必须做好充分的准备。首先，会议组织者必须确定会议日期和地点并提前通知与会者。

【技能训练句型】

You know, the meeting is scheduled from 2:00 p.m. this afternoon. And I've chosen a good place for it. It's in West Lake Hotel.

会议定在下午两点钟举行。我已挑好地点，在西湖酒店。

【知识点2】在会议要开始时，会议主持人常常会提高自己的声音，与会者就会停止交谈，准备开会。

【技能训练句型】

宣布会议开始的表达方式有：

Ladies and gentlemen, shall we get started?

先生们，女士们，我们开始吧？

Please take a seat. The meeting is about to start.

请就座。会议马上就要开始了。

May I have your attention, please?

请大家注意一下，好吗？

Attention, please!

请注意!

【知识点3】如果会议当中没有女士,会议主持人就只用gentlemen,如果会议主持人不清楚是否有女士在场,直接用everyone或者everybody也就是我们通常说的"所有人"!

【技能训练句型】

OK, everyone!

好了,所有人(注意)!

The meeting is about to start.

会议马上就要开始了。

Please be seated.

请就座。

【知识点4】一个成功的会议,一般都要设定一个议程。

【技能训练句型】

会议主持人可以这样表达:

As you can see from our agenda, we need to look at 3 items today, and they are ...

从我们的议程安排可以看出,今天要讨论三个问题,它们是……

I suggest we take a look at them one by one.

我建议一个个来讨论。

当然,与会者可以根据议程的重要性来决定会议讨论的顺序。

【技能训练句型】

I suggest we take the items in this order.

我建议按这样的程序进行。

Could we take the third item first?

我们可以先从第三项开始吗?

I think it's very important for us to look at the last one first.

我认为先看最后一项是很重要的。

【知识点5】往往一次会议的终结意味着另一个会议的开始,一个问题的深入会导致多个问题的出现,这些都有可能使我们进入一个无休止的会议的循环往复。会议主持人会询问记录人员上次会议谈到哪里。这时会议主持人会说:"Where were we last time?"

【知识点6】开会时经常会遇到跑题的情况,所以会议的主持人最好能在会议一开始就确定会议的目标和最终要达到的效果,否则,会议就会失去原本的意义,会议主持人一定要时刻提醒与会者。

【技能训练句型】

表示会议目的可以这样表达:

The goal for our meeting is to ...

今天会议的目的是……

Our aim is to ...

我们的目的是……

I've called this meeting in order to ...

223

会议的主题是……

会议主持人提醒与会者时可以这样表达：We have to get down to business.

【知识点7】在会议中会议主持人征询他人的意见是很常见的，也是使与会者各抒己见、避免冷场的一种好办法。

【技能训练句型】

How do you find things over the bargain?

你觉得这笔买卖怎么样？

How do you see things like this?

你对这类事怎么看？

What do you reckon, Tom?

你是怎么考虑的，汤姆？

Have you got any comments on this new plan?

你对这个新计划有何评论？

Do you have any particular view on the present market?

你对目前的市场有什么特殊的见解？

【知识点8】召开会议就是要集思广益，找到最佳方案，从而做出最有利的决定。所以，在会议中，与会者在发言时必须要做到观点明确、简洁和具体。

【技能训练句型】

In my view, the business talk is very successful.

在我看来，这次业务洽谈非常成功。

Don't you think this design is rather beautiful?

你不觉得这个设计很漂亮吗？

Personally, I believe quality is still a great problem.

我个人认为质量依然存在很大问题。

I'd just like to say your arrangement is satisfactory.

我想说您的安排令人满意。

Well, I must say it would be better to pack the goods in wooden cases.

我认为用木箱子包装更好。

The way I see it, goods at lower prices are not certainly popular items.

在我看来，低价格的产品并非畅销。

【知识点9】若与会者对某项计划还没有什么看法时，也必须清楚地表明。

【技能训练句型】

I have nothing to say about this plan.

我对这个计划没有什么可说的。

I really don't know what to think about this transaction.

我确实不知道怎么考虑这笔生意。

【知识点10】当然，有时与会者会对某项计划持截然不同的观点。为避免言语冲突，在表达自己的看法时可以避免直抒己见。

Chapter 16 Business Conference

【技能训练句型】

I'd prefer not to say anything about the issue.

对这件事我宁愿不发表任何意见。

I'd rather not say anything about the new plan.

对新计划我宁愿不发表任何意见。

That's an interesting idea, but it's not for me to say.

这是个有趣的想法,不过这不是我说了算。

I'd rather not commit myself on that, if you don't mind.

如果你不介意,我倒希望不对此发表意见。

【知识点11】会议总是冗长的,与会者各抒己见,但往往会花去大量时间。在商务活动中,时间就是金钱,因此要讲求工作效率。所以,会议主持人在确认会议已取得原定效果的前提下,应该及时得体地结束会议。

【技能训练句型】

Let's leave the details to our next meeting.

我们可以把细节问题留到下一个会议。

I'm afraid we have to finish here.

恐怕今天就到此为止。

Let's call it a day.

今天就到这儿吧。

OK, time to wrap it up.

该结束了。

Part D Practice

I. **Complete the Following Dialogues**

(1)

A: Is the room ready for the meeting?

B: Yes. I've put the ___1___ book and some spare copies of the ___2___ on the table including pens and papers.

A: Well, everyone is going to Mr. Brown's speech. Have you ___3___ the microphone?

B: Yes. It's OK.

A: Good. We'll have some foreign guests to attend the meeting. What have you got then?

B: I've ___4___ for an ___5___ to be present.

A: Then how would you ___6___ our guests?

B: I've prepared name cards to be ___7___ on the conference table for guests to sit by.

A: Nice work. I hope our organization of the meeting will be ___8___.

(2)

A: Do you have any points, Tom?

B: Well, I must ___1___ I'm still a bit ___2___ about this plan. Electronic products trade is always a ___3___ affair.

A: I think electronic products trade is ___4___ to be a booming business soon. What do you ___5___, Bill?

C: It seems to me that our first job is to find out what it's ___6___ to cost us to get started, and what kind of return we can ___7___ over the next four years.

D: You are right.

A: Good. Now let's put it to the ___8___.

II. Role-plays

Task 1

The teacher divides students into groups. Each group is suggested to be 5 students. Make dialogues and role-play them.

Hold a business conference according to the following hints: Student A is the manager of a company. Now you are presiding over a conference at which a discussion is held about whether to carry out a proposed plan or not; Student B, Student C are for the plan; Student D and Student E are against the plan.

Task 2

Short conversations.

Suppose you are a secretary of a company. You are asked to prepare for the coming conference. Now you report your work to the boss and answer the boss's questions.

III. Guided Talking

Work in pairs.

Use the minutes of the meetings below to practice with your partner.

HENG XING SILK TRDING CO.

Minutes of Meeting of Branch Managers

Dec. 8, 2023

Presiding: Mr. White, President

  Present: Mr. Wang, Personnel Manager

        Mr. Wu, Sales Manager

        Mr. Li, Technical Manager

Minutes:

After calling the meeting to order at 3:00 p.m., the President asked Mr. Wu for a brief report. Mr. Wu explained that profits had dropped recently owing to the high rate of inflation. He pointed out that the Purchasing Department was now having to pay double for supplies of raw materials.

Chapter 16 Business Conference

The President asked Mr. Wang to comment. Mr. Wang suggested that they ship their goods down the Yangtze River from Wuhan. He felt that would reduce costs considerably.

Mr. Li pointed out that if they did that, they would have to revise their schedules to allow for the longer time it would take.

Mr. Wu wondered if there wasn't a risk of delays. He felt the volume of traffic on the Yangtze River was very heavy.

Mr. Wang believed that delays would certainly be very bad for public relations. He felt they couldn't afford to lose customers through delayed deliveries.

There was no agreement on this issue.

The meeting was adjourned at 4:30 p.m.

Respectfully submitted

Janet Olliphant, Secretary

1. Ask how to take notes at the conference.
2. Explain how to take steps.

IV. Creative Discussion

The teacher divides the class into groups for discussion. Each group chooses a representative after discussion. The student who expresses well will be the winner.

Topic:

Sometimes you are asked to make a speech at the conference. Will you feel nervous to speak in front of the crowd?

Please discuss with your partner about how to overcome nervousness to make a good speech at the conference.

Chapter 17

Sales Promotion

Learning Objectives
Upon completion of this chapter, you will be able to

- acquaint yourself with the process of sales promotion.
- learn how to persuade others and talk about one's intention.
- conduct the activities related to sales promotion.
- make yourself more knowledgeable in more fields.
- make the past serve the present and develop the new from the old.[1]

---

1 古为今用，推陈出新。

Part A Situational Dialogue

Sales Call

(Rose, from Sales Department of Sunrise Health Products Company, calls at a toy factory and is talking with Jack to push the sale of their products.)

Rose: Good morning. I'm from Sunrise Health Products Company. We are a major manufacturer of massage chairs. <u>I wonder if you could spare me a few minutes to listen to my brief introduction of our products.</u>[1]

Jack: I'm sorry, but this is a toy factory. Do our staff have to make the lovely toys on your chairs?

Rose: Are you joking?

Jack: <u>So could you tell me what on earth your massage chairs have to do with us?</u>[2]

Rose: Certainly, quite a lot. Recently many workers have suffered from neck pain and back pain, haven't they?

Jack: Yes, they have.

Rose: <u>Your staff are stressed out and they have to work on the assembly line for a long time.</u>[3] <u>No wonder they are not very well.</u>[4] By the way, what do they usually do with their pains?

Jack: Go to the massage hospital after work.

Rose: Your factory is located in the suburbs, <u>so you are a long way from the town, aren't you?</u>[5]

Jack: Er, yes. It's about seven kilometers away from downtown.

Rose: So it's not convenient for your workers to cure their disease, is it?

Jack: You said it.

Rose: I'm sure that the pains will have a great effect on your staff's working efficiency if that's the case. So why not try our massage chairs?

Jack: Yes?

Rose: They are designed to stimulate the circulation of blood and relax muscles.

Jack: Then?

Rose: It can rub their necks and upper backs. At the same time, your workers don't need to travel a long way to cure their pains.

Jack: Sounds good. May I have a try?

Rose: Of course. (*Let the manager sit in the chair.*)

Jack: (*After a while*) Wow, it feels so good.

Rose: Your staff will save much money paid for a chiropractor if you buy some of our massage chairs.

Jack: Could you show me how to operate it?

Rose: No problem. First you have to plug it in. There is a control panel on this armrest.

Jack: A control panel?

Rose: Yes, press the "Power" button to turn it on and off. Next you can press the "Mode" button to choose a mode. In this model, we have different modes including "Rub" and "Pound".

Jack: "Rub" and "Pound"? Oh, now I do feel as if someone is rubbing my back with his hand. So it must be in "Rub" mode.

Rose: That's true. (*Press the "Pound" button.*) You will feel as if someone is pounding you with a hammer lightly if you choose "Pound" mode.

Jack: Wonderful!

Rose: If your staff is free from pains, they will be happy and work more efficiently.

Jack: It sounds great!

Rose: Are you in favor of what I said? And do you have any interest in our massage chairs and intend to place some orders?

Jack: What you said is really attractive. But I'd like to think it over before I make the final decision.

Rose: Well, I'll call again in a day or two. Here is my card. Could you give me a ring whenever you need me?

Jack: Thank you. I will.

Communicative Scene 2

Describing the New Product to the Customer

(Juliet, specializing in women's clothes in America, comes to trade with Mr. Wang, the sales manager. She is talking with him about the features of a new product.)

Wang: Welcome to China, Juliet.

Juliet: It's my pleasure to visit your company. I hope we can do business together.

Wang: So do I. Have you seen our catalogue?

Juliet: Oh, yes. I've gone over the catalogue and the pamphlets enclosed in your last letter.

Wang: What do you think of our latest product?

Juliet: I'm very favorably impressed.

Wang: So happy to hear that. In fact, it's a revolutionary new product we've just developed. The yarn is carefully selected for quality and woven very tightly in this fabric. So far it has been sold in a number of areas abroad. They sell like hot cakes.

Juliet: Sounds good. How many colors are available for this item?

Wang: We have two standard colors. What's your favorite color?

Juliet: The darker one as it will cater more to the elders.

Wang: I agree with you. If the quantity is 5,000 sets or more, you may choose any color you like.

Juliet: Do you have any samples here?

Wang: Yes, they're in the showroom. Would you like to have a look?

Juliet: I'd love to.

Wang: Let me take you to the showroom.

Juliet: That's very kind of you.

Wang: It's my pleasure. This way, please. (*A few minutes later*) Here is our showroom. Almost all of our company's products can be seen here.

Juliet: Oh, you have a large collection of samples. Do you get many overseas buyers here?

Wang: Yes, quite a lot. They like to keep up-to-date, so we change our display pieces every month.

Juliet: What's the percentage of overseas markets in proportion to domestic markets for your products?

Wang: The ratio is about 7 overseas to 3 domestic.

Juliet: I see.

Wang: Juliet, please step this way. Our latest models are over there.

Juliet: Oh, look at this one. I like this rose pattern. It makes us feel warm and romantic.

Wang: That's true. And also this kind of material is very easy to wash.

Juliet: Really?

Wang: Yes. Just put it in your washing machine and then dry it. It doesn't need any extra care.

Juliet: That'll be very convenient. How much is a yard?

Wang: 50 yuan per yard. But it depends on quantity.

Juliet: Are these available now?

Wang: We have available stocks for some of the items displayed because they are now in great demand. You'll have to wait a week before we can supply you with the rest. Before you leave, would you place some orders?

Juliet: Mmm...I think your price is higher than that of other companies. And your latest product is new to the consumers of our country. You know, it is not easy to open up a new market.

Wang: That's true, but when we compare prices, we'd better take quality into consideration first. <u>Everyone in the trade knows that our product is of superior quality to those from other companies.</u>[6] I can assure you that our price is practical and reasonable. <u>So we are sure that our product will stand a good chance with your clients.</u>[7]

Juliet: Well, if you can make a discount, I intend to consider the order.

Wang: We can offer a 10% discount for orders over 1,000 pieces.

Juliet: OK, I'm willing to give your latest model a try. When is the earliest we can expect delivery?

Wang: By the end of the month.

Juliet: All right. But delivery dates must be kept.

Wang: Yes, of course. <u>We always give priority to export orders.</u>[8] No need to worry.

Juliet: Then when can we work out a deal?

Wang: Would tomorrow morning be convenient?

Chapter 17 Sales Promotion

Juliet: Yes, that'll be fine.

Communicative Scene 3

Talk about the Advertising Campaign

(Juliet would like to do business with Mr. Wang's company. Now she is talking with Mr. Wang about the advertising campaign.)

Juliet: Mr. Wang, I'm deeply impressed by your new product and I'd like to do business with you. But now my main concern is business promotion. You know, there are a lot of ways to push sales. So I'm wondering if you could tell me something about your company's advertising campaign for the new product.

Wang: Sure. Our product enjoys a good reputation here, but it is quite new in your country. So market positioning must be considered first. We must carry out market research, then decide who are the most probable buyers.

Juliet: You're quite right. We should set the target customer before publicizing the product.

Wang: And we think advertising, price and free samples are the most important when we introduce a new product. First we need to advertise the product. We must make the new product known to the consumers.

Juliet: I couldn't agree with you more.

Wang: We think the next thing is what media we should use and when we should place advertising in the media.

Juliet: Media? Only by showing the goods in an attractive way can the consumers pay for them.⁹

Wang: Yes, media. Very often in a campaign, two or more media are used together. The purpose of our advertising is to draw the local customers' interest and keep hold of their attention, so that they may do something in return.

Juliet: What media would you like to choose?

Wang: We think television advertising has a bigger impact on the choice the customers make in buying products. For example, the advertisers often use famous people to make the customers believe the product is worth buying.

Juliet: Truly.

Wang: And also the television covers a large number of audiences, so advertising on television can reach a lot of people.

Juliet: But advertisement on TV will cost a lot of money.

Wang: I suppose it's worth doing so long as the result is satisfactory.

Juliet: That sounds reasonable. And when shall we make this advertisement?

Wang: How about the beginning of this summer?

Juliet: All right. I suggest that besides television, we use other channels to advertise the product at the same time.

Wang: What are they?

Juliet: How about advertising the product in newspapers, magazines, direct mail, Internet and radio?

Wang: That's great. Through advertisements on various media, we can point out the different characteristics about our new product and get more people to learn about the product and change their views. We are also trying our best to sell on line.

Juliet: Nowadays, online sales are becoming a popular way to push sales.[10]

Wang: We'll try to find the most effective way to let customers know our site and new products.

Juliet: Good. By the way, as a new foreign product, we cannot set a very low price. Or it will cut the value of the product in our customers' mind.

Wang: Absolutely. And because we are facing fierce competition from the existing similar product in your market, we may well need to hold a news conference to introduce our product.

Juliet: Don't worry. I'll contact the journalists from some important media, potential clients and salespersons later on to join the news conference.

Wang: Great! We had better get down to business.

Words and Expressions

1. massage	n.	按摩	
2. efficiency	n.	效率	
3. stimulate	v.	刺激，激励	
4. circulation	n.	循环	
5. rub	v.	摩擦	
6. chiropractor	n.	按摩关节（尤指脊椎）以治病者	
7. panel	n.	仪表板	
8. armrest	n.	扶手	
9. pound	v.	连续重击	
10. feature	n.	特点	
11. yarn	n.	纱，线	
12. fabric	n.	织物	
13. weave	v.	织（纱、线）成布等	
14. ratio	n.	比例	
15. campaign	n.	（为达到某一特殊目标所做的一连串有计划的）活动	
16. business promotion		促销	
17. market positioning		市场定位	
18. publicize	v.	宣传	
19. fierce	adj.	强烈的，剧烈的	

Notes

1. I wonder if you could spare me a few minutes to listen to my brief introduction of our products.
   我想占用你几分钟的时间，简单介绍一下我们的产品。
   spare 提供（时间、金钱等）给某人或为某种目的匀出，分出
   例句：
       Can you spare me a few litres of petrol?
       你能分给我几公升汽油吗？
       I can't spare the time for market research.
       目前我抽不出时间做市场调查。

2. So could you tell me what on earth your massage chairs have to do with us?
   那么，你能跟我说说到底按摩椅与我们公司有什么关系？
   have sth. / nothing / not much / a great deal, etc. to do with 与……有（无、没多少、有很大等）关系
   例句：
       His instruction had something to do with my decision to do business.
       他与我决定从商有关系。

3. Your staff are stressed out and they have to work on the assembly line for a long time.
   你们公司的员工工作压力大，而且他们得在流水线旁工作很长时间。
   stress out 使紧张，使感到压力
   例句：
       Interviews always stress me out.
       面试总让我感到紧张。

4. No wonder they are not very well.
   难怪他们的身体状况不太好。
   no wonder 难怪
   例句：
       No wonder your trial order was so late.
       难怪你的试订单来得那么迟。

5. So you are a long way from the town, aren't you?
   那么你们离市里有很长一段距离，是不是？
   be free from 无……的；摆脱了……的
   例句：
       You are free from blame.
       你没有过错。

6. Everyone in the trade knows that our product is of superior quality to those from other companies.
   同行都知道我们产品的质量优于其他公司。
   ① superior *adj.* 优越的
   ② be superior to 比……更好，比……更优越

③ be inferior to 比……劣、差

例句：

He thinks he's superior to us because his father is CEO.

他认为父亲是CEO，他就高人一等。

7. So we are sure that our product will stand a good chance with your clients.

所以我们确信我们的产品很有希望获得你们客户的欢迎。

stand a chance 有希望，有可能

例句：

She stands a good chance of getting promotion.

她很有希望晋升。

8. We always give priority to export orders.

我们一直对出口订单给予优先。

give priority to 最优先考虑

类似的短语还有：

place / put high / top priority on

attach high priority to

give first priority to

9. Only by showing the goods in an attractive way can the consumers pay for them.

只有以一种吸引人的方式展示产品，消费者才可能购买。

副词only置于句首，强调方式状语、条件状语、地点状语、时间状语等状语时，主句要进行部分倒装。如果被only所强调的状语为状语从句，该状语从句不倒装，只对主句进行倒装。

10. Nowadays, online sales are becoming a popular way to push sales.

当今，网上交易正在成为推销产品的十分流行的方式。

online sales 网上交易 push sales 促销

例句：

You must push your wares if you want better sales.

如果你想要有好的销路，必须推销你的商品。

*11. enclose 把……装入信封（或包裹等），附入

例句：

A cheque is enclosed herewith.

随信附上支票一张。

*12. cater to 满足某种需要或要求

例句：

Some tabloid newspapers cater to low taste.

有些小型报纸迎合低级趣味。

*13. cater for 提供，迎合

例句：

TV programs usually cater for all tastes.

电视通常提供各种不同趣味的娱乐节目。

Part B Practical Key Sentences

1. selling

（1） Expressing something sells well 表达某物卖得好

The feedback shows these handicrafts have a ready market in Asia.
反馈显示这些手工艺品在亚洲很畅销。

替换表达：

　　Our bikes are very popular in Asia on account of their superior quality and competitive price.

　　This product is one of the best sellers in Asia.

（2） When expressing something doesn't sell well, we can say 当表达某物卖得不好，我们可以说

Promoting the sale of your cars has proved unsuccessful.
推销你方的汽车证明不成功。

替换表达：

　　There is a poor market for your razors.

　　We've spared no effort and spent money in pushing the sales but the result is disappointing.

2. reason

And because we are facing fierce competition from the existing similar product in your market, we may well need to hold a news conference to introduce our product.
因为面对在你们国家市场上现已存在的类似产品的激烈竞争，我们也需要召开一个新闻发布会来介绍我们的产品。

替换表达：

　　Our bikes are very popular in Asia on account of their superior quality and competitive price.

　　One possible cause of the decline seems to be their large and increasing trade deficit, which means that all foreign imports have been reduced.

　　I'll buy the endowment policy, for it enables me to save money for my old age.

　　Since there is a growing demand for this product, please ensure the supply is sufficient.

3. persuasion

That's true, but ... 不错，但是……

That's true, but when we compare prices, we'd better take quality into consideration first.
不错，但是当我们比较价格时，最好先考虑产品的质量，不是吗？

替换表达：

　　But surely you can see when we compare prices, we'd better take quality into consideration first.

　　Yes, but you must admit when we compare prices, we'd better take quality into consideration first.

That might be right, but you didn't get the main point when we compare prices, we'd better take quality into consideration first.

4. suggestion

How about advertising the product in newspapers, magazines, direct mail, Internet and radio?

通过报纸、杂志、直接邮购、网络、广播来宣传我们的产品怎么样？

替换表达：

What about making yourselves known by TV ads?

I suggest that besides television, we use other channels to advertise the product at the same time.

We would like to recommend here a few popular items available for immediate shipment.

A transaction at this price is recommended.

5. intention

（1）Asking about somebody's intention 询问某人的打算

Do you have any interest in our massage chairs and intend to place some orders?

你对我们的按摩椅感兴趣吗？有没有想订几台我们的按摩椅？

替换表达：

Your intention is to help advertise the products, isn't it?

Do you have any intention of carrying out a market survey?

Does this sales representative plan to pay regular visits to these customers?

Are you thinking of making all efforts to promote the sale of your products?

（2）Stating your intention 说明你的打算

If you can make a discount, I intend to consider the order.

如果你们给予打折，我会考虑试着下订单的。

替换表达：

I would like to buy a large quantity of your goods if your price is competitive.

We have every intention to establish business relations with your company if you can spend a sum of money on advertisement on TV.

6. liking

I like this rose pattern.

我喜欢这种玫瑰花的图案。

替换表达：

I love advertisements with catchphrases in them.

I really enjoy attending business talk.

I have a fancy for this sales drive.

I'm keen on the new formulas you are advertising.

I'm crazy about the work of samples and propaganda.

Part C Integration of Theory and Practice

1. **sales promotion 促销**

   【知识点】促销的关键目标是提供信息、刺激需求和突出价值。促销必须向市场提供有什么产品、产品的特色以及如何使用等信息。专业的推销人员具备关于推销过程的全面知识。这个过程包括开发潜在客户、接近客户、介绍和演示产品、处理用户的反对意见、完成交易，即锲而不舍地跟踪一笔交易。

2. **prospective customer 潜在的客户**

   【知识点】在接近客户之前，推销人员要先开发潜在客户，即辨认出哪些是最有购买意向的企业和人群。在企业间的交易中，选定可能的用户之后，推销人员就要接触该企业的决策者，接下来是产品介绍和演示、推销人员调试和操作设备、回答问题以及承接订货。产品介绍并没有定规，它也许更接近于一个非正式的谈话，在谈话间推销人员介绍产品的特色和用途，潜在客户或许对此感兴趣。

   【技能训练句型】

   A: You can now do all your cooking in beautiful Ceramic Ware—cook and serve food in the same lovely dishes! Boil, fry, roast, bake—do it all in Ceramic Ware. Freeze food in the same dishes, if you wish. These beautiful utensils, made of the same amazing ceramic used in missile cones, can go from freezer to stove to table. You then slip them into the dishwasher or the sink with the other dishes. Never slave at scouring pans again.

   B: Sounds good.

3. **salesperson 推销员**

   【知识点】专业的推销人员应该具备良好的品性，应当具有广博的知识，应当很好地支配自己的时间，应当对自己的工作和产品充满激情。他们的推销宣传应该以产品的实用性和会带给客户何种益处为根本，而不是仅仅介绍产品本身或产品的外在形式。在面对客户时，要事先想好客户可能会感兴趣的话题，要能使气氛活跃起来，言语上不能过火或者过于刻板。在谈话中，推销人员可以从轻松的话题开始，灵活自然地过渡到推销的正题上。

   优秀的推销员除了要有说服力、自信心和洞悉顾客心理的能力外，还要能经常介绍公司的最新或最畅销的产品。可以说 "This is our newest product." 或 "This is our most recently developed product."（这是我公司最新产品。）甚至还可以强调 "They are of the newest patterns that can be obtained in town."（这个款式目前在市面上绝无仅有。）面对令人眼花缭乱的产品，特色是顾客考虑的要素之一。所以，把 "Its durability will be an agreeable surprise to you."（它的耐久性将让您吃惊）常挂嘴边是必要的。

4. **showroom 展室**

   【知识点】多数客户都秉持"眼见为实"的审慎做法，所以带客户参观样品展览室，可以帮助客户建立对公司产品的信心。你不妨主动提出带客户参观样品展览室。参观样品展览室是你向客户大力推销公司产品的大好时机。你必须针对参观时客户感兴趣的产品重点解说。当客户对某个环节有疑问或心存疑虑时，推销员要充满信心，措辞有力，详细说明公司产品的优点，这样才能吸引客户，促成交易。

【技能训练句型】

A: Would you like to have a look at our showroom?

B: I'd love to.

A: This way, please.

B: Oh, you have got a large collection of sample medicines.

A: We make two kinds of things: medicines to fight disease and products for health care. Look, that's a new product we've just developed.

B: What's it about?

A: It is manufactured with traditional Chinese medicinal herbs. It can cure sporadic hair loss and baldness. This series of drugs has been exported to many countries. And the demand is getting greater and greater.

5. advertisement 广告

【知识点】广告是一种很好的推销宣传公司产品的方式，但是每一个公司都必须确定哪一种广告媒介最适合自己的产品。做出这种判定的影响因素，一是媒介的费用，二是目标对象是否可接触到该媒介。

【技能训练句型】

A: What kind of advertising will you do for us?

B: Many kinds. We can announce your superior quality through mass media including radio, TV, or newspaper. We can print it on posters and send them to citizens by direct mail. We can imprint it on thousands and thousands of ceramic mugs and caps. All these will create a large market for your products.

6. online sales 网上交易

【知识点】网上交易主要是以网络为载体或传播媒介，对产品和服务进行宣传推销，利用电子商务的各种手段，达成买卖的虚拟交易过程。网上交易的市场范围超越了传统意义上的市场范围。能跨越国界进行交易，使得国际贸易进一步多样化。互联网为企业提供了全球范围的商务空间，能跨越时空，组织世界各地商务人士参与同一项目的运作，或者利用跨境电子商务平台向全球的消费者展示并销售新上市的产品。

【技能训练句型】

Nowadays, online sales are becoming a popular way to push sales.

当今，网上交易正在成为十分流行的推销产品的方式。

Part D Practice

I. Complete the Following Dialogues

(1)

A: Our new products have been sold in a number of areas abroad. They sell like ___1___ cakes.

B: The exhibits in the showroom certainly look ___2___.

Chapter 17 Sales Promotion

A: I'm sure they will sell well in your market, too.

B: I'm willing to ___3___ your products a try, but your delivery must be ___4___ to sample.

A: Certainly. It's our ___5___ in business to honor the contract and keep our promise. Here is some technical data. We also have a video which ___6___ the operation of our latest products.

B: That'll be ___7___ great help.

A: If you like, I can ___8___ a meeting with our technician, who can give you an ___9___ understanding of our products.

B: Good. I'm looking forward ___10___ meeting him.

(2)

A: Did you see our catalogues?

B: Yes.

A: How do feel about our new product?

B: I'm favorably ___1___. Your catalogues say that you have more than 20 ___2___ with over 100 designs, right?

A: Yes. I hope this is a big enough collection for you to ___3___ from.

B: Well, we think the Christmas teddy bears are cute. You know teddy bears are very ___4___ here, and the holiday season is coming.

A: Yes, I know. And I'm sure our well-made teddy bears will ___5___ your satisfaction.

B: What materials are they made of?

A: We have a variety of ___6___ such as cloth, velvet, linen, flannel, etc. You can order whichever you like.

B: Great. What ___7___ do you have?

A: Usually we have 5 sizes, mini, small, ___8___, large and extra large. We can also have the toys made to customers' ___9___. So if you have your own designs and ask for special sizes, please ___10___ us know.

II. Role-plays

Task 1

The teacher divides students into groups. Students make dialogues and role-play them.

Discussion is held between the host and the visitor about the samples of products according to the following hints.

Student A plays the host, Mr. Fang, the sales manager of a carpet company. Student B is Jack, a businessperson from Austria. Student A's role: As a sales manager of a carpet company, you are now having a talk with a businessman from Austria about your products, trying to persuade him to buy your products. Student B's role: You are a businessperson from Austria. This is your first visit to China. You are not sure whether you can close a deal or not. After visiting the showroom, you find some items very attractive. So you ask a few questions.

Task 2

Short conversations.

Suppose you meet an old customer, Mr. Brown, who comes to your company. Mr. Brown want to do business with your company again, so you discuss about how to push sales with him.

III. Guided Talking

Work in pairs.

Zhang Hua from ABC Company comes to MIG Health Products Company which his own company hasn't established business contact with before. First he persuades Mr. White, the manager in MIG Health Products Company to listen to his promotion. Then he tries his best to describe the strong points of his company's new product. For example, it has fine quality and reasonable price. Finally the manager agrees to give ABC Company's new product a try.

IV. Creative Discussion

The teacher divides the class into groups and asks them to discuss, then choose the representatives of each group after discussion. The student who expresses well will be the winner.

Topics:

1. Promotion, especially sales promotion, is very important in our daily life. What tips have you got? Please discuss with your partner about how to make promotion effectively.

2. Talk about your experience in online sales.

Chapter 18

Interview

Learning Objectives
Upon completion of this chapter, you will be able to

- talk about job applications and interviews.
- learn some etiquettes when attending an interview.
- know how to perform well at an interview.
- strengthen confidence in the path, theory, system and culture of socialism with Chinese characteristics.[1]

---

1 加强中国特色社会主义道路自信、理论自信、制度自信和文化自信。

Part A Situational Dialogue

At the Reception Desk

(*Mr. Liu has just graduated from the university. Looking for a job, today he will take part in an interview. He walks towards the receptionist, Miss Gao, who welcomes the applicants.*)

Liu: Good morning.

Gao: Good morning, sir. What can I do for you?

Liu: I'm coming for an interview at nine o'clock this morning. I received a call the day before yesterday, informing me of my interview.

Gao: I see. So can I have your name, please?

Liu: Sure, my name is Liu Feng.

Gao: (*Taking a quick glimpse at the name list.*[1])

Oh, yes, your number is 6. Would you please sit there and wait a moment? I'll call your name when it is your turn.

Liu: OK, thank you.

(*About twenty minutes later, Miss Gao gestures to Mr. Liu.*)

Gao: Mr. Liu, it's your turn now. Our interviewers are waiting for you in Room 201. Please come this way!

Liu: OK! You are so kind, thank you!

Gao: Don't mention it. Good luck to you!

Liu: Thank you very much.

Gao: You're welcome.

At the Interview

(*When Mr. Liu enters the interviewing room, the personnel manager, Miss Lin and her colleagues are waiting for him.*)

Liu: Good morning. My name is Liu Feng.

Lin: Good morning, Mr. Liu. Nice to meet you, I'm Lin Qing from Personnel Section. Just sit down, please.

Liu: Thank you, Miss Lin.

Lin: I see by your resume that you have just graduated from college. Please tell me something about yourself.

Liu: I've just graduated from Peking University, and I studied Economics, with an emphasis on International Trade. ²

Lin: How were your scores at university?

Liu: They were excellent. I worked hard and I made fine records in almost every examination. I've got scholarship on merit.³ You can see it from my resume.

Lin: And you know our company is a very large international trading company. It has offices in over 10 countries. You would be using mainly English on this job, so how do you describe your English ability?

Liu: I think I have a good command of English.⁴ I'm proficient in both written and spoken English.⁵ I have passed CET-6 and I got high scores in almost every exam.

Lin: Well, I can see it from your resume. How do you think the education you've received will contribute to your work in this company?⁶

Liu: My specialization at the university is just in line with the areas your company deals with.⁷ I'm sure I can apply what I have learned to the work in your company.

Lin: What kind of personality do you think you have?

Liu: I'm not sure what information you'd like to know about me. Well, I approach things very enthusiastically, I think, and I don't like to leave something half-done. It makes me nervous. I can't concentrate on something else until the first thing is finished.⁸ In all, I think I'm an ambitious, self-motivated person and I always keep my promise.⁹

Lin: Well, I really appreciate that. Would you describe yourself as outgoing or more reserved?¹⁰

Liu: Well, I'm not really sure, maybe partly both. Sometimes I want to be by myself, but most of the time I prefer being with a group of people. I was very active in my university club.

Lin: Are you more of a follower or a leader?¹¹

Liu: I don't try to get in front of people and lead them, particularly. I'd rather cooperate with everybody else, and get the job done by working together.

Communicative Scene 3

The Interview Continued

(Miss Lin exchanges opinions with her colleagues sitting beside her.)

Lin: Why did you choose our company? There are so many foreign trading companies in this city.

Liu: Because yours is one of the most effective and respectable companies in our city. You provide your employees with an open, team-based environment. I am also aware that you provide a mentor for all new employees. I'll embrace any opportunity to work with a mentor and I think working in this company would provide me with more opportunities to use my knowledge.[12]

Lin: But you have no experience, why should I hire you?

Liu: Lack of experience doesn't mean inability. Theoretically, I have learned what international trade is and how it works. And I feel strongly that my enthusiasm, diligence and adaptability could compensate. I sincerely believe that I'm the best person for the job. Please give me a chance to prove my ability!

Lin: How about overtime work? You know, sometimes we are so busy, so you have to work overtime. Do you have any complaint if you have to work on the night shift?

Liu: Of course not. I think it's a natural thing.

Lin: Although you haven't asked anything about the salary, I think you'd like to know it. What salary are you expecting?

Liu: I would accept the starting salary in your company of my qualification. But I hope raises are given according to my ability. Your firm has a reputation of compensating employees fairly and I trust you would do the same in my case.[13]

Lin: OK! Is there anything else you'd like to ask me before we terminate the interview?

Liu: When can I know whether I'm accepted or not?

Lin: We'll notify you of our decision by early next week if you're wanted.[14] But we'll have to take you on three months' probation first. That's our usual practice.

Liu: I understand.

Lin: All right. Thank you for coming today, Mr. Liu.

Liu: Thank you for giving me the opportunity, Miss Lin. I hope to see you again.

Lin: Good luck to you.

Liu: Thank you, Miss Lin. Goodbye.

Words and Expressions

1. glimpse	n.	一瞥，一看
2. Personnel Section		人事部
3. scholarship on merit		学业成绩优良奖学金
4. proficient	adj.	精通的，熟练的
5. specialization	n.	专业
6. enthusiastically	adv.	热心地，热情地
7. ambitious	adj.	有雄心壮志的
8. self-motivated		自我激励的，主动的
9. mentor	n.	导师
10. embrace	v.	接受，拥抱
11. theoretically	adv.	理论地，从理论上来讲
12. diligence	n.	勤奋，勤勉

13. adaptability	n.	适应性
14. compensate	v.	补偿
15. overtime work		加班
16. night shift		夜班
17. qualification	n.	资格
18. probation	n.	试用期

Notes

1. Taking a quick glimpse at the name list.
   快速地看了一下名单。
   glimpse at 匆匆看一下，瞥一下
   例句：
   > He took a glimpse at himself in the mirror.
   > 他瞥了一眼镜子中的自己。

2. I studied Economics, with an emphasis on International Trade.
   我学经济，主修国际贸易。
   emphasis on (upon) 强调，重点
   例句：
   > This is a new economic policy, with a greater emphasis on reducing inflation.
   > 这是一项更加强调降低通货膨胀的新经济政策。

3. I worked hard and I made fine records in almost every examination. I've got scholarship on merit.
   我很努力学习并几乎在每一场考试里都取得了好成绩。我是奖学金的获得者。
   ① make fine records 得高分
   ② prize fellow 奖学金获得者

4. I think I have a good command of English.
   我觉得我英语学得很好。
   have a good command of 在……方面很在行，精通
   例句：
   > He has a good command of French.
   > 他精通法语。

5. I'm proficient in both written and spoken English.
   我英语口语和书面能力都很强。
   be proficient in (at) 精通……
   例句：
   > She is proficient in / at operating the computer.
   > 她精通计算机操作。

6. How do you think the education you've received will contribute to your work in this company?
   你觉得你在学校里受到的教育能够应用到我们公司的工作当中去吗？

contribute to 起促成作用

例句：

The new policy contributes greatly to the commercial growth to the country.

新政策大大地促进了这个国家商业的发展。

7. My specialization at the university is just in line with the areas your company deals with.

我在学校里学的专业和你们公司所处的领域是对口的。

in line with 和……在一条直线（水平线）上的，和……一致的

例句：

The wheel at the back isn't in line with the one at the front.

后轮和前轮没有保持在一条直线上。

8. I can't concentrate on something else until the first thing is finished.

除非一件事做完，否则我无法专心做其他事情。

concentrate on (upon) 集中（思想、精力、注意力等）

例句：

This year the company has concentrated on improving its efficiency.

这家公司今年致力于提高效率。

9. I always keep my promise.

我总是信守诺言。

keep promise 信守诺言

例句：

If you make a promise you should keep it.

假如你做了承诺，就要守信。

10. Would you describe yourself as outgoing or more reserved?

你说自己性格是外向型还是内向型的?

① outgoing *adj.* 好交际的，外向的

例句：

We need an outgoing person to receive our foreign visitors.

我们需要一个善于交际的人来接待我们的外国客人。

② reserved *adj.* 沉默寡言的，含蓄的，内向的

例句：

Bob is very reserved——you never know what he's thinking.

鲍伯相当沉默寡言——你决不会知道他在想什么。

11. Are you more of a follower or a leader?

你是一个从众者，还是一个领导者?

① follower和leader 在这里分别指"跟随者，被领导者"和"领导者"。

② more of 更多的……

例句：

Can I have some more of that apple pie this time?

我可以再来一些苹果派吗?

12. I'll embrace any opportunity to work with a mentor and I think working in this company would provide me with more opportunities to use my knowledge.

    我会珍惜每一个和前辈工作的机会，而且我相信在贵公司工作会给我提供更多的机会学以致用。

    ① embrace v. 接受

    to embrace an opportunity 很高兴有机会……

    ② to provide sb. with sth. 为提供……

    例句：

    These letters should provide us with all the information we need.
    这些信函为我们提供所需要的全部信息。

13. I trust you would do the same in my case.

    我相信你们也会对我一视同仁。

    in one's case 就……情况而言

    例句：

    Jane's bad results were partly due to illness, but in John's case / in the case of John, no such excuse is possible.
    简的成绩不好，部分原因是由于她生病，但就约翰的情况而言，这样的理由却站不住脚。

14. We'll notify you of our decision by early next week if you're wanted.

    如果你被录用，我们会在下周初通知你的。

    notify sb. of sth. 通知某人某事

    例句：

    You will be notified of any changes in the system.
    系统有任何变化你都会接到通知。

 Part B Practical Key Sentences

1. **Please tell me ...**

   Please tell me something about yourself.
   请谈谈你个人的一些情况。

   替换表达：

   Would you mind answering a few personal questions?

   Would you begin by telling me something about yourself?

   Can you tell me something about yourself?

   Would you please say something about yourself?

2. **How are your scores ...**

   How were your scores at university?
   你在大学里成绩如何？

替换表达：

  How were your grades in college?

  What grades did you get at university?

3. What kind of personality ...

What kind of personality do you think you have?

你认为你是什么样的人？

替换表达：

  How would you describe yourself?

  How do you feel about yourself?

面试中询问个性的表达方式还有：

  Would you describe yourself as outgoing or more reserved?

  你性格外向还是内向？

替换表达：

  Do you think you are more outward-looking or more inward-looking?

  Are you more of a follower or a leader?

  Are you a team player?

4. Why do you choose ...

Why did you choose our company?

你为什么选择我们公司？

替换表达：

  Why you are interested in working at our company?

  What made you decide on choosing our company?

  Why do you want to work for our company?

5. Why should we hire ...

Why should I hire you?

我为什么要录用你呢？

替换表达：

  Why should we offer you the job?

  Why are you the best person for the job?

6. What salary ...

What salary are you expecting?

你期望拿到多少薪水？

替换表达：

  What is your expected salary?

  What are your salary expectations?

  If you are accepted, how much salary would you expect?

  How much do you wish to have for your salary?

  What kind of salary are you seeking/looking for?

Part C Integration of Theory and Practice

1. dress for interview success   面试成功的着装

【知识点】职业面试时对着装有一定的讲究，以下是获得面试成功的着装建议。

Men's wear：

（1） Conservative two-piece suit

（2） Necktie should be silk with a conservative pattern

（3） Short hair

（4） Dark shoes

（5） Dark socks

（6） No beards

（7） No rings other than wedding ring

（8） No earrings

Lady's garment:

（1） Conservative suit

（2） Shoes with conservative heels

（3） Conservative socks at or near skin color

（4） Carry a briefcase, not a purse

（5） You'd better have no nail polish

（6） Minimal use of makeup (it should not be too noticeable)

（7） No more than one ring on each hand

（8） One set of earrings only

2. some standard interview questions   标准的面试问题

【知识点】面试的问题常涉及个人信息、教育背景、工作经验、申请理由、工作要求、兴趣爱好和与工作相关的问题。

（1） Personal information（个人信息）：

① Where is your birthplace?

② Are you a resident of Shanghai now?

③ What is your nationality?

④ How large is your family?

⑤ Would you talk about your merits?

⑥ What kind of personality do you think you have?

⑦ Are you a team player?

⑧ Do you handle pressure well?

⑨ What are your greatest strength and your greatest weakness?

（2） Educational background（教育背景）：

① Can you talk about your educational background?

② What department did you study in?

③ What subjects were you doing?

④ How about your scores at college?

⑤ Have you received any honors or rewards at college?

（3） Working experience (工作经验):

① Have you worked as a secretary?

② Could you tell me what was your last job?

③ Did you make any notable achievements or receive any honors in the company?

（4） Reasons for applying (申请理由):

① Why should I hire you?

② Why did you choose this career?

③ When did you decide on this career?

④ What do you know about our company?

⑤ Why are you interested in our company?

（5） Hobbies and interests (兴趣爱好):

① Do you have any hobbies? What is it or what are they?

② How do you spend your spare time?

③ What kind of books are you interested in?

④ What do you usually do when you are free?

（6） Salary (工资):

① How much are you looking for?

② How much do you expect if we offer this position to you?

③ What kind of salary are you worth?

3. how to write a resume 如何写简历

（1） 【知识点】The Content of Your Resume:

① Full name (pinyin and Chinese Characters)

  姓名（拼音及汉字）

  Former name(s) (Maiden, Religious, Professional, Aliases)

  曾用名（婚前姓名、教名、职业名、别名）

② Present address (postal zone)

  现在住址（邮政编码）

  Telephone number

  电话号码

③ Date of birth (day, month, year)

  出生日期（日、月、年）

④ Place of birth (city, province, country)

  出生地点（市、省、国）

  Nationality or citizenship

  国籍

⑤ Sex (female, male)

性别（女、男）

Marital status (married, single, widowed, divorced)

婚姻状况（已婚、未婚、鳏寡、离婚）

⑥ Height and weight and health

身高、体重与健康状况

⑦ What is your present job/occupation?

现有的工作、职业

Post of rank held at present

现在的职位

⑧ Employment record/Experience

经历

Names and addresses of firms or organizations to which you belonged

曾供职过的公司或机关名称和地址

Principal former positions

曾任职过的主要职位

Reasons for leaving

离职原因

⑨ Education (Qualification)

学历

Schools attended (including middle school, technical school, college, etc.)

曾就读过的学校名称（包括中学、技校、大学等）

School transcripts

学习成绩单

⑩ Professional experience and skills

专业技能

除了上述十项内容外，如果应聘者曾有著作、论文出版、发表等，也要一并附上。

（2）【知识点】一份好的简历，应做到以下几点：

① 简明扼要、完整无缺。

要做一份好的简历，首要的一条就是要简明，同时也要注意完整，学习经历和工作经历都要包括在内。

写简历时，如果用表格形式，就不必用完整的文句来述说经历，应尽量写得简要。但对一些学校、单位、公司等的名称，却不可用缩略语，而要写出全称，以免造成不必要的误会。

② 工作经历和资历要详而全。

为了让主试人员对应聘者的工作能力和成绩有一个充分全面的了解，应聘者必须将所任的工作和职务、取得过何种评语和嘉奖，尽量在主试人员面前展示出来。

③ 语言要规范，用词要得当。

所谓语言规范，指的是从语法、拼写、标点各个方面都要正确，符合习惯；同时，在填写简历时要注意实事求是，不可言过其实，但也不要妄自菲薄。

④ 简历表要打印出来。

个人简历表要打印在16开大小的全白纸上。

（3）【技能训练】Sample Resume

Name: Lin Hao

Address: No. 128 Lianghua Road. Gulou District. Fuzhou

Postal: 350001

Telephone Number: 135093729XX

Birth Date and Birth Place: October 13, 2000

Sex: Female

Marital Status: Single

Height: 162cm

Weight: 45kg

Health Condition: Excellent

Education:

    2022.9-2024.6 Dept. of Automation, Graduate School of Tsinghua University

    2018.9-2022.7 Dept. of Automation, Beijing Institute of Technology

English Skills

    Have a good command of both spoken and written English. Past CET-6.
TOEFL: 105; GRE: 330

Scholarships and Awards

    2023.3   Guanghua first-class scholarship for graduate

    2021.3   second-class scholarship

    2020.3   first-class scholarship

Qualifications

    General business knowledge relating to financial, healthcare

    Have a passion for the Internet, and an abundance of common sense

Part D Practice

I. Complete the Following Dialogue

(*A is an applicant, and B is the personnel manager.*)

A: Good morning. Mr. Smith.

B: Good morning, Mr. Liu. Please ___1___.

A: Thank you.

B: I've learnt from your ___2___ that you have just graduated from the college. Please ___3___.

A: I've just graduated from Xiamen University, and I studied commerce, with an ___4___ on foreign trade.

B: How's your ____5____ at university?

A: I got high scores in almost every examination. You can see it from my resume.

B: Do you think your English is quite good? Tell me something about your English education.

A: I think I have a good ____6____ of English. My English teacher has said that my English is quite good, and I scored high in a TOEFL test last year. I am ____7____ in both written and spoken English.

B: Very well. Can I ask you what made you ____8____ our company?

A: A friend of mine works here. And he told me about your company.

B: I see. It's been pleasant talking with you, Mr. Liu. We'll ____9____ you of our decision by next Monday. If you're accepted, we'll put you on six months' ____10____ first. Good luck!

A: Thank you. Mr. Smith. Good bye.

II. Oral Translation

A： 你好，我是人事处经理彼得。

B： 很高兴见到你。

A： 请先谈谈你的学历情况吧。

B： 一年前我从汕头大学毕业。我的专业是英语语言和文学。

A： 你认为你的英语好吗？

B： 是的，我的英语很好。在学校几乎每一次考试我都得高分。在英语专业八级的考试中我也取得了很好的成绩。我还是学生时，就有好几家公司请我去当翻译。

A： 很好。什么原因使你选择我们公司呢？

B： 贵公司有很好的名誉。我想在贵公司工作将会给我提供很多的机会，使我学有所用。

A： 我知道了，和你交谈很愉快。下星期前我们就会通知你结果的。

B： 谢谢。

III. Situational Talks

Task 1

Suppose you are a manager of a company and a job applicant is coming for an interview. You'll ask about his educational background, foreign language abilities and working experience, reasons for applying.

Task 2

You apply for the sales marketing position, but it is very competitive. Please try your best to convince the personnel manager that you are well qualified for the position.

IV. Practical Questions and Answers

Discuss the following questions with your classmates.

1. You are a manager of a certain company. In an interview, you want to know whether the applicant can speak English well or not. How do you ask?

2. You are an applicant for a job in a company. When you are asked why you pick their company, what would you answer?

3. You are working in a small company and the salary is low. When you are asked why you want to change your job, what would you answer?

V. Writing

Try to write a resume according to your own situation.

Work in pairs and write a letter of application.

VI. Creative Discussion

1. The teacher divides the class into groups and asks them to discuss, then chooses the representatives of each group after discussion. The student who expresses well will be the winner.

Topics:

(1) What is the most important thing in choosing a job?

(2) Do you design the presentations yourself?

2. Mock interview.

The teacher and some students will act as interviewers and the students will practice in turn as an interviewee.

Chapter 19

Complaints

Learning Objectives
Upon completion of this chapter, you will be able to

- learn how to make complaints to the seller.
- learn how to settle a claim.
- conduct the activities related to complaints.
- serve the overall, basic and long-term interest of the country.[1]

---

1 立足于国家整体利益、根本利益和长远利益。

No Spam Please!

(Jenny logged in a website and signed up, yet never expected the endless spam. She pours out her experience to her friend.)

Jenny: This almost drives me mad!

Shelley: What's up?

Jenny: My mailbox is stuffed with Spam.

Shelley: What for?

Jenny: I browsed the eBay[1] and was interested in an article of a cyber store, so I signed up for more information about their commodity.[2]

Shelley: So they served you information as you wished...

Jenny: OK, but later I didn't like their solicitation, and have requested numerous times to be taken off the mailing list, and they have promised to do it each time but I still get mail...

Shelley: Understandable, so you got hooked by them.

Jenny: Yes, but now after hundreds of requests via fax and phone, they act like I'm the one harassing them...

Shelley: I think you can get yourself removed out of the Spam list with certain instructions given on the Internet.[3] When a consumer no longer wishes to get mail, the company has an obligation to stop sending the mail.

Jenny: I tried, thousands of times...they are just liars. These people are basically refusing to do that. One guy told me "I removed your name myself the day you called". Everything remains. I got mail again yesterday!

Shelley: Gosh... so frustrating...so what are you going to do?

Jenny: Nothing but tit for tat. They continue to lie and I keep getting mail so I will continue to call, fax and e-mail until they stop. If they don't want calls in the middle of the night, they shouldn't send me mail with their cell phone numbers on it, right?

Commercial Fraud

(*A women made a call to Complaints Center to expose a commercial fraud.*[4])

Clerk: Complaints Center. Can I help you?
Madame: Ah... afternoon, it's terrific for me to have somewhere to complain.
Clerk: Glad to serve you, Madame, what is it?
Madame: Well, Horizon Travel Company duped us. Two years ago, <u>my husband and I attended their presentation on timeshares.</u>[5]
Clerk: Didn't you refuse to buy anything?
Madame: How couldn't we buy? <u>The sales men persisted for several hours sweetening with all manners of inducements</u>[6] and they promised us free trips to Vegas. At last I bought their timeshare points.
Clerk: So you got the free trips?
Madame: No, the free trip is fixed on certain days. <u>Unforeseen problems came up with our child,</u>[7] so we gave it up. But the nuisance is that recently I called to book a trip and found I have no points left at all.
Clerk: How come?
Madame: I don't know, I thought I had accumulated points since I had never used it, but I was told I actually lost them for paying to be in the club. Their representatives had never mentioned the surprise maintenance fees on a membership. <u>If all that had been stated up front that I would not have signed anything.</u>[8]
Clerk: OK, I have noted down your complaint. We will accept your complaint and transfer the case to relative administrations as soon as possible.
Madame: Thank you. I will never again attend one of these fiascos. I knew it sounded too good to be true!

Wrong Shipment

(*Stevenson complains about the wrong shipment. The secretary of his business partner receives his complaint.*)

Stevenson: Morning, I'd like to speak to Mr. Li, your manager of Sales Department.
Secretary: Sorry. He is on vacation now. I'm his secretary responsible for his work during his absence. Can I help you?

259

Stevenson: I'm Stevenson from Holland. I have a complaint to make.

Secretary: What is it?

Stevenson: OK, I'll explain the problem briefly. It's about our order No. 1326 placed 2 months ago. We have received the articles, yet when we opened the carton, we found 1/4 of them contained completely different articles. Obviously you packed the wrong articles and this troubles us a lot.

Secretary: I'm sorry to hear that. I'll go into this matter. If it's really our fault, we'll send you the replacement immediately.

Stevenson: For the time being, we'll hold these wrong articles at your disposal. <u>So it's peak season for the ordered articles,</u>⁹ we need the goods urgently. If we fail to receive the articles in two weeks, <u>we have to cancel that part of the order and ask for refund.</u>¹⁰

Secretary: Even if we made the mistake as you mentioned, it's impossible for us to ship it and let it arrive in 2 weeks.

Stevenson: In that case, <u>you have to make the shipment by airfreight instead of original sea freight.</u>¹¹ By the way, we'll not share the difference between the 2 freight charges.

Secretary: But before I'm clear about this matter, I have no way to talk about shipping the replacement. Please send us the inspection report and pictures by fax or e-mail, I'll let you know the result as soon as possible.

...

Secretary: I'm sorry, we indeed made a mistake in packing through a confusion of numbers. Since it's our fault, we'll dispatch the right goods by airfreight and pay the difference between freight charges as you will. You know, <u>the freight charge cannot even be covered by the cost of the articles,</u>¹² but we really need your support in that new market.

Stevenson: Business is business. We appreciate your cooperation very much.

Communicative Scene 4

Product Defectiveness

(Mr. White files a complaint against the product defectiveness. Mr. Wang, the representative of the local producer, claims the responsibility and promises to improve QC.)

White: Mr. Wang, we have long been satisfied with the quality of your product, but I am shocked this time.

Wang: What for? Something is wrong with our product?

White: We just received the shipment of our order No. 3261. We discovered the defective percentage is nearly 5%, far beyond the stated 2%. What's wrong?

Wang: How can that be? <u>Every batch is produced to identical standards in design and performance</u>¹³ and was inspected by QC department before being sent out.

White: Seeing is believing. Here are the inspection reports.

Wang: (*Embarrassed*) OK, as your agent here, we're really sorry for that. <u>The Spring Festival is coming and the manufacturer has to run up the order in only one month.</u>[14] Haste makes waste. <u>Maybe this batch of product slipped through the normal examination.</u>[15]

White: So what shall we do?

Wang: We'll send a team immediately to the manufacturer to notify them of the problems and take action to rectify the situation.

White: I mean about our loss...

Wang: We'll also try to negotiate with the suppliers on your behalf, and get the fair compensation from them within the shortest time.

White: I hope you can solve this problem as soon as possible. The defective rate must be kept within 2%.

Wang: I promise we'll improve the quality control. We'll send personnel to supervise on-site. To avoid the same problem, we assure you that we'll inspect the goods more thoroughly and strictly.

White: The most important is to have a qualified supplier. If the situation cannot be rectified, we suggest that you look for another supplier.

Wang: No problem.

Words and Expressions

1. stuff		v.	塞满
2. spam		n.	junk mail 垃圾邮件
3. browse		v.	浏览
4. cyber store			网上商铺
5. sign up			签约，注册
6. solicitation		n.	恳求，征求；诱发；教唆；询价
7. harass		v.	扰乱，骚扰，（使）困扰
8. obligation		n.	义务
9. tit for tat			针锋相对
10. fraud		n.	欺骗
11. dupe		v.	欺骗，愚弄
12. timeshare		n.	分时度假
13. sweeten		v.	变甜；说好话
14. inducement		n.	刺激物
15. stated		adj.	规定的
16. up front			预先
17. membership		n.	会员
18. fiasco		n.	惨败，大失败
19. for the time being			暂时
20. at one's disposal			由某人做主

21. refund		n.	偿还额，退款
22. defectiveness		n.	有缺陷，缺乏
23. batch		n.	一批
24. run up			赶制
25. haste makes waste			欲速则不达
26. rectify		vt.	矫正，调整
27. compensation		n.	补偿，赔偿
28. on-site			现场

Notes

1. I browsed the eBay.

   我在易趣网上购物中心闲逛。

   ① eBay *n.* 易趣，购物网

   ② browse through 浏览

   例句：

   I was browsing through a newspaper when I spotted your name.

   我们通过报纸得知贵公司。

2. I signed up for more information about their commodity.

   我注册以希望得到更多的有关他们产品的信息。

   ① sign up (for) 经报名参加（课程学习）

   ② sign in / (out) 签到/签名登记离开

   例句：

   Remember to sign in at the reception.

   记得到报到处登记。

3. I think you can get yourself removed out of the Spam list with certain instructions given on the Internet.

   我想按照网上的说明，你应该能够自己退出他们的联系人列表吧！

   removed from (a place) / (a job) 迁移/开除

   例句：

   Our office has removed from Boston to New York.

   我们的办公地址从波士顿迁到了纽约。

   The merciless boss removed poor Tony from his beloved position.

   无情的老板开除了可怜的托尼，他离开了钟爱的岗位。

4. A women made a call to Complaints Center to expose a commercial fraud.

   一位女士致电投诉中心投诉一桩商业欺诈。

   Complaints Center

   投诉受理中心

5. My husband and I attended their presentation on timeshare.
   我和丈夫参加了他们分时度假项目的推介会。
   timeshare 分时度假（又称vacation ownership或 holiday ownership），最初是指人们在度假地购买房产时，只购买部分时段的产权，几户人家共同拥有一处房产。共同维护、分时使用的度假形式，后来逐渐演变成每户人家在每年只拥有某一段的度假地房产使用权，并且可以通过交换系统对不同房产的使用权实行交换。
   国际上一度通行的惯例是：将一处住宿设施（如饭店、公寓、度假别墅等）的住宿单元每年的使用期分为52周，将52周中的51周分时销售给顾客。每个单位的分时度假产品，就是在约定的时期内（一般为20~40年）每年在这一住宿单元中住宿一周的权利。

6. The sales men persisted for several hours sweetening with all manner of inducements.
   那些推销员缠了我们几小时，以各种各样的优惠来讨好我们。
   ① manners *n.* 方式，方法
   例句：
   　　I object to being repeatedly dropped on in this manner.
   　　我反对用这种方式屡次被挑中。
   ② manners *n.* 礼貌，礼仪
   例句：
   　　She has good / no manners.
   　　她很有/没有礼貌。
   　　Where are your manners?
   　　你的礼貌哪儿去了？（指某人，尤指孩子，不懂礼貌）

7. Unforeseen problems came up to our child.
   我们的孩子出了点意外。
   ① come up 出现或发生
   例句：
   　　Your name came up in our conversation once or twice.
   　　你的名字在我们的谈话中被提到了一两次。
   ② come up to sth. 比得上，达到
   例句：
   　　This doesn't come up to the standard of your usual work.
   　　这次你们的工作有失水准。

8. If all that had been stated up front that I would not have signed anything.
   要是预先说明（要交纳会员费）的话，我才不会签约呢！

9. So it's peak season for the ordered articles.
   所以，现在是我们所订货品的销售旺季。
   ① peak season 销售旺季
   ② reach your peak 达到巅峰时期
   例句：
   　　Most athletes have reached their peak by the time they're 20.

大多数运动员20岁时已达到巅峰时期。

10. We have to cancel that part of the order and ask for refund.
    我们不得不撤销这部分订单并要求退款。
    ① refund *n.* 退款
    ② allow (make) no refund 不予退款
    ③ give (pay) a refund 给付退款

11. You have to make the shipment by airfreight instead of original sea freight.
    你们必须以空运代替原先的海运出货。
    ① airfreight *n.* 空运
    ② seafreight *n.* 海运
    ③ freight charge 运费
    例句：
    We'll not share the difference between the two freight charges.
    我们不会分担两种运费的差价。
    ④ share *v.* 分担
    share responsibility 分担责任
    share the cost 分担费用

12. The freight charge cannot even be covered by the cost of the articles.
    运费甚至不抵货款。
    ① cover for sb. 代替（某人的工作）
    例句：
    Who's going to cover for you when you're on holiday?
    度假期间谁接替你的工作？
    ② cover sth. up 掩饰，隐瞒
    例句：
    The whole thing was very well covered up and never reached the newspapers.
    整个事情都被巧妙地隐瞒起来，始终没有在报纸上曝光。

13. Every batch is produced to identical standards in design and performance.
    每一批货都是按照相同的设计和性能标准来生产的。
    ① performance *n.*（机器或汽车的）性能
    例句：
    The car's performance on mountain roads was impressive.
    这辆汽车在山路上表现出的性能给人留下深刻的印象。
    ② performance *n.*（工作或活动中的）表现
    例句：
    Jodie's performance in the exams was disappointing.
    乔迪的考试成绩令人失望。

14. The Spring Festival is coming and the manufacturer has to run up the order in only one month.
    春节就要来了，厂家不得不在一个月内赶完所有的订单。

run up a bill 积欠账款
例句：
> She ran up an enormous phone bill.
> 她积欠了很多电话费。

15. Maybe this batch of product slipped through the normal examination.
也许这批货漏检了。
① slip *v.* 滑倒；下降
例句：
> Sales slip sharply last year.
> 去年的销售量急剧下降。

② slip through the net 漏网，未受到有关部门的处理

Part B Practical Key Sentences

1. **I have a complaint to make**

   I want to file (make) a complaint.
   我要投诉。
   替换表达：
   > I complain that…
   > I complain about…
   > I'm not satisfied with…
   > Really, I'm fed up with your…
   > I've just about had enough of that.
   > For God's sake, could you keep silent for a while?

2. **submit a complaint**

   You'd better settle down the mess before she lodges an official complaint.
   最好在她没有正式起诉之前，就把乱子摆平。
   The BBC received a stream of complaints against this program.
   BBC（英国广播公司）源源不断地收到了对这个节目的投诉。
   替换表达：
   > The buyer files a complaint against the poor quality of exercises machines.
   > Many consumers lodge complaints against the safety of the toys.

3. **grounds for complaint**

   The loss we suffered in this business gives us the grounds for complaint.
   这笔生意损失惨重，我们当然有理由投诉。
   Our main complaint is the poor standard of the service.
   我们投诉主要是因为服务质量差。

替换表达：

The reasons for complaint is that the products slipped through the normal examination.

The cause for complaint is due to the discovery of high percentage of defective products.

4. going into the matter

We'll study the letter of complaint and inquiry into the case.

我会关注投诉函并调查这件事情。

替换表达：

I'll examine this matter thoroughly and give a refund if necessary.

Let's investigate the complaints and solve the problem as soon as possible.

Part C Integration of Theory and Practice

在商务活动中，买卖双方来电抱怨的情形时有发生，抱怨的问题也多种多样。

1. 在接到货物之前，买方可能会抱怨出货速度太慢。

【技能训练句型】

George: We need to know if you shipped our order no. SW-012 by the end of July. Have you sent out the shipping advice?

我必须知道你们是否已于七月底装出我们的订单SW-012，何时可以给我们出货通知？

Lily: Sorry, this order will be delayed to August 15.

抱歉，这张订单要延迟到8月15日。

2. 买方抱怨出货速度太慢时，卖方要能提出适当理由，并和买方协商，否则买方可能会要求取消订单或者要求卖方改空运出货并负担空运费。卖方发货延迟的理由有很多：

【技能训练句型】

① 船期不对。There is no vessel available this week.

② 生产荷载过大。The production line is over booked / due to too tight a schedule.

③ 生产期内公共假日过多。There are too many holidays this month.

④ 不良率太高。The defective rate is too high.

⑤ 进口原料逾期。The imported raw material has been delayed for two weeks.

3. 【知识点】如果是买方过失，例如信用证开出较慢，卖方就不需要负责任。

【技能训练句型】

George: How about the order now? Our customer needs the goods urgently.

我们的订单现在如何了？我们的顾客急需这批货。

Lily: We understand, but we can't make the shipment without receiving payment.

理解您的处境，但是我们要先收到货款才能出货。

4. 【知识点】如果延迟出货是由不可抗力事件造成的，例如天灾、战争、罢工等，则双方都无责任，此状况下就由买卖双方共同负担所有损失。

Chapter 19　Complaints

【技能训练句型】

George: I'd like to know what's the reason causing the delay in the shipment of our order No. 2423.
我想知道什么原因造成了我方第2423号订单延迟出货。

Lily: As you know, our factory is in the middle of Taiwan and recently there was a serious earthquake that happened there. Our factory has been damaged and we need time to have the factory repaired first.
如您所知，我们工厂在台湾中部，最近那儿发生严重的地震，我们工厂被震坏，需要一些时间修复。

5.【技能训练】接到货物后，买方可能会抱怨以下一些问题：

① Some parts are damaged.
一些零件坏损。

② The quantity is different from that shown on your packing list.
数量与包装表上显示的不符。

③ The color is lighter than that of the sample.
颜色比样品浅。

④ The size is too small to use.
尺寸太小，无法用。

⑤ Some parts are not what we ordered.
有些零件不是我们订购的。

⑥ The defective rate is too high.
不良率太高。

6.【知识点】针对买方收到货物后的赔偿要求，卖方可以先请客户退回不良样品。

【技能训练句型】

Since we did 100% inspection before shipment, we are wondering why the problem happened. Anyway, please send back some defective samples for our evaluation.
由于我们出货前都做100%检验，我们奇怪为何会发生这种问题。无论如何，请先寄回一些不良样品以供评估。

7. 卖方收到不良样品后，先分析原因，再了解问题，之后再确定责任的归属，是买方、卖方、保险公司还是运输公司？如果是卖方的责任，就应依照合同给予赔偿，并提送更正报告。

Part D　Practice

I. Complete the Following Dialogues

(1)

A: I would like to know if you have shipped our order No. 443? When will we be able to get the ___1___（出货通知）？

267

B: Sorry, the shipment has to be put off, because of the shortage of the ___2___ （原材料）, the high ___3___ （缺陷率）on our production, and the delay on ___4___ （模具）, and the serious ___5___ （人力短缺）.

(2)

A: What about the ___1___ （打样样品）we ordered from you?

B: I'm sorry. We're unable to make them according to your ___2___ （规格）.

A: Oh! Why didn't you inform us earlier?

B: We had thought we could make it...Well, we'd like to suggest you use ___3___ （替代品）. It's ___4___ （相当）to your original sample in quality, function and efficiency, but has slightly different ___5___ （外观）. Will that be acceptable to you?

(3)

A: What causes ___1___ （延期发货）of our order No. 285. I've been ___2___ （如坐针毡）for the last few weeks. How's everything going ___3___ （你方）?

B: There was a typhoon ___4___ （袭击）our city last week. Several container cranes at the harbor were damaged. This caused a severe jam ___5___ （装载工作）.

(4)

A: I have a complaint to make about our order No. 443. We found that the quality is different from that of ___1___ （确认样品）.

B: I'm sorry to hear that. Can you give us more details about the problem?

A: Yes, of course. We found that

(1) ___2___ （颜色较浅）than that of the sample.

(2) ___3___ （尺寸）is too small to use.

(3) the quantity is different from that shown on your ___4___ （装箱单）.

(4) ___5___ （一些零件）are not what we ordered.

II. Role-plays

Task 1

Carry out a conversation about a complaint.

Student A refers to paragraph A, and student B refers to paragraph B.

Paragraph A: You placed an order with a company last month. Now you have received the shipment of that order, yet found that some cartons are broken and some parts are damaged. So, the quantity is not enough now. You make a call to that company to complain and ask for more replacement.

Paragraph B: You accepted an order last month. You have delivered the ordered articles to the buyer. Now you receive the complaints from the buyer on the shortage of quantity caused by the defectiveness. You tell the customer there is a carton of spare parts attached with the shipment and you can send more replacements if needed.

Here are some useful expressions:

(1) ABC company, can I help you?

(2) This is ...

(3) We received ..., we found ...

(4) Don't worry. There is ...

(5) What if ...

Task 2

Make up a conversation about a complaint.

Student A refers to paragraph A, and student B refers to paragraph B.

Paragraph A: You work in a "dot com" company and recently you have to work overtime frequently. You have grumbles about this, and complain to your colleague.

Paragraph B: You work in an IT company and recently you and your colleague have to work for more hours per day due to a new task. Your colleague complains about the overtime. You just initiate a talk with him.

Here are some useful expressions:

(1) What's the problem? You have a long face.

(2) I have to work overtime recently and I have no time to ...

(3) I can understand you ... but ...

III. Conversation Activity

Topic: Who is next?

Purpose: Practice Complaining and Persuading

Participants: Whole class

Procedures:

1. The whole class stands up and moves around.

2. Each student takes turns to act both as a customer and then as a shop assistant.

3. The teacher (customer) sets the ball rolling by making a complaint and then asking one student (assistant) to offer the excuses and solutions. The student (assistant) can either accept or refuse the complaint, but he/she must make the customer feel satisfied.

4. After satisfying the customer, the assistant turns to be the customer and hunts for the next assistant in the class.

5. Repeat the above process among the class.

IV. Actual Practice

1. Complain to the given people in the given situations.

(1) You want to return a pair of new pants because you found a hole in them.

(2) Ask a waitress to bring you water with ice because the water she gave you is warm.

(3) You are eating in a restaurant and someone begins to smoke next to you, ask him / her to stop.

2. Respond to these complaints in the restaurant.

(1) Miss, can you ask the cook to heat this food up? It's too cold.

(2) Excuse me, but do you mind if you speak a little softer? I can't speak with the people at my table.

(3) Waiter, there aren't enough chairs for us here.

V. Creative Discussion

Try to write a resume according to your own situation.

Work in pairs and write an applicant's letter of application.

VI. Creative Discussion

The teacher divides the class into groups for discussion. Each group chooses a representative after discussion. The student who expresses well will be the winner.

Topic:

There is an expression in English that "The customer is always right" when a dispute appears between the customers and the sellers. There is also another expression that "Business is business", that is, no sellers would like to lose money in business. How do you keep the balance between satisfying customers and making money?

Chapter 20

Banquet and Parting

Learning Objectives
Upon completion of this chapter, you will be able to

- get familiar with the process of having a banquet.
- know how to communicate with foreigners at the banquet.
- know how to make a toast at the banquet.
- conduct welcome and farewell speeches at the banquet.
- aim high, be practical and realistic.[1]

1　志存高远，脚踏实地。

Part A Situational Dialogue

Communicative Scene 1

At the Table

(Mr. Smith and his colleagues are invited by Ms. Liu, board chairman of the enterprise corporation to a dinner at a restaurant.)

Liu: Good evening, Mr. Smith! Welcome to our dinner party.

Smith: Good evening, Chairman! Thank you for inviting us to dinner.

Liu: You're welcome! First, please allow me to introduce my colleague to you. Mr. Smith, This is Wang Hong, the production manager of our company. And this is Mr. Smith, Vice General Manager of American Electronic Company.

Wang: Pleased to meet you, Mr. Smith.

Smith: It's my pleasure, too.

Liu: Now that everybody knows everybody else,[1] shall we sit and talk?

(They all take seats.)

Smith: I was told that they serve good food here in this restaurant.

Liu: Yes, the food here is excellent. And the service here is also beyond comparison.

Liu: Mr. Smith, I wonder if you have a particular preference?

Smith: Well, when in Rome, do as the Romans do.[2]

Liu: Then I hope that our selection of dishes this evening will be to your liking.[3]

Smith: We have heard a great deal about the famous Chinese dishes and we are looking forward to tasting them.

Liu: So you may also want to use chopsticks as we Chinese do? Of course, you may still use knife and fork if you don't feel confident with chopsticks.

Smith: I'll try chopsticks, but I'm afraid if I use them all the way through, I'll come back to the hotel with a half empty stomach. So, I'll also use knife and fork in case I have problems taming my chopsticks.

(All laugh.)

Liu: And what do you like to drink?

Smith: We'd like to have Chinese drinks. But we haven't got the faintest idea of the Chinese drinks. Would you please recommend me some?

Liu: Yes, of course. We have some famous brands of alcohol, such as Moutai, Wuliangye, Jiannanchun, Kongfu Jiajiu, and so on. And we also have some good red wine and white wine,

Chapter 20 Banquet and Parting

    such as Changyu Red Wine and Great Wall White Wine. Which do you prefer?

Smith: They say that Moutai tastes quite good.

 Liu: Yes. It is one of the most famous liquors in China. It's good indeed. It never goes to the head.

Smith: OK! I'd like to try it.

(*Dinner is served.*)

 Liu: Here are the Chinese cold dishes. <u>Please help yourself and make yourself at home.</u>[4]

Smith: Thank you. These dishes are all delicious.

 Liu: I'm glad you like it. May I help you to some more?

Smith: Thank you, just a small helping.

 Liu: Have some Beijing roast duck, this is one of Beijing's famous delicacies.

Smith: Yes, please. Oh, how delicious! It's tender and crisp. I've never tasted anything like that.

 Liu: Really? So please have some more.

Smith: Thank you. From what I heard about your banquets, there are many more courses to come. So I think I'd better go easy at the beginning.

 Liu: Mr. Smith, you seem to be quite an expert at chopsticks.

Smith: Thank you for encouraging me.

 Liu: How about some prawns?

Smith: Yes, please. It's tasty too.

 Liu: <u>You seem to have a good appetite.</u>[5] (Joking) <u>This calls for a drink.</u>[6] To your health, cheers!

 All: Cheers!

Smith: By the way, what do you say in Chinese for "<u>Bottoms up</u>[7]"?

 Liu: We say "Gan Bei".

Smith: <u>Well, I wish to propose a toast to our friendship and cooperation, Gan Bei!</u>[8]

 Liu: You are learning fast, Mr. Smith. Gan Bei!

Smith: This one is really palatable. What is it?

 Liu: I don't know its English name, but in Chinese we call it "suji", which literally means "vegetarian's chicken".

Smith: Suji? Er, incredibly tasty!

 Liu: Let me help you to some seafood hot pot, the specialty of this restaurant.

Smith: Please. I'm fond of sea food. It's fresh and tasty. And it looks beautiful.

 Liu: Yes, <u>Chinese cuisine places stress on color, aroma and flavor all at the same time.</u>[9] Oh, would you like to have some Jiaozi?

Smith: What is it?

 Liu: It is a kind of boiled dumpling stuffed with minced meat and vegetable.

Smith: Sounds interesting. I'd like to have some.

Smith: <u>This Specially Flavored Chicken really works up my appetite.</u>[10]

 Liu: <u>It seems we have the same taste.</u>[11] Help yourself to some more, please.

Smith: Thank you, but I have to watch my weight.

Make a Toast

(Almost an hour has passed since the dinner started. Chairman Liu clears her throat and stands up with a glass of wine in her hand. Everyone stops talking and turns towards her.)

Mr. Smith,

Ladies and gentlemen:

I don't want to spoil your enjoyment of this evening's festivities with a long and boring speech, but I would just like to say a few words.

On behalf of our company,[12] I would like to say how delighted to have Mr. Smith and his colleagues with us tonight. As the saying goes, "What a joy it is to have friends coming from afar!"[13] Our distinguished guests come from the other side of the earth, so our joy tonight is beyond expression.[14]

I'm glad to tell you that this trip of our American friends has been very fruitful—we've struck a deal worth 30 million dollars and reached an agreement for long-term cooperation, which has sown the seeds for a bright future of our business relations. The only regret is that your stay is too brief, so I look forward to another chance to receive you in China.

I'd like to take this opportunity to propose a toast to the friendship between our two companies, to the prosperity of our two companies, to a pleasant journey tomorrow. Cheers!

All: Bottoms up!

(All the people stand up and raise their glass, then take a sip of wine and clap.)

A Reciprocal Reception

Chairman Liu,

Distinguished guest, ladies and gentlemen:

Thank you for your kind words, Chairman Liu. I'd like to take this opportunity to express our sincere thanks to your nice welcome and hospitality.

I believe we have accomplished a great deal during our brief stay. We have concluded a deal worth 30 million dollars and reached an agreement for long-term cooperation. More importantly, we have seen and talked with your people. We have dined with you, drunk with you, bargained, worried and laughed with you. In all this, our respect has grown, our friendship warmed. We have certainly achieved more than we hoped, and I'd like you all to know that we are most appreciative of your efforts in making this possible.

Tomorrow, my colleagues and I are leaving your beautiful city, but we will remember this pleasant visit all the time. And I hope that one day you can also visit our city so that we can reciprocate your warmness and hospitality.

Now, may I propose a toast? Here is to our hosts, to your good health, and, of course, to our friendship and our mutual cooperation. Cheers!

All: Cheers!

(*Warm flutters of applause. And the next course is served. The dinner goes on for another twenty minutes or so, as does the lively flow of conversation.*)

Words and Expressions

1. board chairman		董事长
2. preference	n.	偏爱，偏爱的东西
3. chopsticks	n.	筷子
4. knife and fork		刀叉
5. tame	v.	驯服
6. helping	n.	（食物的）一份
7. delicacy	n.	佳肴
8. tender and crisp		又脆又嫩
9. prawn	n.	对虾
10. tasty	adj.	美味的
11. cheers	v.	干杯（举杯敬酒之用语）
12. palatable	adj.	可口的，美味的
13. vegetarian	n.	素食（主义）者
14. incredibly	adv.	不可思议地
15. seafood hot pot		海鲜火锅
16. specialty	n.	特色菜
17. cuisine	n.	烹调
18. aroma	n.	芳香；香味
19. flavor	n.	味道
20. dumpling	n.	团子
21. minced meat		肉馅
22. Specially Flavored Chicken		怪味鸡
23. watch my weight		注意我的体重
24. clear her throat		清清喉咙
25. spoil	v.	损坏
26. festivity	n.	欢乐气氛
27. sip	v.	啜

28. reciprocate	v.	回报
29. hospitality	n.	好客
30. flutter	v.	拍打

Notes

1. Now that everybody knows everybody else, ...

   既然大家都互相认识了，……

   now that 既然，由于

   例句：

   > Now that John's arrived, we can begin.
   >
   > 约翰来了，我们可以开始。

2. When in Rome, do as the Romans do.

   入乡随俗（谚语）。

   亦可说：Do in Rome as the Romans do.

   英语中常用的含有Rome的谚语还有：

   All roads lead to Rome.

   条条大路通罗马。

   Rome was not built in a day.

   罗马非一日建成。

3. Then I hope that our selection of dishes this evening will be to your liking.

   那么我期望我们今晚选择的菜肴你们能够喜欢。

   to one's liking 对某人的胃口，合某人的意

   例句：

   > Was the meal to your liking, madam?
   >
   > 太太，饭菜合您的意吗？

4. Please help yourself and make yourself at home.

   请自便，就像在自己家里一样。

   make oneself at home 随便（像在家里一样），不要拘礼

   例句：

   > Make yourself at home while I get some coffee.
   >
   > 随便坐吧，我去倒杯咖啡。

5. You seem to have a good appetite.

   你看来胃口不错。

   在餐桌上一般不评论客人的胃口或体重，以免冒犯客人，但开玩笑时可用这个句子，此处为开玩笑。

   have a good/healthy appetite 胃口好，食欲很好

6. This calls for a drink.

   这值得干一杯。

① call for 要求，提倡

例句：

President Xi called for jointly building the Belt and Road Initiative, and push forward the building of a community with a shared future for mankind.

习主席号召积极共建"一带一路"，推动构建人类命运共同体。

② call for 需要，值得

例句：

Are you getting married? This calls for a celebration.

你要结婚了？这值得大大庆祝一番。

7. Bottoms up!

干杯！

中西方文化不同，西方一般不提倡一饮而尽的干杯 Bottoms up或Gan Bei!

敬酒时的用语，最好说Cheers!

8. Well, I wish to propose a toast to our friendship and cooperation, Gan Bei!

那么，我想提议为了我们的友谊和合作，干杯！

propose a toast to 提议为……干杯

例句：

I propose a toast to the health of all the guests.

我提议为所有来宾的健康干杯！

9. Chinese cuisine places stress on color, aroma and flavor all at the same time.

中国菜肴强调色香味俱全。

place stress on 强调

例句：

The teacher places particular stress on the need for accuracy.

教师特别强调准确的重要性。

10. This Specially Flavored Chicken really works up my appetite.

这怪味鸡使我胃口大开。

work up my appetite 使我胃口大开

11. It seems we have the same taste.

看来咱俩的口味相同。

to one's taste 合乎某人的口味

例句：

Oh, they look delicious, I'm sure they will be to my taste.

菜看起来味道很不错，一定会对我的口味。

12. on behalf of our company... 我代表本公司……

on behalf 代表，为了，因为

例句：

The president can't be here today, so I'm going to speak on his behalf.

今天总裁不能来，我将代表他发言。

13. What a joy it is to have friends coming from afar!

（谚语）有朋自远方来，不亦乐乎！

14. Our distinguished guests come from the other side of the earth, so our joy tonight is beyond expression.

我们尊贵的客人来自地球的另一边，所以我们今晚的欢喜是无法形容的。

① distinguished 尊贵的，杰出的

② a distinguished writer 一个杰出的作家

③ distinguished guests 贵宾

Part B Practical Key Sentences

1. **welcome to ...**

   Welcome to our dinner party.

   非常乐意邀请你加入我们酒会。

   be welcome to ... 可以随意……

   You are welcome to attend the business conference.

   欢迎参加商务会议。

   替换表达：

   Welcome to China!

   Welcome to our country!

2. **take a seat**

   Shall we sit and talk?

   请坐下谈。

   这个句型用于邀请客人入席。

   替换表达：

   Will you take this seat, please?

   Be seated, please.

   Please sit here on my right.

   Shall we go into the dining-room?

   Shall we go this way to the dinner table?

   Come on. Let's go into the dining-hall.

3. **make yourself at home**

   Please help yourself and make yourself at home.

   别客气，请随便吃。

   这个句型用于用餐时让客人放轻松，可以使客人感到宾至如归。还可以用以下几种表达法：

   Please help yourself to whatever you like.

   Enjoy yourself!

Please don't stand on ceremony!

4. Let me help you to ...

Let me help you to some seafood hot pot.

我给您来点海鲜火锅。

这个句型为餐桌上主人向客人让餐时常用的句型。

① help sb. to sth. 给某人拿/取某物

Let me help you to the roast duck.

我给您夹块烤鸭。

② help oneself to 自己亲自拿或取某物

Please help yourself to a steak.

请来一块牛排。

常用的让餐的表达法还有：

Would you like to have some more... (roast duck, beef, fish)

May I help you to some more...

5. this calls for a drink

This calls for a drink. To your health, cheers!

值得喝一杯。为您的健康，干杯！

这句话用于餐桌上敬酒。

替换表达：

  Now, let's drink a toast to our guests.

  I wish to propose a toast to... (our cooperation)

  Let me propose a toast to... (our good relationship)

  Let's drink to... (the success of our talks)

6. go to someone's head

（酒）上头，使某人醉

It never goes to the head.

不会使人醉。

The wine went straight to my head.

我很快感到酒力上头了。

I've had a drop too much.

我有点醉意。

Part C Integration of Theory and Practice

1. the congratulatory words   祝语

  【知识点】在演讲结束时，常用一些表示祝贺或祝福的话语，使气氛达到高潮。以下是一些常用的祝贺语：

【技能训练句型】

I hope this gathering will help keep our friendship till the end.

希望这次聚会能使我们的友谊地久天长。

Now, let us propose a toast on this happy occasion. Here's to our friendship!

现在，在这欢乐的时刻，让我们举杯庆贺，为我们的友谊干杯！

We take our hats off to you. Good luck and God bless you.

我们向您致敬！愿您福星高照，愿上帝保佑您。

We wish you the very best of luck in your future.

我们祝您一帆风顺、万事如意！

May the friendship between our two countries be further developed and consolidated.

愿我们两国之间的友谊进一步发展和巩固。

All our best wishes for you.

衷心祝你万事如意。

Best wishes to you.

祝你万事如意。

2. ordering the food 点菜

【知识点】点菜在中西方也有较大的不同。在中国讲究客随主便，通常是由主人点菜。而西方人则认为点菜是能否享受饮食的第一步，所以总是请客人点菜。接待国外的客人时，许多客人对当地的饮食可能并不熟悉，所以点菜的时候问客人喜欢吃什么菜是一种礼节。

【技能训练句型】

What kind of food do you like?

What drinks do you like?

Do you like Chinese food?

What would you like to have?

3. different eating habits 不同的饮食习惯

【知识点】东西方的饮食习惯也有极大的不同。比如西方人喜欢吃生菜，即使肉类、鱼类等食物也煮得很生。他们认为煮得太熟会破坏食物的营养价值，蔬菜也大多生吃。因此在吃西餐时，服务员一般都会询问客人所点的菜要做成什么样子。西方对食物的生熟程度一般分为五种：rare（半熟），medium rare（中等偏生），medium（中等熟），medium well（中等偏熟），well-done（熟透）。

【技能训练句型】

How would you like your steak?

Do you want your steak well-done, medium or rare?

Rare, please.

4. etiquette of eating western-style food 西餐礼仪

【知识点】（1）吃西餐时使用刀叉，一般是右手持刀，左手执叉。每道菜吃完后，将刀叉并拢平放在盘里，以示吃完。如未吃完，应摆成八字或交叉放着，刀口应向内。（2）喝茶或咖啡时，应右手拿杯把，左手拿盛杯的小碟。（3）在吃西餐时，应把餐巾铺在双膝上。中途离席时，应把餐巾放在椅子上，如放在桌上则意味着你不想吃了。餐巾应用来擦嘴，不能用来擦汗。

5. menu   菜谱

【知识点】中国人在请客时要准备很多菜，还要说"菜不多，请多包涵"之类的客气话。而英美人招待客人则一般只准备三四道菜。

英美人请客比较正规的菜谱如下。

第一道：开胃食品（appetizer）——汤、果汁或色拉。

第二道：主菜（main course）——往往是一种肉或鱼，配以土豆、蔬菜、调味品等。

第三道：甜食（dessert）——冰淇淋、水果馅饼或布丁等。

6. different kinds of wine   不同种类的酒

【知识点】酒在宴会中也是不可或缺的。一般来说，英国人爱喝啤酒、葡萄酒和白兰地，美国人则爱喝葡萄酒、啤酒等。美国人喝的葡萄酒（grape wine）带较重的酸味，所以又称这种酒为dry wine。有的英美人爱喝酒精含量较高的酒，如brandy，whisky，他们把这类酒称为liquor。

wine通常分为以下四类：

（1） still wine 没有气体的酒　　例如：Dynasty 王朝葡萄酒

（2） sparkling wine 有气体的酒　　例如：champagne 香槟酒

（3） fortified wine 掺加烈酒的酒　　例如：sherry 雪梨酒

（4） distilled wine 经过蒸馏的酒　　例如：brandy 白兰地

Part D Practice

I. Complete the Following Dialogues

A: I hope that the dishes tonight will be ___1___ your liking.

B: Thank you. These dishes are all delicious. They really work ___2___ my appetite.

A: Here are some cold dishes. Please help yourself and make yourself ___3___ home.

B: Thank you!

A: I'm glad that you have a good appetite. This calls ___4___ a drink. Cheers!

B: ___5___ our health, Gan Bei!

B: The wine also tastes quite good.

A: Yes, Moutai is one of the most famous liquors in China. It never goes ___6___ the head.

A: You seem to be quite an expert ___7___ chopsticks.

B: Thank you! I have practiced it for two months before I came to China.

A: Really? I'd like to propose a toast ___8___ your progress in using chopsticks. Cheers!

B: Cheers! Oh! This duck is not only tasty and fresh, but also beautiful!

A: Yes, Chinese cuisine places stress ___9___ color, aroma and flavor all at the same time.

B: I like it very much. Let's help ourselves ___10___ some more, please.

II. Oral Translation

Task 1

Translate the following sentences into English orally.
（1）我建议为我们的主人干杯。
（2）我代表所有在座的中国人说几句话。
（3）你们的特色菜是什么？
（4）我给您再夹些菜好么？
（5）为这，我们得喝一杯。为您的健康，干杯！
（6）这个火锅使我胃口大开。
（7）恐怕我得注意我的体重了。
（8）这种食物正合他的口味。
（9）谢谢你们的好客。
（10）那就入乡随俗吧。
（11）你有没有一些个人的喜好呢？
（12）希望今天的菜肴你能喜欢。
（13）请您自便吧。
（14）这种酒不会上头的。
（15）我对中国菜一点都不了解。

Task 2

Translate the following dialogue into English orally.
A: 谢谢你请我们赴宴。
B: 你们能出席我们的宴会，我们深感荣幸。我们入座吧。
A: 好的。听说这儿的菜很好吃，服务也无可比拟。
B: 是啊，你可以试一下。你有没有什么个人的喜好呢？
A: 没有，还是入乡随俗吧。
B: 我们再喝点酒吧？
A: 够了，我有点醉意了。
B: 那再喝点汤吧，请不要客气。

III. Oral Practice

Task 1

Work in pairs.

You are hosting a dinner for your partner. Serve your partner with the following Chinese food:

(1) shredded pork with spicy sauce（鱼香肉丝）

(2) sour spicy soup（酸辣汤）

(3) sweet and sour spare-ribs（糖醋排骨）

(4) prawn cooked with soy sauce（红烧明虾）

(5) specially flavored chicken（怪味鸡）

Task 2

Work in groups and practice proposing toasts and responding to toast to the following:

(1) friendship

(2) health

(3) family

(4) cooperation

(5) progress in speaking Chinese

IV. Situational Talks

Students work in pairs and make dialogues according to the following situation:

The hosts: Mr. Wang and his colleagues. Mr. Wang is the manager of Changyu Company.

The guests: Mr. Brown and his colleagues, who come from Australia. Mr. Brown is the vice manager of Crane Company.

They are at a welcoming banquet. Mr. Brown and his colleagues have just arrived. Their purpose of the journey this time is to investigate the cooperation possibility between the two companies.

(1) Dinner is ready. The host invites his guests to take a seat at the table and then make a toast to welcome them.

(2) Try to make a welcoming speech and thank you speech.

V. Creative Discussion

The teacher divides the class into several groups to discuss the questions below:

1. What are the common topics at the table? What kinds of topics should be avoided?

2. List the table manners.